KW-305-382

The European Union

Also edited by John McCombie and Carlos Rodríguez González

ISSUES IN FINANCE AND MONETARY POLICY

The European Union

Current Problems and Prospects

Edited by

John McCombie

and

Carlos Rodríguez González

palgrave
macmillan

Selection and editorial matter © John McCombie and
Carlos Rodríguez González 2007
Individual chapters © contributors 2007

All rights reserved. No reproduction, copy or transmission of this publication
may be made without written permission.

No paragraph of this publication may be reproduced, copied or transmitted
save with written permission or in accordance with the provisions of the
Copyright, Designs and Patents Act 1988, or under the terms of any licence
permitting limited copying issued by the Copyright Licensing Agency, 90
Tottenham Court Road, London W1T 4LP.

Any person who does any unauthorized act in relation to this publication may
be liable to criminal prosecution and civil claims for damages.

The authors have asserted their rights to be identified as the authors of this
work in accordance with the Copyright, Designs and Patents Act 1988.

First published 2007 by
PALGRAVE MACMILLAN
Houndmills, Basingstoke, Hampshire RG21 6XS and
175 Fifth Avenue, New York, N.Y. 10010
Companies and representatives throughout the world

PALGRAVE MACMILLAN is the global academic imprint of the Palgrave
Macmillan division of St. Martin's Press, LLC and of Palgrave Macmillan Ltd.
Macmillan® is a registered trademark in the United States, United Kingdom
and other countries. Palgrave is a registered trademark in the European Union
and other countries.

ISBN–13: 978–0–230–00799–4
ISBN–10: 0–230–00799–6

This book is printed on paper suitable for recycling and made from fully
managed and sustained forest sources.

A catalogue record for this book is available from the British Library.

Library of Congress Cataloging-in-Publication Data
    International Conference on the "Development in Economic Theory and
        Policy" (2nd: 2005: Bilbao, Spain)
        The European Union: current problems and prospects/edited by
    John McCombie and Carlos Rodríguez González.
        p. cm.
        Selected papers from the Second International Conference on the
    "Development in Economic Theory and Policy", held in Bilbao, July 7–8, 2005.
    Includes bibliographical references and index.
        ISBN–13: 978–0–230–00799–4 (cloth)
        ISBN–10: 0–230–00799–6 (cloth)
        1. European Union countries—Economic policy—Congresses. 2. Fiscal
    policy—European Union countries—Congresses. I. McCombie, J. S. L.
    II. Rodríguez González, Carlos. III. Title.
    HC240.I644 2005
    337.1'42—dc22   2006051594

10   9   8   7   6   5   4   3   2   1
16   15   14   13   12   11   10   09   08   07

Printed and bound in Great Britain by
Antony Rowe Ltd, Chippenham and Eastbourne

UNIVERSIT⟩   ⟩LYMOUTH

9007547800

Contents

List of Tables

List of Figures

Notes on the Contributors

José Albiac is researcher at the Economics Department of CITA (Government of Aragón). He completed his PhD in agricultural economics at the University of Illinois. His research interests include natural resources, economics, agricultural and environmental policies, and modelling.

Nigel F. B. Allington is Bye Fellow and Director of Studies in Economics at Downing College, Cambridge University and a member of the Julian Hodge Applied Macroeconomics Institute, Cardiff University. His most recent journal publication is 'One Market, One Money, One Price?', *International Journal of Central Banking*, 2005 (with P. Kattuman and F. Waldmann).

Rui Henrique Alves is Invited Lecturer in the Faculty of Economics at the University of Porto, Portugal, where he teaches European economics, international economics and macroeconomics. For some years, he has also been adviser to the Porto Derivatives Exchange in the area of training and education. Rui holds an MSc degree in economics and is currently finishing his PhD thesis in European economics. His main areas of research include political and economic organization of the European Union, fiscal federalism, fiscal policies and macroeconomic effects. He has published a book and several articles concerning these areas.

Jesús Ferreiro is Associate Professor in Economics at the University of the Basque Country in Bilbao. He has a PhD degree from the University of the Basque Country. His research interests are in the areas of macroeconomic policy, incomes policy, labour market institutions and foreign direct investments. He is the author of a number of papers on those subjects in refereed Spanish and foreign journals (*Journal of Post Keynesian Economics, Economie Appliquée, International Review of Applied Economics, European Planning Studies*, among others) and of chapters in edited books.

Davide Furceri is currently a PhD student at the University of Illinois at Chicago. He received a Laurea degree in statistics and economics from the University of Palermo (Italy) in 2001, and an MSc in economics from the Coripe (Italy) in 2002. His research interests are in the areas of macroeconomics, international economics and European integration. He is the author of a number of papers on these subjects in refereed Italian and international journals.

Jochen Hartwig is a researcher at the Swiss Institute for Business Cycle Research and lecturer at the University of St Gallen and at the Swiss Federal Institute of Technology, Zurich. Apart from his empirical work, which focuses on international data comparability and macroeconometric modelling, his research aims at advancing post-Keynesian analysis. He has published in, amongst others, the *Review of Political Economy*, the *Journal of Economics and Statistics* and the *History of Economic Ideas*.

Eckhard Hein is a Senior Researcher for Macroeconomic Policies at the Macroeconomic Policy Institute (IMK) in the Hans Boeckler Foundation, Duesseldorf, and a Visiting Lecturer at Carl von Ossietzky University, Oldenburg, Germany. Among his most recent publications are co-edited books on *Wages, Distribution, Employment and Growth – International Perspectives* (2006, Palgrave Macmillan) and *Macroeconomic Policy Coordination in Europe and the Role of the Trade Unions* (2005, ETUI), as well as (co-)authored papers on post-Keynesian theories of distribution and growth and on German and European macroeconomics in *Banca Nazionale del Lavoro Quarterly Review*, *European Journal of the History of Economic Thought*, *International Review of Applied Economics*, *Metroeconomica* and *Structural Change and Economic Dynamics*.

John McCombie is Director, Centre for Economic and Public Policy, University of Cambridge, and is Fellow in Economics at Downing College, Cambridge. He has previously held positions at the University of Hull and the University of Melbourne. His research interests include the study of national and regional growth disparities, economic growth and the balance-of-payments constraint, and criticisms of the aggregate production function and conventional measures of the rate of technical progress.

Juan Ramón Murua is Professor of Economics in the Applied Economics Department of the University of the Basque Country, UPV-EHU. He completed his PhD in agricultural economics at the University of the Basque Country and CITA. His main research interests include agricultural and rural policies, land use, forestry and agricultural marketing.

Torsten Niechoj is a Research Fellow at the Faculty of Social Sciences at the University of Goettingen, Germany. His fields of research include European integration and actor- and institution-centred theories. He is co-editor of a book on *Macroeconomic Policy Coordination in Europe and the Role of the Trade Unions* (2005, ETUI) and one of the editors of *Intervention, Journal of Economics*.

Carlos Rodríguez González is a Lecturer in Economics at the University of the Basque Country and has a PhD from the same University. His research interests are in the area of foreign direct investment and monetary policy. He is the author of several papers and has recently published *The Pattern of Inward FDI Geographical Distribution: Can Developing Countries Base their Development on these Flows?* (Palgrave Macmillan, 2006).

Margit Schratzenstaller is a researcher at the Austrian Institute of Economic Research in Vienna, Austria. She teaches at the University of Vienna and at the University of Applied Sciences in Vienna. Before that, she held positions as a research assistant and as a post-doctoral researcher at the Universities of Giessen and Goettingen, Germany. Her research interests are tax and budget policy, particularly in the fields of capital taxation and tax competition, fiscal federalism and gender budgeting.

Felipe Serrano is Professor in Economics at the University of the Basque Country in Bilbao. He is the Head of the Department of Applied Economics V at the University of the Basque Country. His research interests are in the areas of social security, the welfare state, labour market, innovation and economic policy. He has been an adviser to the Spanish Parliament on the process of reform of the social security system. He is the author of a number of books and papers (in journals such as *Economies et Sociétés, Informacion Comercial Española, European Planning Studies, Journal of Income Distribution, International Review of Applied Economics, Journal of Post Keynesian Economics, International Papers in Political Economy*), and has edited books on those subjects.

List of Abbreviations

APBR	Augmented Permanent Balance Rule
BEA	Bureau of Economic Analysis
BEPGs	Broad Economic Policy Guidelines
BLS	Bureau of Labor Statistics
CAP	Common Agricultural Policy
CCBT	Common Consolidated Base Taxation
CEDP	Common External and Defence Policy
CEPR	Centre for Economic and Policy Research
CITA	Centro de Investigación y Tecnología Agroalimentaria (Agrifood Research and Technology Centre)
COGI	cost of goods index
COLI	cost of living index
CPI	Consumer Price Index
CPI-U	Consumer Price Index – all urban consumers
CPI-U-RS	Consumer Price Index research series using current methods
EATR	effective average tax rates
ECB	European Central Bank
ECJ	European Court of Justice
EDP	Excessive Deficit Procedure
ELI	entry level item
EMS	European Monetary System
EMTR	effective marginal tax rates
EMU	Economic and Monetary Union/European Monetary Union
ETR	effective tax rates
ETUI	European Trade Union Institute
EU	European Union
EUCIT	European Corporate Income Tax
FDI	foreign direct investment
Fed	The Federal Reserve Bank
FISIM	financial intermediation services indirectly measured
GDP	gross domestic product
GNP	gross national product
GVA	gross value added
HST	Home State Taxation
ICT	information and communication technology
IFS	Institute for Fiscal Studies

IHS	Institut für Höhere Studien
IMF	International Monetary Fund
NAIRU	non-accelerating inflation rate of unemployment
NBER	National Bureau of Economic Research
NCM	'new consensus' macroeconomics
NIPAs	National Income and Product Accounts
NMS	new member states
OECD	Organisation for Economic Co-operation and Development
OMS	old member states
p.a.	per annum
PAYG	pay-as-you-go
PBR	Permanent Balance Rule
PPP	purchasing power parity
PSE	producer support estimate
R&D	research and development
SGP	Stability and Growth Pact
WTO	World Trade Organization
ZEW	Zentrum für Europäische Wirtschaftsforschung

1
Introduction

John McCombie and Carlos Rodríguez González

In spite of, or perhaps because of, the adoption of a common currency for the majority of the European Union (EU) countries and the implementation of the Stability and Growth Pact, the recent economic performance of the EU as a whole has been exceptionally weak, especially with respect to unemployment. (A notable exception is the UK.) This is irrespective of whether we compare the economic performance of the EU of the last two decades with the so-called Golden Age of 1950–73 or whether we compare the EU with the US.

The chapters in this book are a selection of papers on the EU from the Second International Conference on 'Developments in Economic Theory and Policy'. This was held in Bilbao on 7–8 July 2005 and was organized under the auspices of the Department of Applied Economics V of the University of the Basque Country, Spain, and the Centre of Economic and Public Policy, Department of Land Economy, University of Cambridge, UK. The contributions focus on various economic issues and problems that currently face the EU countries, and they make important contributions to a number of important ongoing debates.

Eckhard Hein and Torsten Niechoj set the scene in their chapter which considers the Broad Economic Policy Guidelines (BEPGs). These guidelines were first introduced in 1993 and represent the overall policy model for EU member countries to be adopted putatively to generate rapid and sustained growth. Yet, by any standard, they must be considered a failure. Hein and Niechoj pose the question: 'Is this because the BEPGs have been incorrectly implemented, or is it that the BEPGs are themselves at fault?' To answer this, they first trace the origins of the BEPGs and discuss how they are presently drawn up. They next go on to assess the underlying economic policy model on which the guidelines are based. When they consider the impact of the guidelines, they come to the pessimistic conclusion that the

1

BEPGs have conspicuously failed in their remit to foster growth and employment. However, this is not, they argue, because the guidelines have been incompletely or wrongly implemented; the answer is that the guidelines are ill conceived and Hein and Niechoj call for their abandonment. They propose an alternative policy mix that they believe is necessary for the economic revitalization of the EU.

The failure in 2003 by the European Council to begin the Excessive Deficit Procedure against Germany and France was widely seen as throwing the Stability and Growth Pact (SGP) into disarray, and some have questioned whether or not this sees the end of the Pact. Nigel Allington and John McCombie examine the events leading up to the crisis and the current problems facing the SGP. They conclude that the position taken depends upon the underlying theory on which the judgement is based. Those subscribing to the New Macroeconomic Consensus model are rather more sanguine than those who view the crisis from a more Keynesian framework. They assess a number of proposals that have been advanced in an attempt to rehabilitate the SGP.

Chapter 4 by Davide Furceri presents some econometric evidence on the impact of the Maastricht Treaty (and its convergence criteria) on the convergence or otherwise of GDP per capita and sectoral productivity. He analyses the rate of convergence for different time periods: namely, before and after the Maastricht Treaty and before and after the introduction of the Stability and Growth Pact. The results indicate that they have not affected the real convergence process at the aggregate level, except for the five years from 1992 to 1997. Moreover, there is a wide diversity of experience between the sectors and it is only some sectors, notably agriculture, industry and construction, that are responsible for the lack of convergence at the aggregate level.

Jochen Hartwig in Chapter 5 raises the important question as to whether the difference in GDP growth rates between the EU15 and the US are as large as those generally believed and indicated by using the OECD National Accounts. According to OECD data, the US grew between 1980 and 1997 at a rate that was 0.3 percentage points faster than the EU15. This increased to 0.9 percentage points over the period 1997–2004. However, Hartwig shows that nearly all of the latter difference can be explained by changes in the deflation methods used to convert nominal to constant price data which were introduced in the US after 1997, but not in the EU. This means that the view that major changes in policy are necessary if the US's growth rates are to be matched is not necessarily valid.

The increasing integration of the EU national economies, together with the accession of ten new member states in May 2004 to the European

Union, have led to increasing competition between the EU countries in their accompanying tax rates. The chapter by Margit Schratzenstaller deals with this important development in the EU. She gives special consideration to the question of whether or not a 'race to the bottom' can be observed in company taxation rates in the EU, and selected problems of company taxation in the EU are also discussed. Chapter 6 concludes with a survey and a discussion of the proposals and current initiatives pursued at the EU level to harmonize and co-ordinate company taxation in the EU against the background of these problems.

Felipe Serrano and Jesús Ferreiro discuss the important question of how state pensions should be financed in the EU in the light of the ageing structure of the population. This mirrors the debate that has recently been taking place in the US over whether the ageing of the population requires a move away from an unfunded system (where social security payments are financed from taxation) to a funded and privatized system. A preference for the funded system is based on the assumption that the economic returns are higher and that it will lead to a rise in savings. However, Serrano and Ferreiro put forward cogent reasons as to why the unfunded system is preferable.

Juan Ramón Murua and José Albiac consider the case for the complete abolition of the Common Agricultural Policy (CAP). The CAP has become a bone of contention between the member states, especially between those with relatively efficient and those with relatively inefficient agricultural sectors. However, they make a persuasive case that the 'gradual and inevitable decline in the importance of the agricultural sector and the . . . problems [mentioned in their chapter] relating to the CAP are not sufficient reasons to scrap the common agricultural policy or drain it of all content'. Just as the US has retained an active agricultural policy, so should the EU. The only valid reason, they consider, for the abandonment of the CAP is to curtail the EU budget, but such a move would be totally inappropriate, especially following the incorporation of the new countries into the EU where agriculture has such an important role in their economies.

The book concludes with a chapter by Rui Henrique Alves which concentrates on broader political and economic issues facing the EU. He argues convincingly that whatever the deficiencies of the economic union, the lack of a pan-European political union has even more severely limited the EU's influence in the world. He proposes that this can only be overcome by a more radical restructuring of the EU along more federal lines, but with due cognizance taken of the problems posed by nationalism.

He considers that the changes currently proposed by the European Constitution are unlikely to be sufficient to give the EU a strong voice in the international economic and political arenas. It would also require a move on the economic front towards a form of fiscal federalism. Alves ends by noting that 'the success of such a model would largely depend upon achieving a sentiment of true European citizenship'. Given the various histories of the member states, this may actually prove difficult to achieve.

As a final word, we would like to thank the University of the Basque Country, the Basque Government and the Bilbao Bizkaia Kutxa for providing financial support for the conference, and we thank all the participants and contributors.

2
Guidelines for Sustained Growth in the European Union? The Concept and Consequences of the Broad Economic Policy Guidelines[*]

Eckhard Hein and Torsten Niechoj

Introduction

For several years now, various economic policy measures have been employed at the EU level in an attempt to stimulate sustained growth and employment. Since 1993, the key EU economic policy document in this regard has been the Broad Economic Policy Guidelines (BEPGs). They provide an over-arching model for European economic policy and the policies of the member countries. Structural reforms and a supposedly 'stable' macroeconomic framework are intended to ensure the achievement of the Lisbon Strategy's goal of making the EU the world's most competitive and dynamic economy by 2010.

However, these efforts have hitherto met with little success. The EU and, in particular, the European Monetary Union (EMU) have been lagging behind the US since the mid-1990s and have been suffering from slow growth and high unemployment. Is this because the BEPGs have been incorrectly implemented, or is it that the BEPGs are themselves at fault? In order to answer this question, we begin by describing how the BEPGs came about in the first place and the goals which they were designed to pursue. We then provide an overview of the current procedure for drawing up the BEPGs, before analysing their underlying economic policy model. Having set the scene in this way, we move on to establish the extent to

[*] This chapter is a completely revised and updated version of an earlier German paper which has been published in *Wirtschaft und Gesellschaft*, 31(1) (2005), pp. 11–40. We would like to thank the participants in the conference 'Developments in Economic Theory and Policy' in Bilbao, 7–8 July 2005, for stimulating comments.

which the BEPGs have achieved their intended goals and consider whether it is actually possible for them to attain such goals. We show how, far from promoting dynamic growth, the implementation of the recommendations contained within the BEPGs has resulted in a restrictive policy that, in fact, acts as an obstacle to achieving the goal of fostering growth and employment.

The background

At the end of the 1980s, the difficulty encountered by some currencies in keeping within the exchange rate fluctuation limits set by the European Monetary System (EMS) led to plans for a new single European Union monetary policy that was to be complemented by some elements of supra-national economic policy co-ordination. In 1989, the report of a working group led by the then President of the Commission, Jacques Delors, called for the creation of an independent central bank committed to achieving price level stability (Delors Report, 1989, pp. 21–3). In the report, however, this was not matched by an integrated economic policy at the supra-national level: all that was proposed was a form of loosely binding co-ordination.[1] Co-ordination should take place above all in the area of fiscal policy, in order to ensure that it does not have a negative influence on monetary policy. The report also proposed that, while budgetary policy would continue to be the responsibility of the member countries, national budgets should be monitored with a view to limiting the extent of budget deficits. In addition, the report called for a regular joint evaluation of economic development and guidelines for economic policy (Delors Report, 1989, pp. 16–21).

The negotiation and development of the ensuing monetary union framework took place almost entirely without public debate. The EMS had already led to the establishment of a network amongst the central banks, and despite the official insistence on the parallel development of economic and monetary convergence, individual governments left the negotiations mainly in the hands of their finance ministries. The result was that key policy decisions were taken by a small circle of monetary committee experts or the council of central bank presidents. This accounts for the extremely high level of consensus among the parties involved, all of whom shared the opinion that a single currency area would require an independent central bank in order to ensure price level stability, as well as institutional means of limiting member countries' budget deficits (Dyson, 1999).

There was, however, disagreement regarding the nature and the extent of the EU-level economic policy co-ordination or management that should accompany monetary union. A first proposal of the Commission which attempts to bring together the member countries' views up to 1990 concentrates mainly on the monetary policy aspects of integration. The proposals concerning economic policy co-ordination are much more restricted in scope, although they are undoubtedly more comprehensive and specific than the proposals subsequently made by the individual governments. The Commission identifies three instruments or processes for the implementation of a common economic policy (Proposal by the European Commission, 1993 [1990], p. 199). First, it calls for common and country-specific guidelines pertaining to national budgets, wage policy and structural policy to be drawn up and reviewed, thereby providing a blueprint for the subsequent BEPGs. Second, it proposes a regular joint evaluation of economic development as a concrete means of pursuing the Treaty's goal of harmonizing the economic policies of the member countries. Third, the Commission calls for the creation of a Community support programme offering budgetary support or special loans to countries experiencing financial difficulties.

The subsequent French proposal needs to be understood in the context of an approach to economics that has traditionally tended to place greater emphasis on government control (Dyson and Featherstone, 1999, pp. 221–30). In line with this *gouvernement économique* approach, the French suggested that the Council of Ministers should co-ordinate member countries' economic policies and should be empowered to cut a country's allocation from the EU's common budget if it failed to comply with the Council's recommendations. Furthermore, as a matter of common interest, economic policy should be jointly evaluated on a regular basis. In addition, while the main goal of monetary policy would remain the pursuit of price level stability, it should also support the EU's overall economic policy (Proposal by the French Government, 1993 [1991], pp. 343–4). Nevertheless, and as a result of Mitterrand's failed experiment with an expansive fiscal and monetary policy in 1982, the French government's proposals adhere to the fundamental principles of the consensus concerning price level stability and budget consolidation.

The German proposal for the Maastricht Treaty follows an economic policy approach that focuses on price level stability, in keeping with the Bundesbank's established tradition. Unlike the French proposal, it makes no mention of placing constraints on monetary policy in order to support the EU's overall economic policy. In contrast to the other proposals described above, the German alternative devotes a lot of attention to German *Ordnungspolitik* issues, such as free price formation in markets and privatization. It is true that the German proposal also considers economic policy co-ordination to be a matter of common interest, but it refrains from talking of economic policy 'guidelines', preferring instead to use the term 'orientations'. Moreover, the specific details of this co-ordination are confined to the prevention of budget deficits. The proposal does provide for cuts in a country's allocation from the EU's common budget as the sanction of choice, but only in case of a country failing to pursue an appropriate budgetary policy (Proposal by the German Government, 1993 [1991]).

The Dutch Presidency's proposal of 28 October 1991 contains the first formulation of what would later become the convergence criteria (Proposal by the Dutch Presidency, 1993 [1991], p. 230). Like the German proposal, it envisages a central bank modelled on the Bundesbank, and it also follows the German position in setting no fixed deadline for joining the monetary union, stating instead that countries may only join once they have met the convergence criteria. However, it also reflects the positions of the Commission and the French government through the inclusion of extensive passages concerning economic policy co-ordination which, in addition to mentioning budgetary control, also refer to the regular drafting of economic policy guidelines.

The Dutch compromise proposal brought the divergent views closer to an agreement, and the ultimate results of the negotiations are well known. The independence of the European Central Bank (ECB) is enshrined in the Maastricht Treaty and is complemented by co-ordination procedures aimed mainly at controlling budget deficits (Treaty of Maastricht, 1992, Art. 103–9).[2] Despite Germany's opposition, the stronger term of economic policy 'guidelines' (as opposed to 'orientations') was chosen (Treaty of Maastricht, 1992, Art. 103 or Art. 99 of the current consolidated version of the EC Treaty) and the Treaty established an automatic mechanism for joining the monetary union (Treaty of Maastricht, 1992, Art. 109j or EC Treaty, 2002, Art. 121).

How did these results come about? Clearly, a monetary union without the region's key currency, the Deutschmark, would have been unthinkable, and this put Germany in a strong position in the negotiations. Furthermore, the high level of independence enjoyed by the Bundesbank compared to central banks elsewhere in Europe was seen as a model for the planned European Central Bank not only by the Bundesbank but also by the central banks in other countries. Consequently, there was widespread support right from the start for a strong ECB and for a budgetary control system. But the Germans suffered a defeat with regard to the degree of planned co-ordination when they were forced to agree to the use of guidelines, thereby paving the way for the BEPGs. These concessions can be attributed to the fact that, after reunification, the German government was very keen to use monetary union as a clear and unequivocal sign of Germany's place at the heart of Europe, and was therefore prepared to compromise (Dyson and Featherstone, 1999, pp. 363–9; Garrett, 2001, pp. 118–23). Pressure from the European Commission and France thus led to the legal enshrinement in the Maastricht Treaty of a new procedure for economic policy co-ordination in the form of the BEPGs (EC Treaty, 2002, Art. 99).[3]

Procedure and drafting

The first BEPGs of 1993 were drafted by the Commission and only had a few pages. Their main topic was the co-ordination of fiscal policy, and a supplementary document also dealt with structural reforms and wage policy. The Council of Ministers amended the Commission's document to include extracts from the White Paper on Growth, Competitiveness and Employment (European Commission, 1993). The first BEPGs followed the same fundamental approach to economic policy that has continued to be adopted to the present day: a combination of a 'stable macroeconomic framework', low inflation and balanced budgets, together with structural reforms designed to foster growth and employment.

Although reference to the situation in individual member countries is made as early as 1994 in the Commission's draft versions of the BEPGs and from 1995 onwards also in the version approved by the Council of Ministers, it was not until the 1998 BEPGs that country-specific recommendations were explicitly made for the first time, while more detailed country-by-country recommendations were only made from 1999 onwards. In 1994, the Commission started monitoring the extent to which the previous year's proposals had been complied with, and from 1996 it began to include an assessment of implementation of its proposals for the BEPGs. By 1997 it was issuing its own brief report on the implementation of the BEPGs, and this report started to appear in more detailed form from 2000 onwards. In 1998, the sections dealing with structural reform of the goods, services and labour markets were expanded and complemented by observations regarding the financial markets. The year 2000 saw the addition of passages relating to the knowledge society and the ageing of the population. Furthermore, following the decision taken at the Barcelona European Council, the scope of the recommendations contained in the BEPGs since 2003 has been expanded to cover a three-year period rather than just the following year (European Commission, 2002; Broad Economic Policy Guidelines, 2003). These medium-term recommendations are to be expanded and updated annually, and this happened for the first time in 2004 (Broad Economic Policy Guidelines, 2004).

Contrary to expectations, in 2005 the procedure has changed again as a reaction to the ongoing debate on the Lisbon strategy of the 2000 summit. Aiming at a reduction of unemployment and a rising participation rate in the labour market, the results of the Lisbon strategy were mixed and not satisfactory after five years. Therefore the Commission prepared a relaunch by streamlining and simplifying the procedures (European Commission, 2005). This Commission document served as a basis for the presidency conclusions of the Brussels Summit in 2005. One of the main effects of the strategy revision is the integration of the BEPGs and the Employment Guidelines into one document, the so-called Integrated Guidelines for Growth and Jobs (Integrated Guidelines, 2005).

From 2005 on, the governance cycle starts with the new Integrated Guidelines being drafted by the Commission in April of the three-year period's first year, endorsed by the European Council in June and adopted by the Council of Ministers afterwards. In autumn the member countries have to draw up newly introduced National Reform Programmes for three years describing their reform measures in order to meet the demands of the Integrated Guidelines. Each year the member countries will report on the implementation in National Lisbon Reports and the Commission will present a Progress Report covering all countries' development. If necessary, annual updates of the Integrated Guidelines will be published by the Commission.

Other bodies participate in this process in an advisory role: for example, the Economic and Financial Committee and the Economic Policy Committee. Preparatory work undertaken by the member countries is also incorporated, and the European Parliament issues an opinion on the Commission's draft of the BEPGs as part of the Integrated Guidelines. The BEPGs are therefore a Commission policy document that has been discussed with, and agreed by, several other bodies. Furthermore, it contains recommendations pertaining to all policy areas and all other co-ordination procedures are required to deliver results that are in line with the content of the BEPGs. It is thus a document that represents the economic policy consensus (or perhaps it would be more accurate to say 'compromise' on economic policy) at European level and is approved by the Council of Ministers as the body representing the governments of the EU member countries. The member countries are committed to implementing the recommendations contained in the BEPGs, although in contrast to the budgetary control measures of the SGP, countries that fail to implement them cannot be sanctioned. As such, the BEPGs are a form of 'soft co-ordination' that relies on voluntary compliance by national governments and peer pressure.

The economic policy model underlying the Broad Economic Policy Guidelines

Until 1999, the key goals of the BEPGs were non-inflationary growth and high employment in accordance with Art. 2 of the EC Treaty. Since the Lisbon Summit, however, the goals agreed on in Lisbon have been adopted. In the 2003–5 version of the BEPGs the wording is identical with the central passage of the Lisbon strategy. The main object is 'to become the most competitive and dynamic knowledge-based economy in the world capable of sustainable economic growth with more and better jobs and greater social cohesion' (Broad Economic Policy Guidelines, 2003, p. 59; see also European Council, 2000). This orientation also underlies the BEPGs as part of the Integrated Guidelines.

The main idea of the BEPGs is that structural reforms should be used to boost growth potential. According to the BEPGs, 'sound' macroeconomic conditions should enable the economy to realize this potential. The resulting growth would in turn lead to more and better jobs. It can thus be said that in the year 2000 the BEPGs have given concrete expression to the complementary relationship between macroeconomic policy and structural reforms for the first time. This is very explicit in the current version which is divided into two sections: section one contains macroeconomic guidelines concerning the macroeconomic framework, and section two covers microeconomic guidelines dealing with the proposed structural changes.

The core elements of the structural reforms are deregulation and liberalization of goods, services, financial and labour markets, on the one hand (Broad Economic Policy Guidelines, 2005; Integrated Guidelines, 2005, pp. 3–4, 7–11), and investment in research and development (R&D) and innovation policy, on the other hand (Integrated Guidelines, 2005, pp. 12–16). Furthermore, measures should be taken to expand the labour supply, increase the adaptability of the workforce, and improve education.

In order for the (supposedly) higher growth potential resulting from these structural reforms to be transformed into actual growth, it is argued that 'sound macroeconomic conditions' should prevail. These conditions are defined by the BEPGs as a stable monetary framework, fiscal discipline and modest wage increases (Integrated Guidelines, 2005, pp. 1–2, 5–6). The BEPGs consistently stipulate a clear assignment of the macropolitical players in the fields of monetary, fiscal and wage policy and the instruments at their disposal to the economic policy targets. This approach strengthens the ECB's focus on its primary goal, the creation of price stability; although, once this has been ensured, the central bank is also supposed to support the EU's economic policy. The task of fiscal policy, meanwhile, is to achieve a super-cyclically balanced budget. Wage growth should not exceed the sum of inflation and trend productivity growth and should take into account workplace productivity.

The BEPGs assume that the ECB's monetary policy automatically concurs with the recommendations and have nothing further to say on the matter. They fail to question the ECB's target of 'medium-term inflation below but close to 2 %' (ECB, 2003, p. 89), which is, in fact, quite restrictive for a heterogeneous economic area with different growth rates and markedly divergent inflation rates; and neither do they make any criticism of the asymmetrical and ultimately growth-unfriendly policy pursued by the ECB in the past.[4]

In accordance with the SGP, the BEPGs require fiscal policies to ensure that, in the medium term, member countries have either balanced budgets or budget surpluses. On the one hand, this is intended to ensure that national fiscal policies are protected against future recessions and are in a position to allow the automatic stabilizers to take full effect; while on the other hand, it should free up financial resources to address the funding problems associated with demographic change and the ageing of the population. Despite the fact that greater public investment in research, education and infrastructure is urged, the recommendations do not mention borrowing as a means of financing this spending. On the contrary, budget management in order to obtain sustained surpluses will involve reducing public debt to zero in the long run. This implies a rejection of what was until recently widely accepted as the 'golden rule' of fiscal policy: that is, the principle of borrowing to fund the public capital stock. Despite the fact that the BEPGs demand that the automatic stabilizers should be allowed to take effect and that pro-cyclical policies should be avoided, they make no attempt to question the consolidation measures required by the SGP during recessions. The BEPGs rather require that those member countries which have not reached their budgetary objectives should reduce their cyclically-adjusted deficits by 0.5 per cent of GDP each year and should pursue greater improvements in good times. It is not noticed that if such cuts were to be made in a recession phase of the economic cycle they would have a marked pro-cyclical effect and would in fact exacerbate the recession.

According to the BEPGs, wage developments have to contribute to macroeconomic stability. It is therefore argued that wage trends in member countries should be consistent with price level stability and trend productivity. Further explanations make clear that this is an upper limit and not a target. Wages should reflect workplace productivity; in other words, there should be greater wage differentiation than there has been in the past. And, even more important, wages should allow for a rate of profit that enhances productivity, capacity and employment. In places, the BEPGs talk positively about the role of the collective bargaining parties and even adopt a decidedly favourable tone with regard to collective wage bargaining: for example, they recommend that the bargaining parties should agree to pursue a policy of wage moderation via the Macroeconomic Dialogue, a forum established by the Cologne Process in order to achieve a consensus among the players in the fields of monetary, fiscal and wage policy. In so doing, the BEPGs favour the corporatist approach to wage bargaining and, notwithstanding all their proposals regarding clauses allowing companies to diverge from collective agreements and regarding the decentralization of wage bargaining, they still support the principle of the bargaining parties being responsible for negotiating wages. However, they completely fail to take into account the fact that a policy of promoting company-level wage settlements and wage differentiation actually undermines the bargaining parties' ability to act strategically in order to ensure wage trends that meet macroeconomic requirements, whatever these may be.

Contrary to former issues of the BEPGs, the recent one does not deal with the question of policy co-ordination. In the previous BEPGs, however, a better co-ordination of monetary, wage and fiscal policy was demanded in order to achieve wage restraint, avoid public deficits and implement structural reforms (Broad Economic Policy Guidelines, 2003, pp. 67–8). As such, co-ordination means gaining a commitment by the players to the programme outlined in the BEPGs, including the clear assignment of economic policy goals to the individual macropolitical players and the instruments at their disposal. The BEPGs do not understand co-ordination to mean that the players from different policy areas are heavily dependent on each other in order to achieve their policy goals. This means that the BEPGs ignore the fact that the effects of individual policies are interdependent and that it is therefore impossible for one policy area's goals to be achieved without co-ordination with the other players.

In summary, it can be said that for more than a decade now the policy mix recommended by the BEPGs for the EMU has followed an economic policy model that Arestis, McCauley and Sawyer (2001) aptly describe as 'new-monetarist'. Its theoretical basis is a mixture of new-classical, monetarist and new-Keynesian economic policy assignments (Hein, 2002a). It can be broadly summarized as follows: it is assumed that the private sector is stable in the long run and that discretionary economic policies have a destabilizing effect. Inflation is a monetary phenomenon and the central bank can bring down inflation without any real costs in terms of growth or employment. Unemployment fluctuates around an equilibrium level determined by supply-side factors that is known as the NAIRU (non-accelerating inflation rate of unemployment) and can only be reduced by creating more flexible labour markets. Fiscal policy has no long-term effect on growth and employment and should therefore be subordinated to the goal of price level stability.

Macroeconomic effects

Since the BEPGs have been largely responsible for determining the direction of economic policy within the EU for a period of some ten years, we will analyse the macroeconomic effects of the associated policy model. We are, of course, not suggesting that the recommendations contained in the BEPGs have always been implemented to the letter; however, we do believe that they provide a very accurate reflection of the fundamental direction followed by economic policy in the EU, or at least in the EMU. Therefore, the evolution of macroeconomic target variables and some indicators of the policies implemented in the EMU countries between 1994 and 2003 will be compared with the period from 1984 to 1993 (see Table 2.1). This will enable us to compare two ten-year periods that both include a recession towards the end. Trends in the EMU will also be contrasted with developments in the USA, which constitutes an economic area with a single currency that is comparable in size to the EMU. Although the BEPGs apply to all the EU member countries, our empirical analysis

Table 2.1   Real GDP growth, unemployment and inflation in the EMU and the USA, annual averages for 1984–93 and 1994–2003 (%)

	EMU		USA	
	1984–93	1994–2003	1984–93	1994–2003
Real GDP growth	2.7	2.1	3.3	3.3
Unemployment rate	8.7	9.6	6.6	5.1
Inflation rate (private consumption)	4.5	2.1	3.8	2.4

Source: OECD (2004).

will be confined to the EMU countries that have, since 1999, been subject to the centralized single monetary policy of the ECB as well as the SGP's regulations regarding fiscal policy.

There is a broad consensus that the key macroeconomic target variables are economic growth, high employment and price level stability. As far as GDP growth is concerned, it can be seen from Table 2.1 that the overall figures for the EMU were lower between 1994 and 2003 than for the period 1984–93. Meanwhile, the USA experienced a consistently stronger average growth rate in both periods. The unemployment figures reflect this falling GDP growth in the EMU countries and the fact that growth was lower than in the USA. Average unemployment rose from the first to the second period, whereas in the USA the average unemployment rate fell considerably. As far as the real target variables of growth and unemployment are concerned, the EMU countries' performance since the introduction of the BEPGs has undergone a marked deterioration both in comparison with the previous ten years and with the USA. On the other hand, there has been an improvement with regard to the nominal target variable of price level stability. The average annual inflation rate in the EMU countries more than halved in the second compared to the first period, and is slightly below the US average in this period. Overall, it can be said that since 1994, the USA has been much more successful than the EMU countries in achieving a combination of high growth, low unemployment and low inflation.

What are the reasons for the EMU countries' unsatisfactory performance? Is it that the extent of the structural reforms called for by the BEPGs and the speed of implementation were insufficient? Or were the recommendations for the macropolitical players ultimately counterproductive? Based on a comprehensive data set assembled by Baker *et al.* (2004) which covers indicators for labour market institutions and social security systems in 20 OECD countries between 1960 and 1999, Hein and Truger (2005c) calculated a total index of the rigidity of labour market institutions and the welfare state and compared its development with that of the unemployment rate in the countries in question. This global index covers employment protection, the benefit replacement rate, benefit duration, union density, the degree of co-ordination of wage bargaining and the tax wedge. Much of the more recent mainstream literature on labour market theory predicts that these partial indicators will, to a greater or lesser extent, have a negative influence on employment (Nickell, 1997; Nickell and Layard, 1999). Figure 2.1 compares the changes in the total index of institutional sclerosis from 1980/84 until 1995/99 with the associated changes in unemployment rates in 20 OECD countries.

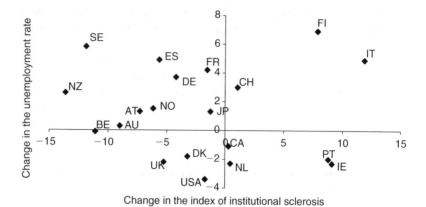

Figure 2.1   Change in the unemployment rate and in the total index of institutional sclerosis from 1980/84 to 1995/99 (20 OECD countries)
Source: Hein and Truger (2005c) p. 16.

Although the data on labour market institutions and the social security system only cover the first part of our second time period under consideration, it becomes clear, on the one hand, that there is significant variation in the extent to which 'structural reforms' have been implemented in the EMU countries. The rigidity of the labour market and social security systems in Finland (Fl), Italy (IT), Portugal (PT) and Ireland (IE) increased significantly, while it remained more or less the same in the Netherlands (NL) and decreased considerably in Germany (GE), Denmark (DK), Spain (ES), Austria (AU) and Belgium (BE). On the other hand, it is also clear that, on the whole, there is no unequivocal relation between the change in rigidity of labour market institutions and the welfare state on the one hand, and the change in the unemployment rate on the other.

There is thus no conclusive proof that structural reforms have a systematically positive influence on economic performance.[5] Therefore, it makes sense to consider whether the causes of the EMU countries' unsatisfactory macroeconomic performance can be traced to the macroeconomic policy approach recommended in the BEPGs. In the following paragraphs, some indicators for monetary, wage and fiscal policies will therefore be analysed (Table 2.2).

As far as monetary policy is concerned, we consider the relationship between the real short-term interest rate and the real GDP growth rate. While it is true that the central bank only directly controls the short-term nominal interest rate, it nevertheless also determines the real short-term interest rate, owing to the fact that it sets its nominal rate with an eye to

Table 2.2   Indicators for monetary, wage and fiscal policies in the EMU and the USA, 1984–93 and 1994–2003

	EMU		USA	
	1984–93	**1994–2003**	**1984–93**	**1994–2003**
Monetary policy				
Real GDP growth rate minus short-term real interest rate (percentage points)	−2.3	−0.1	0.0	1.2
Wage policy				
Growth in nominal compensation per employee (%)	5.2	2.3	4.4	3.5
Growth in nominal unit labour costs (%)	4.4	1.5	2.9	1.7
Labour income share (% of GDP at factor costs)	70.7	67.6	68.6	67.5
Fiscal Policy				
Number of years with a pro-cyclical fiscal policy	7	4	5	2
Real public investment as a share of real GDP (%)	2.9	2.5	3.3	3.1

Sources: European Commission (2004); OECD (2004).

inflation. If the real interest rate is above the real GDP growth rate, this will be unfavourable for growth and economic activity, because it encourages investment in financial assets as opposed to real assets.

Even between 1984 and 1993, the average difference between GDP growth and interest rates in the USA was 0.0 percentage points, indicating a markedly less restrictive monetary policy than in the future EMU countries, where monetary policy was dominated by the German Bundesbank and the average difference stood at −2.3 per cent. Although both economic areas witnessed a trend towards a more expansive monetary policy over the whole period 1994–2003, monetary policy in the USA did much more to promote growth and economic activity than in the EMU. In the USA, the average difference between GDP growth and interest rates during this period was 1.2 per cent, as opposed to −0.1 per cent in the EMU countries. This is even more remarkable because until 1999 the EMU countries were still benefiting from the reduction in their interest rates to the lower level found in Germany, the region's key currency country (Hein and Truger, 2005a). The ECB's more restrictive approach to monetary policy compared to the Federal Reserve (Fed) once again became particularly apparent after the 2001 recession. While the Fed managed to promote a growth-friendly constellation with a positive difference of 1.95 per cent between real GDP growth and short-term real interest rates on average between 2001 and 2003, the ECB proved much more reluctant to act, because in the Euro area this difference remained still slightly negative at −0.04 per cent on average.

The wage policies pursued by the bargaining parties, or the wage settlements arrived at on the labour market, determine the nominal wage rate and hence also nominal unit labour costs, when labour productivity is considered to be given or following an exogenous trend. Insofar as businesses pass on unit labour cost fluctuations directly to prices, wage policy influences inflation. If these changes are not passed on fully, there will also be changes in functional income distribution, which is measured here by the labour income share. A combination of high unemployment, labour market deregulation and the emergence of national competitive social pacts that govern collective bargaining have caused a significant decline in the growth rate of nominal compensations per employee in the EMU countries from 5.2 per cent on average between 1984 and 1993 to an average 2.3 per cent between 1994 and 2003. Therefore, average unit labour cost growth in the EMU countries fell from 4.4 per cent between 1984 and 1993 to 1.5 per cent between 1994 and 2003.[6]

In the USA average annual growth of nominal compensation per employee also declined from the first to the second period, from 4.4 to 3.5 per cent, and hence to a much lesser extent. A reduction was also seen in the nominal unit labour cost growth, albeit a more modest one than in the EMU, from 2.9 to 1.7 per cent. In both regions, modest wage increases made a key contribution to the sharp fall in inflation described above (Table 2.1). While wage trends in the EMU countries between 1984 and 1993 were at times still clearly inflationary and thus not conducive to stability, in the period between 1994 and 2003 they no longer posed a threat to low inflation, and neither did they put the achievement of the ECB's inflation target at risk from 1999 onwards.[7] Even the fact that unit labour cost growth has risen slightly above the 2 per cent mark since 2001 is more a consequence of the fall in productivity growth resulting from the cyclical downturn than of a wage policy that fails to promote stability (Hein and Truger, 2005b). Consequently, wage trends could have allowed for a much more expansive monetary policy than that pursued by the ECB without unleashing inflationary pressures.

Another consequence of the wage restraint practised in the EMU countries since 1994 has been a further fall in the labour income share from an average of 70.7 per cent between 1984 and 1993 to 67.6 per cent between 1994 and 2003. While the labour income share in the USA also fell from 68.6 to 67.5 per cent, this decline was far less pronounced than in the EMU. In the EMU countries, a lower proportion of the fall in unit labour cost growth was passed on to commodity prices than in the USA, as can be seen from a comparison of the annual averages for inflation and unit labour cost growth in Tables 2.1 and 2.2. If the propensity to consume out of labour income exceeds the propensity to consume out of profit income, it can be assumed that the redistribution to the detriment of labour will have a negative impact on consumer demand, which is the largest element of aggregate demand. This will also negatively affect GDP growth, unless the redistribution in favour of profits leads directly to increased investment, or the improvement in price competitiveness on international markets achieved by wage restraint leads to a major increase in export surpluses. It is clear that neither of the above has happened in the EMU since 1994, or at least not to a sufficient degree.

The extent to which fiscal policy exerts a stabilizing or destabilizing influence on the economy can be assessed by comparing changes in the output gap and the structural budget balance (Figures 2.2 and 2.3).

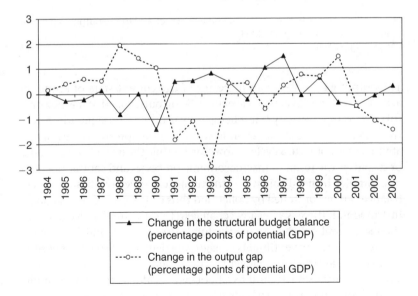

Figure 2.2 Change in the structural budget balance and in the output gap to previous year in the EMU, 1984–2003
Source: OECD (2004).

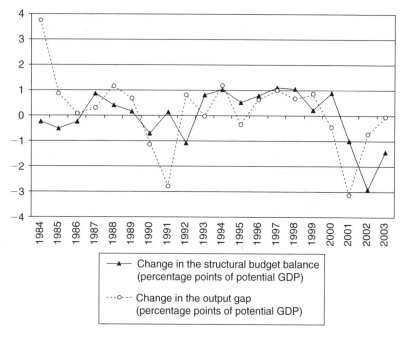

Figure 2.3   Change in the structural budget balance and in the output gap to previous year in the USA, 1984–2003
Source: OECD (2004).

The output gap serves as an indicator of the current state of economic activity. If it is positive, then capacity is being outstripped; if it is negative, this means that capacity is not being fully utilized. Consequently, a positive change in the output gap indicates a cyclical upturn, whereas a negative change points to a cyclical downturn. While the overall budget deficit or surplus is the result of macroeconomic processes and cannot therefore be controlled by fiscal policy, the structural (i.e., cyclically adjusted) budget balance can be controlled by policy and thus can be seen as a fiscal policy instrument. If there is a negative change in the structural budget balance, then structural deficits rise or structural surpluses fall, and fiscal policy provides an expansive stimulus to aggregate demand. If there is a positive change in the structural budget balance, then structural deficits fall or structural surpluses rise, and fiscal policy provides a restrictive stimulus to demand. If the structural budget balance remains the same when there is a change in the output gap, then fiscal policy is neither expansive nor restrictive and the automatic stabilizers are simply left to take effect.

Between 1984 and 1993, fiscal policies in the future EMU countries, which at this time were not yet subject to co-ordination, were pro-cyclical in seven out of ten years in this period. In four of these years (1985, 1986, 1988, 1990) they acted to reinforce a recovery and in three years they accentuated a cyclical slowdown or recession (1991, 1992, 1993). Between 1994 and 2003, the fiscal policies of the member countries were now 'co-ordinated', initially as part of the EMU convergence process and latterly through the SGP, and this served to make it somewhat less pro-cyclical. It was only pro-cyclical in four of ten years in this period, reinforcing a cyclical recovery in two years (1995, 2000) and accentuating a downturn in a further two years (1996, 2003). However, fiscal policy, too, fares poorly in comparison with the USA. While between 1984 and 1993, US fiscal policy was pro-cyclical in five years, only exacerbating a downturn on one occasion (1991); between 1994 and 2003 it was only slightly pro-cyclical in two years, reinforcing a cyclical slowdown in 1995 and 2000. However, the cyclical downturn in 2001 was met with decisive expansive measures even before the year was out. Particularly during the 1990s US fiscal policy constituted an example of budget consolidation without pro-cyclical measures, and, as is well known, the US achieved budget surpluses at the end of the upturn.

If we accept that public spending on infrastructure, education, and so on is a key requirement for private investment, and if we use public investment as a share of GDP as an indicator of the extent to which fiscal policy fosters growth, then once again the USA fares better than the EMU countries. Throughout the whole period investigated, the share of public investment in GDP in the US remained comfortably above 3 per cent, showing only a slight reduction from 3.3 per cent on average to 3.1 per cent between the two ten-year periods. In the EMU countries, on the other hand, the figure was lower than in the USA for the entirety of the study period, and fell from an average of 2.9 per cent between 1984 and 1993 to an average of 2.5 per cent between 1994 and 2003. Consequently, not only did the EMU's convergence process and the SGP's drive to achieve budget consolidation force countries to implement more pro-cyclical fiscal policies, but it also had a particularly negative impact on public investment and hence damaged future growth prospects.

In summary, differences in the macroeconomic policy mix offer a plausible explanation for the growth slowdown and the increase in unemployment in the EMU since 1994 and for the divergent macroeconomic performance of the EMU countries and the USA (see also Solow, 2000; Fritsche *et al.*, 2005). Even in the period 1984–93, the US approach to monetary and fiscal policy and its wage trends did much more to promote economic activity and growth than macropolicies in the European countries included in this study did. This difference was accentuated between 1994 and 2003 as a result of the EMU convergence process and the Maastricht macroeconomic regime encapsulated in the BEPGs. The economic policy recommendations contained in the BEPGs can thus be described as inadequate and largely counterproductive.

Conclusions

The BEPGs, which were created as a policy instrument for fostering growth and employment and intended to act as a counterbalance to purely monetary integration, have failed to fulfil this remit. This is not because their policy recommendations have been incompletely or wrongly implemented; rather, it is the fault of the policy recommendations themselves and the economic policy model on which they are based. We have shown how, over the last ten years, this model, which is based on structural reforms and strict assignment of the macropolitical players and the instruments at their disposal to individual goals, has resulted in a consistently poorer macroeconomic performance in the EMU countries compared with the preceding ten years and with the USA. In order to revitalize the EMU economies it will be necessary to abandon the policy-mix of the BEPGs. The implementation of an alternative policy model is required which is based on the co-ordinated deployment of monetary, wage and fiscal policies with a view to achieving steady growth and high employment, whilst at the same time maintaining price stability. Within such a policy-mix monetary policies take responsibility for growth and employment, nominal wage policies take care of stable inflation, fiscal policies stabilize effective demand in the short and long run, and public investment supports the growth potential of the economy.[8]

Notes

1 The co-ordination concept proposed in the Delors Report had been around for quite some time. The Treaty of Rome (1957, Art. 6) had already called on the member countries to coordinate their economic policies.
2 In 1996, the European Council further strengthened the co-ordination of national budgets when it introduced the Stability and Growth Pact.
3 Other more general legal points of reference for economic policy co-ordination are Articles 2, 4 and 98 of the EC Treaty.
4 For a more detailed critique of the ECB's policy, see, for example, Allsopp and Artis (2003), Bibow (2002, 2003), Hein (2002b) and Janssen (2005).

5 For more on the relationship between labour market and welfare state institutions, on the one hand, and employment, on the other hand, see Baker *et al.*
(2004) and the other papers in Howell (2004).
6 For more on the causes and consequences of the modest wage increases in the
EMU countries, see Hein and Schulten (2004) and Hein, Schulten and Truger
(2006).
7 It should be noted that the combined figures for the EMU countries hide considerable differences with regard to national unit labour cost and inflation
trends (Hein and Truger, 2005a). Thus, since the mid-1990s, unit labour cost
growth and inflation in Germany have been significantly below the EMU
average. This has meant that the EMU's largest member has been exposed to
major deflationary pressures, as recognized by the IMF (2003), and has also
been heavily constrained in its ability to achieve economic growth owing to
the fact that, now that nominal interest rates are the same across the EMU,
real interest rates in Germany are significantly higher than in the other EMU
countries (Hein and Truger, 2005c; Hein, Schulten and Truger, 2006).
8 For further details see Hein and Truger (2005b) and the other papers in Hein
et al. (2005).

References

Allsopp, C. and Artis, M.J. (2003) 'The Assessment: EMU, Four Years On', *Oxford Review of Economic Policy*, 19(1), 1–29.
Arestis, P., McCauley, K. and Sawyer, M. (2001) 'An Alternative Stability Pact for the European Union', *Cambridge Journal of Economics*, 25, 113–30.
Baker, D., Glyn, A., Howell, D.R. and Schmitt, J. (2004) 'Labour Market Institutions and Unemployment: A Critical Assessment of the Cross-country Evidence', in Howell, D.R. (ed.), *Fighting Unemployment: The Limits of the Free Market Orthodoxy* (Oxford: Oxford University Press), 72–118.
Bibow, J. (2002) 'The Monetary Policies of the European Central Bank and the Euro's (Mal-)performance: A Stability Oriented Assessment', *International Review of Applied Economics*, 16, 31–50.
Bibow, J. (2003) 'Is Europe Doomed to Stagnation? An Analysis of the Current Crisis and Recommendations for Reforming Macroeconomic Policymaking in Euroland', Levy Economics Institute, Working Paper No. 379, New York.
Broad Economic Policy Guidelines (2003) '2003–2005 period', published by Directorate-General for Economic and Financial Affairs of the European Commission, Series: *European Economy*, 74(4), Brussels.
Broad Economic Policy Guidelines (2004) 'The 2004 Update of the broad eco-nomic policy guidelines (for the 2003–2005 period)', published by Directorate-General for Economic and Financial Affairs of the European Commission, Series: *European Economy*, 75(4), Brussels.
Broad Economic Policy Guidelines (2005) 'Broad Guidelines for the Economic Policies of the Member States and the Community (2005–2008)', in *Integrated Guidelines for Growth and Jobs (2005–2008)*, Communication to the Spring European Council, Brussels, 7–24.
Delors Report (1989) *Report on Economic and Monetary Union in the European Community*, submitted by the Committee for the Study of Economic and Monetary Union (on 12 April 1989), Brussels.

Dyson, K. (1999) 'Economic and Monetary Union in Europe. A Transformation of Governance', in Kohler-Koch, B. and Eising, R. (eds), *The Transformation of Governance in the European Union* (London and New York: Routledge), 98–118.

Dyson, K., and Featherstone, K. (1999) *The Road to Maastricht: Negotiating Economic and Monetary Union* (Oxford: Oxford University Press).

EC Treaty (2002) 'Treaty Establishing the European Community. Consolidated Version', *Official Journal*, C 325, 24 December.

ECB (2003) 'The Outcome of the ECB's Evaluation of its Monetary Strategy', *Monthly Bulletin*, June, 79–92.

European Commission (1993) *White Paper on Growth, Competitiveness and Employment: The Challenges and Ways Forward into the 21st Century* (Brussels: European Commission).

European Commission (2002) *Communication from the Commission on Streamlining the Annual Economic and Employment Policy Co-ordination Cycles*, Series: COM(2002) 487 final (Brussels: European Commission).

European Commission (2004) Annual Macro Economic Database, April (Brussels: European Commission).

European Commission (2005) Communication to the Spring European Council, *Working Together for Growth and Jobs: A New Start for the Lisbon Strategy*, Series: COM (2005) 24 (Brussels: European Commission).

European Council (2000) *Presidency Conclusions*. (Lisbon), 23 and 24 March, http://ue.eu.int/ueDocs/cms_Data/docs/pressData/en/ec/00100-r1.en0.htm (last access: 24 January 2005).

Fritsche, U., Heine, M., Herr, H., Horn, G. and Kaiser, C. (2005) 'Macroeconomic Regime and Economic Development: The Case of the USA', in Hein, E., Niechoj, T., Schulten, T. and Truger, A. (eds), *Macroeconomic Policy Coordination in Europe and the Role of the Trade Unions* (Brussels: European Trade Union Institute, ETUI), 69–107.

Garrett, G. (2001) 'The politics of Maastricht', in Eichengreen, B. and Frieden, J. (eds), *The Political Economy of European Monetary Unification* (Boulder, CO: Westview Press), 111–30.

Hein, E. (2002a) 'Koordinierte Makropolitik in der EWU – zur Notwendigkeit und zu den Problemen der Umsetzung', *WSI Mitteilungen*, 55(5), 251–9.

Hein, E. (2002b) 'Monetary Policy and Wage Bargaining in the EMU: Restrictive ECB Policies, High Unemployment, Nominal Wage Restraint and Inflation Above the Target', *Banca Nazionale del Lavoro Quarterly Review*, 55, 299–337.

Hein, E., Niechoj, T., Schulten, T. and Truger, A. (eds) (2005) *Macroeconomic Policy Coordination in Europe and the Role of the Trade Unions* (Brussels: ETUI).

Hein, E., and Schulten, T. (2004) 'Unemployment, Wages and Collective Bargaining in the European Union', *Transfer: European Review of Labour and Research*, 10, 532–51.

Hein, E., Schulten, T. and Truger, A. (2006) 'Deflation Risks in Germany and the EMU: The Role of Wages and Wage Bargaining', in Hein, E., Heise, A. and Truger, A. (eds), *Wages, Employment, Distribution and Growth: International Perspectives* (Basingstoke: Palgrave Macmillan), 67–92.

Hein, E. and Truger, A. (2005a) 'European Monetary Union: Nominal Convergence, Real Divergence and Slow Growth?', *Structural Change and Economic Dynamics*, 16, 7–33.

Hein, E. and Truger, A. (2005b) 'Macroeconomic Coordination as an Economic Policy Concept – Opportunities and Obstacles in the EMU', in Hein, E.,

Niechoj, T., Schulten, T. and Truger, A. (eds), *Macroeconomic Policy Coordination in Europe and the Role of the Trade Unions* (Brussels: ETUI), 19–67.

Hein, E. and Truger, A. (2005c) 'What Ever Happened to Germany? Is the Decline of the Former European Key Currency Country Caused by Structural Sclerosis or by Macroeconomic Mismanagement', *International Review of Applied Economics*, 19, 3–28.

Howell, D.R. (ed.) (2004) *Fighting Unemployment. The Limits of the Free Market Orthodoxy* (Oxford: Oxford University Press).

IMF (2003) *Deflation: Determinants, Risks and Policy Options – Findings of an Interdepartmental Task Force* (Washington, DC: IMF).

Integrated Guidelines (2005) *Integrated Guidelines for Growth and Jobs (2005–2008)*, Communication to the Spring European Council, Brussels.

Janssen, R. (2005) 'Policy coordination in the Macroeconomic Dialogue of Cologne: Experiences from the ETUC', in Hein, E., Niechoj, T., Schulten, T. and Truger, A. (eds), *Macroeconomic Policy Coordination in Europe and the Role of the Trade Unions* (Brussels: ETUI), 213–36.

Nickell, S. (1997) 'Unemployment and Labor Market Rigidities: Europe Versus North America', *Journal of Economic Perspectives*, 11, 55–74.

Nickell, S. and Layard, R. (1999) 'Labour Market Institutions and Economic Performance', in Ashenfelter, O. and Card, H. (eds), *Handbook of Labour Economics* (Amsterdam: Elsevier), 3,029–84.

OECD (2004) *Economic Outlook*, 75 (Data on CD-ROM), Paris.

Proposal by the Dutch Presidency (1993 [1991]) 'Draft Treaty on Economic and Monetary Union, 28 October 1991' in Krägenau, H. and Wetter, W. (eds), *Europäische Wirtschafts- und Währungsunion. Vom Werner-Plan zum Vertrag von Maastricht* (Baden-Baden: Nomos), 224–31.

Proposal by the European Commission (1993 [1990]) 'Entwurf eines Vertrages zur Änderung des Vertrages zur Gründung der Europäischen Wirtschaftsgemein-schaft im Hinblick auf die Errichtung einer Wirtschafts- und Währungsunion', SEC (90)2500, 10 December, in Krägenau, H. and Wetter, W. (eds), *Europäische Wirtschafts- und Währungsunion. Vom Werner-Plan zum Vertrag von Maastricht* (Baden-Baden: Nomos), 194–203.

Proposal by the French Government (1993 [1991]) 'Vorschlag einer Änderung des EWG-Vertrages im Hinblick auf die Errichtung einer Wirtschafts- und Währungsunion', 25 January, in Krägenau, H. and Wetter, W. (eds), *Europäische Wirtschafts- und Währungsunion. Vom Werner-Plan zum Vertrag von Maastricht* (Baden-Baden: Nomos), 343–7.

Proposal by the German Government (1993 [1991]) 'Vorschlag einer Änderung des EWG-Vertrages im Hinblick auf die Errichtung einer Wirtschafts- und Währungsunion', 25 February, in Krägenau, H. and Wetter, W. (eds), *Europäische Wirtschafts- und Währungsunion. Vom Werner-Plan zum Vertrag von Maastricht* (Baden-Baden: Nomos), 331–4.

Solow, R.M. (2000) 'Unemployment in the United States and in Europe: A Contrast and the Reasons', *Ifo-Studien*, 46, 1–12.

Treaty of Maastricht (1992) 'Treaty on the European Union', *Official Journal*, C 191, 29 July.

Treaty of Rome (1957) *Treaty Establishing the European Community*.

3
'Nonsense Upon Stilts': An Assessment of the European Stability and Growth Pact and How it Might be Reformed[1]

Nigel F.B. Allington and John McCombie

Introduction

In an interview with *Le Monde* in 2002, the then European Union President, Romano Prodi, caused a sensation by claiming that the Stability and Growth Pact (SGP) was 'stupid' because its rules were applied too mechanically. Certainly, there was a democratic deficit within the EU because fiscal rules under the Maastricht Treaty and SGP constrained the fiscal independence of sovereign national governments that were faced with cyclical fluctuations and centralized monetary policy within Economic and Monetary Union (EMU). It is this conflict that lies at the centre of the continuing debate over appropriate EU fiscal-financial rules, how they should be interpreted, and the extent to which the European Council should be able to exercise its discretion over their implementation.

These problems were highlighted in 2003 by the refusal of the European Council to begin the Excessive Deficit Procedure (EDP) against Germany and France, the two worst offenders, which eventually led to the European Court of Justice's judgment effectively suspending the SGP. With this, the question has literally been raised as to whether or not it was 'The End of the Stability Pact?' (de Haan, Berger and Jansen, 2003; Collignon, 2004).[2] The breakdown in budgetary discipline after EMU in 1999 as deficits grew demonstrated the inadequacy of the prevailing institutional arrangements. Furthermore, the reforms settled on in 2005 introduced a myriad of country-specific exemptions from the 'close to balance or surplus' rule. The empirical counterfactual that, without the SGP, budget deficits and debts would have been worse, remains to be settled.

This chapter begins by setting out the rationale for the SGP and the role of fiscal policy in the EU. Next the evolution of fiscal-financial arrangements under the Maastricht Treaty and the SGP are reviewed and the trajectory of budget deficit and debt data analysed. This includes an assessment of cyclically-adjusted deficit data to see whether the recent switch to this measure relieves pressure on those economies at, or beyond, the 3 per cent Maastricht ceiling under the old measure. The inadequacies of the 2005 reforms are examined and the conclusion reached that the SGP is now fatally weakened.

The next section sets up a conceptual framework for assessing whether or not the current fiscal arrangements under the Maastricht Treaty and SGP are transparent, on the grounds that if monetary transparency enhances the effectiveness of monetary policy then, by similar reasoning, fiscal transparency can improve the operation of fiscal policy. Current arrangements fail most of the tests. Following this, we assess some alternative approaches to the SGP. We commence with a discussion of some proposals that the SGP can be rescued with relatively minor changes.

We next compare the SGP rules and an alternative Permanent Balance Rule (PBR) put forward by Buiter and Grafe (2004) in order to show how they differ. This new tax smoothing rule is then assessed and simulations for the 2001 and 2002 budget deficits under the PBR compared with actual deficits for the EU15 and the eastward expansion countries.[3] An augmented version of the PBR is included because this takes account of the projected pension shortfall in the EU. The conclusion reached is that a permanent ratio of tax revenue to GDP has much to commend it, whereas the 'close to balance or surplus' rule has lost its force under relentless reform.

We conclude by considering the more radical Keynesian proposals of Arestis, McCauley and Sawyer (2001) and Arestis and Sawyer (2003).

The rationale behind the Stability and Growth Pact

The SGP was formally adopted in 1997, but it largely represented a clarification and development of the EDP. The latter was one of three economic pillars introduced by the Maastricht Treaty of 1992, the others being the Mutual Surveillance Procedure, and the 'no-bailout' clause. The necessity for these measures reflected concern with the need to ensure stability of national fiscal policies, given that monetary policy was determined supranationally by the independent European Central Bank (ECB). The ECB has the single mandate of reducing inflation to between zero and 2 per cent per annum and there was a perceived danger that unconstrained national fiscal policies could conflict with this. The ECB was seen as central to EU macroeconomic policy to counter the ever-present danger that politicians would stimulate their national economies, especially prior to an election. This would have a temporary effect of reducing unemployment and increasing output, but would be detrimental to price stability and long-term growth. The SGP speeded up the procedures set up under the Maastricht Treaty and strengthened the guidelines, moving the policy-making process to a more rules-based framework. It also effectively gave more power to the ECOFIN (the European Council for Economic and Financial Affairs) and thereby was seen as making the whole process more political.

The Maastricht Treaty set out the conditions for entry to the third stage of EMU and the adoption of the Euro. Macroeconomic stability was emphasized as the over-riding concern in order that growth and employment strategies could be pursued within a non-inflationary environment. Fiscal rectitude became important because the Maastricht Treaty was drawn up during a period when structural budget deficits and government debt were large and rising in many countries, due to their weak economies and the pursuit of allegedly misjudged expansionary Keynesian employment policies. It was held that such budget deficits financed by the sale of government bonds allowed bank lending to rise and this fuelled inflation: the so-called fiscal theory of inflation (Woodford, 2001a).

The major rationale of the SGP, according to Eichengreen and Wyplosz (1998), is to prevent, or at least limit, the moral hazard problem facing national fiscal authorities.[4] Suppose a country runs a large deficit funded by issuing bonds and fails to satisfy its national intertemporal budget constraint.[5] With a common currency, this could not be satisfied by printing money (seigniorage), as might have been the case with a national currency. Suppose, further, that the value of the country's bonds starts to go into freefall. This would cause fears of a default, and could place a strain on the whole EU banking sector, to the extent that these bonds form part of the capital of other countries' banks. There could also be a more general contagion effect if the public begins to perceive the government bonds of other countries to be riskier. In order to circumvent this, the ECB could be compelled to buy up the bonds, thereby increasing inflation. It is true that the ECB is constrained by the 'no-bailout' rule. Nevertheless, it was argued that the pressures could be so great that the ECB would feel that it had no alternative but to circumvent the rule, such as by buying the bonds on the open market. But the adverse effects of this are borne by the EU as a whole, and not just the country concerned. Thus the SGP, along with the EDP, was seen as a necessary bolster to the no-bailout rule. Another argument was that the SGP would encourage policy co-ordination at the EU level. An inappropriate mix of a loose fiscal policy and a tight monetary policy might lead to high real interest rates and low investment together with low growth. But, as we shall see below, the evidence suggests that the numerical limits on the deficits may actually impede co-ordination as they lead to loss of flexibility. As we have noted, the EDP is the central plank of the fiscal framework of EMU. It is this that, *inter alia*, introduced the two fiscal reference values that countries must not exceed: namely, the ratio of the public debt to GDP of 60 per cent and a budget deficit ratio of 3 per cent. Equation (3.1), the government budget constraint, shows how the budget deficit and government debt are linked together:

$$b_t - b_{t-1} = -\left[\frac{\psi_t}{1 + \psi_t}\right] b_t + d_t \tag{3.1}$$

where b_t is the public debt to GDP ratio in period t, ψ_t is the growth of nominal GDP in period t and d_t is the budget deficit to GDP ratio in period t.

While some have argued that the two reference values of 3 per cent and 60 per cent were somewhat arbitrary, one view is that they were derived from the fact that 60 per cent was the average debt ratio of the EU members around the time of the Maastricht Treaty. For the debt to GDP ratio to stabilize, it is necessary that b_t equals b_{t-1} in equation (3.1). This equation shows that under these circumstances a value of 60 per cent for the debt ratio is compatible with growth of nominal GDP of 5 per cent per annum and a budget deficit to GDP ratio of approximately 3 per cent. Given the ECB's target rate of inflation of 2 per cent per annum or less, this implies that a real growth rate of 3 per cent per annum (optimistically taken to be the growth of EU productive potential at the time) would lead to a convergence of debt to GDP ratios at 60 per cent.[6] Alternatively, Buiter, Corsetti and Roubini (1993) suggested that it arose from the 'golden rule' that current expenditure should equal current revenue, and European Community (now EU) public investment equalled almost exactly 3 per cent of European Community GDP over the period 1974–91.

The reference value for the budget deficit was tightened in 2002 so that there was a medium-term budgetary position of the structural deficit being 'close to balance or in surplus'. The aim was that this would improve the chances that the 3 per cent deficit rule would not be exceeded in a typical recession.[7] If this were followed, it would lead to a steadily declining debt ratio to zero which is seen, so the argument goes, as necessary to maintain low interest rates and create an environment that encourages investment and growth (European Commission, 2002). But a zero debt is not necessarily optimal and the SGP takes no notice of the debt ratio a country may have at any particular time or the fact that growth rates and inflation rates differ greatly between countries. The 'New Member States',[8] for example, have higher growth and inflation rates (due partly to the Balassa–Samuelson effect) and a greater need for public infrastructure. Thus, there is a sound case that they should be allowed to run higher deficits.

The preventative element of the SGP would ensure regular surveillance of the budgetary position of Euro members through annual stability reports, and non-Euro members through annual convergence reports. In the event of slippage in the budgetary position, an early warning mechanism would be triggered.

The sanctions imposed as a result of an excessive deficit were to be both automatic and more stringent, injecting a dissuasive element into the SGP. Hence, the 3 per cent budget deficit limit can be exceeded if real GDP falls by 2 per cent or more (as an annual average or over four consecutive quarters), although a fall of between 0.75 and 2 per cent can be considered by the Council in mitigation. Once a member breaking the 3 per cent rule has been confirmed as having an excessive deficit, a non-interest bearing deposit comprising a fixed component of 0.2 per cent of GDP and a variable component of one-tenth of the difference between the actual deficit as a percentage of GDP and the 3 per cent limit must be lodged with the European Commission. If the deficit is not corrected within two years of an excessive deficit having been declared, the Council can turn the deposit into a fine with a maximum annual limit of 0.5 per cent of GDP. Thus to some extent the discretion of the European Commission and Council has been curtailed, if not eliminated. However, there is the important proviso that, as we have noted, there is nothing to prevent the Council from ignoring these considerations, as it did in the case of France and Germany in 2003. The failure of the ECOFIN to vote to proceed that year under the EDP against France and Germany with regard to their budgetary deficits was hardly a surprising result. As many commentators pointed out years ago, it would be politically difficult to discipline the largest countries in the EU. Indeed, as we noted in the introduction, this is seen by many as signalling effectively the end of the SGP in its current form.

One of the problems is that the SGP and the EDP are imposed, monitored and enforced supra-nationally, whereas the fiscal rules have to be implemented at the level of the individual state which leaves plenty of room for conflict. Any influence and constraints that the SGP imposes on national governments cannot produce co-ordination of fiscal policy at the EU level because the policy in one country cannot be constrained by economic conditions in another. The SGP can only have a constraining influence at the present time on the countries of Eastern Europe and the islands of Malta and Cyprus that joined the EU in 2004, and which have to meet the Maastricht convergence criteria before they can join EMU. Those already in Exchange Rate Mechanism II (ERMII) – Estonia, Lithuania and Slovenia – have the most constrained fiscal policies at the moment.

If the SGP is to all intents and purposes at an end, is this to be regretted? Were the rules too rigid and to what extent were they responsible for the EU's persistently high unemployment over the last decade or so? It is noticeable that the success or failure of EU macroeconomic policy is judged almost entirely on the inflation rate and the extent to which the debt ratio is brought down and whether or not the long-term budget deficit is close to zero or in surplus. There is no explicit mention of a target level of unemployment or rate of growth. The key question is whether meeting the monetary and fiscal targets, *per se*, is both necessary and sufficient for minimizing the unemployment rate and maximizing the growth of productive potential.

It is impossible to answer these questions and to judge the prospects for the SGP without first briefly considering the underlying economic theory behind EMU. In the case of the advocates of the SGP, this is the so-called 'new consensus' macroeconomic (NCM) model. It is assumed that the operation of market forces will automatically eventually correct any deviations from the equilibrium or non-accelerating inflation rate of unemployment (NAIRU). The NAIRU is determined by supply-side factors, notably by conditions in the labour market. It is unaffected by the level of effective demand and productive capacity and Say's law is implicitly assumed to hold. Nevertheless, in the NCM model, it is accepted that the NAIRU may differ from country to country, but this is purely due to 'real' or 'institutional' factors, including the degree of flexibility in the labour market. There is no trade-off between inflation and unemployment, except possibly in the very short run, and any attempt to run the economy at a level of unemployment below the NAIRU will only result in accelerating inflation (the time-inconsistency problem). Essentially, monetary policy through (implicit) inflation targeting has become the *sine qua non* of macroeconomic policy and is seen as a necessary and (nearly) sufficient condition for generating maximum economic growth. There is, in effect, only one policy instrument for controlling inflation, and that is the nominal interest rate. Inflation is seen to be determined by excessive demand and hence the interest rate is used as the sole instrument of demand management. However, this policy is impotent against cost-determined inflation and supply shocks. But the answer to this is that markets are seen as essentially competitive and the interest rate should not be used to counter inflation from supply shocks, as it will be ineffective. 'Core' inflation, which explicitly excludes those elements particularly prone to price shocks, such as food and energy, ideally should be targeted (Arestis, McCombie and Mosler, 2006). Monetary policy is too important to be left to the politicians and so the ECB is independent, run by 'experts' as it needs to be seen to be credible.

Any discretionary fiscal policy is seen to be destabilizing, due to the well-known problems of lags, and so on. It is therefore downgraded. In the long run, in the NCM model, any sustained budget deficit would merely lead to financial or real crowding out, and it is held almost as self-evident that government investment is less efficient than private investment. Typical of this view is Issing (2004, p. 10) who argues, 'In the past, in many countries increasing deficits and government debt went hand-in-hand with increasing taxes, sclerotic labour markets and sluggish activity.' Moreover, 'the deterioration of public finances was an important cause behind the poor economic performance of many EU countries since the early 1970s' (European Commission, 2000, p. 9).

According to the 'Ricardian' equivalence hypothesis which is embodied in the NCM model, with perfectly rational individuals, an increase in a budget deficit with its intergenerational effects will lead to no long-term increase of aggregate demand (Barro, 1974), although the assumptions for this to hold are implausibly restrictive. No distinction is made between recurrent and capital government expenditure in calculating the deficit. It also means that governments have to finance public investments out of current receipts and, because of this and interest payments, government expenditure will be lower than tax revenues. Nevertheless, the best fiscal policy is to run a zero deficit in the long run and let cyclical demand shocks be taken care of by automatic stabilizers, with an explicit avoidance of discretionary countercyclical fiscal policy. Estimates suggest that a temporary deficit of 3 per cent ought to be large enough.[9] As a rule of thumb, early evidence suggested that the deficit rises by 0.5 percentage points of GDP for every fall in output below its productive potential of 1 per cent (Eichengreen and Wyplosz, 1998). Thus, a moderately severe recession of 3 per cent would lead to an increase in the deficit of about 1.5 percentage points. If the country were running a structural (or cyclically-adjusted) deficit of 1.5 per cent of GDP, then this would be adequate. If, moreover, the country was at the recommended zero rate then there would be even more scope for the budget deficit to increase in a recession. However, subsequent evidence by Buti, Franco and Ongena (1997) suggests that the elasticity may be as high as 0.8 and 0.9 for the Netherlands and Spain, so that a downturn of 3 per cent would increase the budget deficit by 2.4 and 2.7 percentage points respectively.

Eichengreen and Wyplosz (1998) and Kiander and Virén (2000) have however, *inter alios*, cast doubts on whether the 3 per cent limit may be high enough.

There is substantial evidence that questions the assumptions of the NCM model and the policy conclusions of the NCM model are challenged by the Keynesians, who consequently take a more sceptical view of the SGP. For example, Arestis and Biefang-Frisancho Mariscal (2000) find evidence that the capital stock *does* affect the NAIRU. The results of León-Ledesma and Thirlwall (2002) further show that the natural rate of growth is affected by the growth of aggregate demand. According to the Keynesian view, it is also difficult to ascribe the current high rates of EU unemployment to the absence of a deregulated labour market. The latter needs to explain why France and Germany were able to record some of the fastest growth rates of total factor productivity and lowest unemployment rates in the Golden Age of 1950–73, with labour market institutions largely the same as today. Moreover, it is difficult to attribute today's high unemployment to real wage rigidity as real wages in both France and Germany (and in many of the other EU countries) have been growing slowly relative to productivity growth in many of the past few years (see Baker *et al.*, 2002; Janssen and Watt, 2006).

As far as monetary policy is concerned, Ghosh and Phillips (1998) use an extensive panel data for the IMF countries to show that there are significant non-linearities between inflation and growth. At low inflation rates of between 2 and 3 per cent per annum, inflation and growth are positively correlated, but otherwise they are negatively correlated although the relationship is complex. Consequently, it is not clear that a low and stable inflation rate is the *sine qua non* for sustainable growth. Angeriz and Arestis (2007) have pointed out that the inflation record of those countries which pursue inflation targeting and those that do not are not greatly different. On the question of the putative inefficiency of public investment, Aschauer (1989a, 1989b) suggests the opposite. He finds that public investment actually enhances the productivity of private investment, and the decline in US productivity growth in the early 1970s could have been due to the fall in public investment (see also Munnell, 1992).

The NCM model presupposes that a balanced budget over the cycle is consistent with full employment and discounts the whole of the insights from Keynes's *General Theory*. Moreover, in the evocative phrase of Arestis and Sawyer (2003, p. 36), the SGP requires that 'a one size [of straitjacket] fits all' and there is no reason to think that a balanced budget over the cycle is suitable for all countries. They argue that it imparts a deflationary bias: there is no framework to provide a sufficiently coordinated fiscal policy at the EU level and the EU budget *per se* is very small at 1.01 per cent of EU25 GDP in 2006.

As may be seen from Tables 3.1 and 3.2, the budget deficits and the cyclically-adjusted deficits showed marked variations both between countries and over time. As the ECB has to focus entirely on inflation while the national fiscal authorities have a much broader range of aims, there will be the inevitable potential for conflict.

In the end, the assessment of the best way forward, as we shall see below, depends largely on the view taken of the economic theory under-lying the working of the macroeconomy.

Budget deficits and government debt: the experience since 1992

Given the current problems of the SGP, it is useful to review the situation as it has developed since the Maastricht Treaty. In 1992, the EU15's average debt ratio was almost 60 per cent and this increased to nearly 74 per cent in 1998. However, since then the ratio has declined to 65.5 per cent (2005). Over the whole period, there is evidence that the smaller states have been more effective in controlling their debt ratios than the larger states. From 1998 to 2005, the countries who reduced their ratios by more than 20 percentage points were Belgium, Denmark, Finland, Ireland, Spain and Sweden, and those between 5 and 20 percentage points were Italy, the Netherlands and the UK. The countries that actu-ally increased their debt ratios were two of the largest, Germany (7.4 per-centage points) and France (6.6 percentage points), while the smaller, less developed countries of Greece (16.2 percentage points) and Portugal (7.4 percentage points) had large increases and Austria (1.6 percentage points) had a small increase.

Of course, these figures may be a little misleading because it is easier for a country to achieve a large absolute decline in its debt ratio if its initial value is large. However, using the percentage change does not significantly alter the picture. Thus the SGP has been effective in imposing fiscal dis-cipline on the smaller, but not the larger, states. Further reduction in the debt ratio is seen to be a pressing problem in view of the changing age structure of the population and the weakness of public pensions. But even the proponents of this view realize that the cost of major restruc-turing necessary to improve growth in some countries may lead to large temporary deficits. This may be hampered by the SGP, but the contra-argument is that if the SGP were not in force, other states would follow suit for different reasons and the fiscal framework of EMU would fall apart.

Table 3.1 Budget balance to GDP ratios, 1998–2007

	1998	1999	2000	2001	2002	2003	2004	2005	2006	2007
Austria	-2.4	-2.3	-1.6	-0.1	-0.7	-1.7	-1.2	-1.6	-1.9	-1.5
Belgium	-0.8	-0.5	0.0	0.6	-0.1	0.0	-0.1	-0.1	-0.4	-1.0
Denmark	0.0	1.4	2.3	1.2	0.2	-0.1	1.7	4.0	3.3	3.8
Finland	1.6	2.2	7.1	5.2	4.2	2.3	1.9	2.4	2.2	1.9
France	-2.6	-1.7	-1.5	-1.6	-3.2	-4.2	-3.7	-2.9	-2.9	-2.6
Germany	-2.2	-1.5	1.3	-2.8	-3.7	-4.0	-3.7	-3.3	-3.1	-2.2
Greece	-4.3	-3.5	-4.2	-4.9	-5.0	-5.9	-6.9	-4.4	-3.0	-3.3
Ireland	2.3	2.4	4.4	0.8	-0.4	0.2	1.6	1.0	-0.3	-0.5
Italy	-3.1	-1.8	-0.9	-3.1	-3.0	-3.5	-3.5	-4.3	-4.2	-4.6
Luxembourg	3.2	3.3	5.9	5.9	2.0	0.2	-1.1	-1.9	-1.7	-1.2
Netherlands	-0.6	0.7	2.3	-0.3	-2.0	-3.2	-2.1	-0.3	-0.5	-0.1
Portugal	-3.0	-2.7	-3.0	-4.3	-2.9	-3.0	-3.2	-6.0	-5.0	-4.5
Spain	-3.0	-0.9	-0.9	-0.5	-0.3	0.0	-0.2	1.1	1.1	0.9
Sweden	1.9	2.3	5.0	2.6	-0.5	-0.2	1.6	2.7	1.7	2.2
UK	0.1	1.0	3.8	0.7	-1.7	-3.3	-3.3	-3.2	-3.4	-3.2
Eurozone12	-2.3	-1.3	0.0	-1.8	-2.6	-3.1	-2.8	-2.4	-2.3	-2.1

Source: OECD, Economic Outlook (2006), vol. 79.

Table 3.2 Cyclically-adjusted budget balances to GDP ratios, 1998–2007

	1998	1999	2000	2001	2002	2003	2004	2005	2006	2007
Austria	-2.4	-2.8	-3.0	-0.7	-0.4	-0.7	-0.2	-0.5	-0.8	-0.5
Belgium	0.2	0.1	-0.4	0.2	0.3	1.0	0.8	1.0	0.2	-0.7
Denmark	-0.5	1.1	1.4	0.4	0.4	0.9	2.9	4.5	3.0	3.0
Finland	2.2	2.3	6.4	5.1	4.5	2.7	2.0	2.6	2.0	1.4
France	-1.4	-0.9	-1.5	-2.0	-3.2	-3.6	-2.9	-2.0	-2.1	-1.9
Germany	-1.6	-1.2	-1.9	-3.7	-3.9	-3.3	-2.7	-2.2	-2.1	-1.4
Greece	-3.3	-2.5	-3.7	-5.4	-5.1	-6.3	-7.6	-5.1	-3.5	-3.7
Ireland	2.1	1.3	2.7	-0.9	-1.9	-0.7	1.0	0.7	-0.5	-0.8
Italy	-2.3	-1.3	-2.6	-4.1	-3.7	-3.6	-3.4	-3.7	-3.6	-3.9
Luxembourg	3.8	3.0	4.5	5.2	2.4	1.4	0.0	-0.9	-0.9	-0.7
Netherlands	-1.2	-0.5	-0.1	-2.0	-2.6	-2.4	-0.6	1.3	0.9	0.6
Portugal	-3.2	-3.4	-4.6	-5.5	-3.3	-1.9	-2.0	-4.1	-2.8	-2.5
Spain	-2.1	-0.6	-1.3	-0.8	-0.3	0.3	0.3	1.3	1.3	1.1
Sweden	3.0	2.4	4.2	2.4	-0.4	0.5	2.1	2.9	1.2	1.2
UK	0.2	1.1	1.1	0.3	-1.8	-3.4	-3.6	-3.1	-3.1	-3.0
Eurozone12	-1.8	-1.1	-1.8	-2.5	-2.7	-2.6	-2.3	-1.6	-1.6	-1.5

Source: OECD, *Economic Outlook* (2006), *vol. 79.*

Table 3.3 Government debt to GDP ratios, 1998–2007

	1998	1999	2000	2001	2002	2003	2004	2005	2006	2007
Austria	67.4	69.8	69.5	70.3	71.6	69.5	68.9	69.0	69.2	69.6
Belgium	122.6	119.1	113.4	111.6	108.1	103.2	98.7	98.3	94.6	93.6
Denmark	69.0	63.2	56.3	53.8	54.5	52.8	49.4	43.0	39.6	45.2
Finland	60.8	55.5	52.9	50.9	50.4	52.0	52.5	48.6	48.8	55.2
France	69.9	66.2	65.0	63.6	66.7	71.0	73.4	76.5	75.9	78.1
Germany	62.2	60.8	59.9	59.3	61.6	64.6	67.9	69.6	71.3	72.4
Greece	109.8	113.7	128.1	131.5	130.5	127.3	128.3	126.0	123.4	104.2
Ireland	61.4	50.1	42.6	38.5	36.1	34.5	33.0	31.8	31.7	29.5
Italy	132.5	126.7	121.6	121.1	120.0	117.9	119.4	121.4	122.3	128.6
Luxembourg	6.2	5.6	5.3	6.5	6.5	6.3	6.6	6.0	9.0	11.4
Netherlands	79.5	71.1	63.7	59.5	60.3	61.9	62.3	62.8	62.6	65.2
Portugal	64.9	60.9	60.0	61.5	64.9	66.2	68.4	72.3	74.6	82.7
Spain	74.5	68.5	66.0	61.8	59.9	55.1	53.3	50.4	47.6	44.3
Sweden	81.3	71.3	63.9	62.9	59.8	59.3	58.9	59.3	54.4	59.9
UK	53.7	48.7	45.7	41.1	41.3	41.9	44.1	47.2	50.3	51.0
Eurozone12	76.0	72.3	70.7	70.0	70.0	69.0	69.3	69.4	69.3	69.6

Source: OECD, *Economic Outlook* (2006), vol. 79.

However, it does not seem that the blowouts in the deficits for France and Germany have been for restructuring reasons. One of the major problems facing France and Germany has been their poor economic performance in the real side of the economy. Although France experienced a slight decline in unemployment over the period 1998–2005 (from 11.5 per cent to 9.9 per cent), the figure is still high compared with the US and the UK (5.1 per cent and 4.7 per cent, respectively, in 2005). Germany saw its unemployment increase from 8.1 per cent in 1998 (having been 5.7 per cent in 1992) to 9.1 per cent in 2005. The important question is whether these high unemployment figures are due to supply-side rigidities or lack of aggregate demand. Likewise the growth rates of the two countries have been poor: the average growth of Germany over 1998–2005 has been 1.4 per cent per annum, compared with its average of 2.8 per cent over the period 1981–91. This, itself, is about half the rate achieved in the Golden Age of 1950–73. It is not surprising to find that the budget deficit first breached the 3 per cent rule in 2002 when growth had fallen to 0.1 per cent (it was −0.2 per annum the following year, notwithstanding the additional injection of demand). France performed better with an average rate of growth of 1.9 per cent from 1998 to 2005, but again it had experienced a slowdown to 1.3 per cent in 2002 and 0.9 per cent in 2003.

It is little wonder that, from about 2000, EMU fiscal policy has come under severe strain and this has led to a considerable weakening of the EDP under modifications to the SGP introduced in 2005. Of the 12 members of the Eurozone, four are currently above the 3 per cent budget deficit ceiling or close to it (see Table 3.1). In Germany the deficit in 2005 reached 3.3 per cent, the fourth consecutive year that the reference value had been exceeded. France dipped just below the reference value in 2005 after three consecutive years above it, but both countries are forecast to move comfortably below in 2007 despite the considerable social costs of achieving this adjustment. In the case of Italy, the deficit has been deteriorating since 2001 and the forecasts for 2006 and 2007 are not favourable. But perhaps the worst case of all is Greece, which joined the Euro late in 2002 and misled the European Commission on the size of its budget deficit. The Greek government claimed it had met the deficit criterion when it had consistently overshot the reference value by more than 2 percentage points between 2002 and 2004. Finally Portugal, which just met the criterion in 1998, exceeded it in 2000 and 2001, but managed to rein back the deficit after the EDP had been triggered. Despite a policy of deflation, however, the deficit rose to 6 per cent by 2005.

By late 2002, growing criticism of the SGP from economists and EU governments led the European Commission to strengthen the coordination of budgetary policy by introducing a lighter touch for countries exceeding the deficit that had debt levels below the 60 per cent reference value. Furthermore, 'close to balance or surplus' was to be assessed against cyclically-adjusted data. However, as Table 3.2 makes clear, even when the effect on fiscal balances of any economic downturn have been extracted, the fiscal deficits are still above the 3 per cent limit in Greece, Italy and Portugal, although France and Germany are both comfortably below it. Outside the Euro area, the UK exceeded the reference value for the deficit in 2003 and has continued to do so, even when an adjustment is made for the cyclical component, contravening the Broad Economic Policy Guidelines (BEPGs).[10]

Under the BEPGs the requirement to achieve a budgetary position close to balance or in surplus allows sufficient scope for the operation of automatic stabilizers without breaking the 3 per cent reference value (except in the most severe economic downturns). Additionally, by implying a surplus on the primary account the debt to GDP ratio would fall as nominal income grew.[11] Given that there was no long-run reference value for the debt to GDP ratio, some countries would inevitably move towards the extinction of their debt, while those that started with much higher levels would see little improvement. Table 3.3 shows the debt trajectories over the period 1998–2007 and these indicate that France and Germany will see debt rise above 60 per cent because of growing deficits, although the worst cases are still Greece, Italy and Portugal. However, Portugal's gross debt remains well below 100 per cent. By running large primary surpluses,[12] Belgium has seen its debt levels fall continuously since the start of EMU.

Debt levels must assume even greater importance in fiscal policy deliberations once Europe's ageing population is taken into account. Early retrenchment will become necessary, for example, in Italy and Greece. A recent European Commission report (2001), projecting the effect of ageing populations and associated health care costs on fiscal balances until 2050, estimates that public expenditure will rise by between 1 and 2 per cent of GDP. Figures of this magnitude obviously have serious consequences for budget deficits now and the sustainability of public finances in the longer run. In terms of the NCM model, a budgetary position close to balance or a small surplus thus becomes critical, and with it a corresponding primary surplus and declining debt and interest payments in order to eliminate the time inconsistency problem.

A conceptual framework for fiscal policy

Proponents of the NCM policy advocate inflation targeting by an independent central bank to maintain price stability in an economy (Taylor, 1999; Woodford, 2001b). Furthermore, the empirical evidence shows that the success of the policy depends upon the degree of transparency and accountability with which the central bank operates. For the UK, Geraats (2002) has developed a conceptual framework to describe the monetary policy process and this can be usefully adapted to analyse the operation of fiscal policy in the EU. According to this framework, therefore, fiscal policy must comprise the following elements:

1 Political transparency: there must be clear objectives and institutional arrangements that take into consideration the allocative and distributional aspects of fiscal policy, any inter- and intra-generational transfers that might occur and the role of political transparency in macroeconomic stabilization.
2 Economic transparency: uniformly generated and audited economic data must be used, and the same model should also be used for analysis and forecasting.
3 Procedural transparency: there must be a clear process for making decisions about the operation of fiscal policy in the short and longer term.
4 Policy transparency: fiscal policy decisions must be clearly explained, particularly the reason for any change in the policy, so that expectations are rational.
5 Operational transparency: following unexpected changes in economic conditions, the way in which policy changes should be clear and consistent with the overall objectives of fiscal policy established under (1) above.

How does the SGP perform? Under political transparency the objective has been fiscal policy co-ordination between the member states through ECOFIN, but the SGP has been demonstrated to take precedence insofar as the Council is prepared to exercise the EDP according to the rules. To the extent that the interpretation of the SGP and what constitutes an excessive deficit is now somewhat flexible and obscure, transparency has been lost. As regards economic transparency, the case of Greece shows data provided by EU member states is not drawn up in a uniform way – the purchase of military aircraft does not appear in the Greek accounts, for example – and there is no procedure to audit the fiscal criteria data supplied to the Commission. Recent events make it clear that procedural transparency no longer obtains and that the SGP, although notionally giving more weight to government debt since 2005, does not look ahead to accommodate the recognized shortfall in EU pensions within the existing fiscal-financial rules. Concerning policy transparency, decisions are far from clear and have become less so as changes and reforms have been introduced; indeed, the changes introduced have not been justified on the basis of any verifiable economic logic. With regard to the final point, although fiscal stabilizers to deal with cyclical factors were accommodated by 'the close to balance or surplus' rule (Artis and Buti, 2000), the way in which asymmetric shocks are dealt with on a country-by-country basis now make the overall objective of co-ordinated fiscal policies between member states all but impossible. In mitigation, the evidence seems to suggest that the overall fiscal policy stance has become more anti-cyclical than pro-cyclical since the introduction of the Euro. The current fiscal arrangements therefore comprehensively fail the transparency tests and this should be interpreted as undermining the contribution that the policy can make to national and EU-wide stability.

Proposals for reform

It is generally accepted that the SGP is not functioning adequately and there have been a number of proposals put forward in the light of this. It is difficult not to agree with Collignon (2004) that virtually every possible remedy has been proposed. These range from 'tinkering at the edges' to the need for a radical overhaul.[13] The former include reasonably straightforward changes to the institutions and processes, such as increasing information sharing as this seems to have declined since the formation of EMU (Bini Smaghi and Casini, 2000); having an independent fiscal body to monitor the sustainability of member states' finances (Begg *et al.*, 2002); and, more controversially, taking over the role of the ECOFIN in requiring countries to make adjustments when necessary (von Hagen, 2003).

Low debt countries should be subject to less restrictive limits on their borrowing. These include the suggestion that countries with a debt ratio of below 50 per cent should be exempt from any deficit targets, provided that they have explicit debt targets. Given that nations already set national fiscal rules, the focus of the Commission could be on how well these countries meet their targets. We have already noted that the present system does not differentiate between current and capital government expenditure. It has been suggested that net investment should be excluded from the budget balance (Blanchard and Giavazzi, 2003). It is net, rather than gross, investment, as depreciation is treated as current expenditure. The rationale for this is that as the investment will generate returns over future periods, the net present value should more than compensate for the initial cost of the investment. Alternatively, rules could be designed to allow countries with low debt ratios greater freedom to undertake public capital expenditure. This would require greater transparency to prevent governments engaging in 'creative accounting'.

More radical suggestions include the creation of tradable deficit permits, so that countries that wanted to run large deficits could buy permits from others to do so (Casella, 2001).

A Permanent Balance Rule for EMU countries

Given that a wholly new framework is required, the most impressive suggestion to date has come from Buiter and Grafe (2004) and their alternative PBR is examined below. The major differences between the SGP and the PBR can be demonstrated by analysing their respective theoretical underpinnings. We have already noted that over the medium term all members of the EU, whether they are in EMU or not, must satisfy the SGP rule that the budget deficit should be close to balance or in surplus.

Buiter and Grafe's PBR represents a tax-smoothing approach to fiscal policy as an alternative to the SGP's deficit and debt targets. Barro (1979), for example, shows that a constant tax to GDP ratio is the most efficient way of financing public expenditure. Under the PBR, therefore, the share of taxes in GDP remains constant and tax collection would be maintained at the lowest level consistent with government solvency whilst guaranteeing cyclical stabilization and the minimizing of distortionary taxes. Importantly, the government budget is adjusted for inflation and growth and would be in balance or surplus. Buiter and Grafe define the PBR as: 'that constant value of the share of taxes in GDP whose present discounted value (over an infinite future time horizon) equals the outstanding stock of public debt plus the present discounted value of actual government spending minus government capital income, all taken as shares of GDP' (2004, p. 76).

Buiter and Grafe recommend the PBR for five reasons. First, it ensures government solvency which the SGP does not; second, it is both countercyclical and tax smoothing; third, the effects of inflation and growth on debt are fully accounted for; fourth, no long-run debt target is specified, and, finally, by allowing for public sector investment, it is compatible with the golden rule for public finance. Furthermore, governments would be required to reveal their long-run plans for consumption, investment and welfare benefits. In addition, unlike the SGP, under the PBR a higher debt ratio accompanied by positive nominal growth would actually permit a larger budget deficit because the debt ratio would fall in line with a higher growth rate. The only reason the ratio of debt to GDP matters is because it has implications for the permanent tax rate, and Buiter and Grafe deal with this by introducing an Augmented Permanent Balance Rule (APBR) that incorporates a target for government debt.

Comparing further the SGP and the PBR, a number of points are worth mentioning. The PBR allows countries with higher growth rates to run larger deficits. The SGP constrains all countries by the amended guidelines and, while making lots of exceptions, does not link permissible deficits to growth. The APBR allows countries with deficient capital stock to borrow to raise investment, while the SGP does not. The PBR and APBR both take future pension shortfalls into account through lower debt in the current period to accommodate larger debt through extra pension payments later, whereas the SGP considers past and current gross debt and is not forward looking at all, leaving the pensions crisis to develop without any corrective plan in place. In considering the case of the countries that joined the EU in 2004, their government expenditure for capital and environmental projects will lead to expenditure above the permanent level. The PBR can accommodate this development, but the SGP cannot.

Finally, Buiter and Grafe provide simulations for both the PBR and the APBR with and without provision for future pension liabilities. Germany, for example, had deficits of 2.8 and 3.5 per cent of GDP in 2001 and 2002, whereas under the PBR it should have had a surplus of 0.7 and 0.1 per cent and under the APBR a surplus of 0.3 and a deficit of 0.4 per cent in the respective years. Spain had deficits of 0.1 and 0.1 per cent, but under the PBR these should have been surpluses of 1.2 per cent in each year or, under the APBR, surpluses of 0.3 and 0.2 per cent. And the UK, which had a deficit of 1.3 per cent in 2002, should, under the PBR, have had a deficit of 0.2 per cent, although the deficit could have increased to 1.7 per cent under the APBR. The Netherlands ran too large a deficit in 2002 and Italy did the same in both years under the APBR. In the case of the eastern enlargement countries, almost all of them ran deficits larger than would have been recommended under the PBR. The exceptions are Poland and Hungary in 2001 and Estonia in 2002. But when debt levels (which are low) are taken into account, under the APBR only Lithuania and the Slovak Republic ran excessive deficits, and so did Hungary and Latvia in 2002 if pensions are netted out of the APBR and the Czech Republic in 2001.

A radical Keynesian proposal for reform

The need for a radical reform along Keynesian lines has been articulated, most notably by Arestis and Sawyer (2003) who argue that the SGP has been misconceived from the start. They take the view that there is a need for high levels of aggregate demand to maintain high level of economic activity, and the causation runs predominantly from the former to the latter. Say's law does not hold. Governments can influence aggregate demand through their spending and revenue decisions and the level of public expenditure. The ECB, through pursuing an excessively tight monetary policy with high interest rates, can have an adverse impact on investment and unemployment, which, because of hysteresis, can persist for a long period.

The first change that they would make to the Pact is explicitly to introduce full employment as one of the aims of the SGP (which they would rename as the *Full Employment, Stability and Growth Pact*). They see as one of the real weaknesses of the Pact the separation of monetary policy conducted by the ECB and fiscal policy undertaken by national governments that are subject to the SGP constraints. There is a need for some EU institution that can undertake the necessary co-ordination. They point out that there are huge regional differences in unemployment and that wage bargaining and price determination differ between the EU countries. The 'one size fits all' monetary policy and SGP can each have damaging effects on the national and regional economies.

The money supply is endogenously determined and inflation is essentially the result of the wage bargaining process. Attempts to control inflation through interest rate policy by manipulating aggregate demand can actually have serious supply-side effects. It is purely coincidental that inflation and inflationary expectations have been low with inflation targeting. A major reason has been partly globalization and competition from low wage countries, such as China. Thus, inflation should be controlled through the development of institutional arrangements for centralized European wage bargaining rather than through the manipulation of the interest rate. Given the large disparities in regional unemployment, the enhanced functions of, say, the European Investment Bank are required to ensure that high rates of capital formation are appropriately fostered across the EU regions.

As far as fiscal policy is concerned, there is no reason why the private sector should necessarily generate sufficient demand for full employment and, in these circumstances, the government may well have to run a sustained budget deficit. As purely a matter of national income accounting identities, if the budget deficit is zero then private savings minus investment and the trade deficit (imports minus exports or borrowing from other countries) will have to equal zero.[14] There is no reason, *a priori*, why savings must equal investment. If there were excessive savings, then this would require the country concerned to run a trade surplus and export capital. But there is nothing to ensure that the trade deficits and surpluses between each of the EU member states, and all the states and the rest of the world, would be exactly sufficient to ensure that all the excess savings are mopped up. In fact, the EU is unlikely to be able to run a current account deficit indefinitely, given the sustained increase in foreign debt that this would entail. Indeed, in these circumstances, especially if trade flows are not sensitive to changes in relative prices as empirically seems to be the case, the EU as a whole or a particular EU country (notwithstanding that there is a common currency) could be balance-of-payments constrained (Thirlwall, 1980; McCombie and Thirlwall, 2004).

There is clearly a need for a common EU fiscal policy (the EU total budget is 1 per cent of EU25 GDP and clearly is too small to do the job on its own), but prior to that each country should be permitted to run its own budget deficit. But there are externalities, and so:

> there is then much to be said for co-ordinated fiscal policies, but in the context where that co-ordination is over the stances of active fiscal policies and where the policies themselves are aimed towards the achievement of high levels of economic activity. In view of the arguments of the European Commission (1997, the document known as the MacDougall Report, 1997), such co-ordination of fiscal and monetary policies become paramount.

> (Arestis, McCauley and Sawyer 2001)

It is only where the sub-national authority has little or no tax raising powers (such as the US states) that the danger of bailout becomes real and so fiscal constraints are needed. But in the EU, the national governments have a substantial tax base and can use this as a means to finance borrowing.

Their proposal is that (1) the ECB should be allowed to act as lender of last resort, (2) political constraints on national deficits should be removed and governments should be allowed to set deficits as they see fit, (3) the co-ordination of national fiscal policies should be strengthened, (4) action should be taken to ensure that the monetary authorities are not in pre-eminent positions to dominate EU macroeconomic policy, and (5) there should be an expanded role for an investment bank so that pubic investment can be used to reduce regional disparities.

It is here that we get to the heart of differences between the NCM model and Keynesian approaches. In the former, wage flexibility and a deregulated labour market will ensure that full employment is reached, given fiscal rectitude and low inflation, so agents do not face a signal extraction problem. Thus, the level of savings and investment will be brought into equality (or savings plus the current account deficit will equal investment) automatically at full employment. In this scenario, unemployment is essentially seen as arising from the real wage being too high and not due to lack of effective demand. In the latter, unemployment arises because of lack of aggregate demand for purely Keynesian reasons and the SGP acts to maintain this demand deficiency.

While the Arestis and Sawyer proposal may seem to be radical, that of Collignon (2004) is even more so. He sees that there is an inherent conflict between national and EU interests due to the failure of the principle of fiscal equivalence in the SGP. This, he argues, requires nothing short of an EU government to solve. It is possibly the least practical and most Utopian of all the suggestions that have been made.

Conclusions

We have seen that all parties agree that there is a need for reform of the SGP as a result of 'discipline fatigue' presented by Fatás and Mihov (2002). In the first three years of EMU they find that fiscal policy has been relaxed, and since then the deterioration has accelerated. But opinion differs as to whether this can be accomplished within the existing institutional framework, or whether a far more radical approach is needed. As far as the former is concerned, the Buiter and Grafe (2004) proposal is the most carefully thought-out recommendation. Arestis and Sawyer (2003) take a less sanguine Keynesian viewpoint and see the SGP as being instrumental in generating the high rates of unemployment in Europe and recommend a more radical change. The difference in policy prescription largely reflects differences in the way the macroeconomy is viewed as functioning; in other words, a clash of economic paradigms.

No doubt the EU will muddle through in much the same way as it has done for the last decade or so. Whether this will be sufficient only time will tell. We doubt it.

Notes

1   With apologies to Jeremy Bentham.
2   The suspension of the SGP did not result in the spreads on long-term interest rates widening, indicating that no significant default risk was anticipated (Wyplosz, 2006).
3   Those joining in 2004 were: Cyprus, the Czech Republic, Estonia, Hungary, Latvia, Lithuania, Malta, Poland, Slovenia and the Slovak Republic.

4   Eichengreen and Wyplosz (1998) consider a number of other reasons that
    have been put forward for the SGP and find them of little importance. For
    example, they discount the standard argument that excessive deficits will
    lead to high interest rates and these will spill over into higher interest rates
    in surrounding countries. They point out that European countries borrow on
    the global rather than the national markets.

5   There is the problem that it is not clear over what time period the budget
    constraint is meant to hold.

6   While the ECB has kept inflation close to this value for the first six years of the
    Euro, the value for real growth is unrealistic given that the EU's long-term
    growth rate has been estimated to be 2 per cent per annum (Benalal *et al.*, 2006).

7   The size of aggregate debt and potential economic growth imply that the target
    should be between a maximum deficit of 1 per cent and a small surplus. A
    higher level of debt means greater fiscal consolidation is required and higher
    growth means less need for fiscal consolidation. The medium-term budgetary
    target must be specified annually in the stability programmes of members of
    the Eurozone and convergence programmes by non-Eurozone countries
    (Denmark, Sweden and the UK).

8   See footnote 3.

9   This is based on the assumption that full employment will always be reached
    with a balanced budget.

10 The SGP applied to the Eurozone12 members in addition to the BEPGs
    whereas the UK, Denmark and Sweden simply had to meet the BEPGs.

11 This is predicated on the assumption that the real interest rate is greater than
    the growth of output.

12 The primary surplus is the budget deficit minus interest payments.

13 All these proposed reforms would have to take account of the effect of an
    ageing population on public finances.

14 This follows straightforwardly from the national accounting identity
    $(S - I) + (M - X) + (T - G) \equiv 0$, where S is private savings, I is private invest-
    ment, M is imports, X is exports and T and G are tax revenues and govern-
    ment expenditure. If the government runs a balanced budget, then
    $(S - I) = (X - M)$.

References

Angeriz, A. and Arestis P. (2007) 'Inflation Targeting: Assessing the Evidence', in
    J.S.L. McCombie and C. Rodriguez (eds), *Issues in Finance and Monetary Policy*
    (Basingstoke: Palgrave Macmillan).

Arestis, P. and Biefang-Frisancho Mariscal, I. (2000) 'Capital Shortages,
    Unemployment and Wages in the UK and Germany', *Scottish Journal of Political
    Economy*, 47, 487–503.

Arestis, P., McCauley, K. and Sawyer, M. (2001) 'An Alternative Stability Pact for
    the European Union', *Cambridge Journal of Economics*, 25, 113–30.

Arestis, P., McCombie, J.S.L. and Mosler, W. (2006) 'New Attitudes about
    Controlling Inflation', *Challenge*, forthcoming.

Arestis, P. and Sawyer, M. (2003) 'Macroeconomic Policies of the Economic and
    Monetary Union: Theoretical Underpinnings and Challenges', *International
    Papers in Political Economy*, 10, 1–50.

Artis, M. and Buti, M. (2000) 'Close to Balance or in Surplus: A Policy Maker's Guide to the Implementation of the Stability and Growth Pact', CEPR Discussion Paper No. 2515.

Aschauer, D. A. (1989a) 'Does Public Capital Crowd Out Private Capital?', *Journal of Monetary Economics*, 24, 171–88.

Aschauer, D. A. (1989b) 'Is Public Expenditure Productive?', *Journal of Monetary Economics*, 23, 177–200.

Baker, D., Glyn, A., Howell, D. and Schmitt, J. (2002) 'Labour Market Institutions: A Critical Assessment of the Cross-Country Evidence', Working Paper 2002-17, Center for Economic Policy Analysis, New School University, New York.

Barro R. J. (1974) 'Are Government Bonds Net Wealth?', *Journal of Political Economy*, 82, 1095–117.

Barro, R. J. (1979) 'On the Determination of the Public Debt', *Journal of Political Economy*, 87, 940–71.

Begg, D., Canova, E., De Grauwe, P., Fatás, A. and Lane, P. (2002) *Surviving the Slowdown: Monitoring the Central Bank, no. 4* (London: Centre for Economic and Policy Research).

Benalal, N., Hoyo, J. L., Pierluigi, B. and Vidalis, N. (2006) 'Output Growth Differentials Across the Euro Area Countries: Some Stylised Facts', Occasional Paper 45, European Central Bank.

Bini Smaghi, L. and Casini, C. (2000) 'Monetary and Fiscal Policy Co-operation: Institutions and Procedures in the EMU', *Journal of Common Market Studies*, 38, 375–91.

Blanchard, O. and Giavazzi, F. (2003) 'Improving the SGP through a Proper Accounting of Public Investment', CEPR Discussion Paper, No. 4220 (London: Centre for Economic and Policy Research).

Buiter, W., Corsetti, G. and Roubini, N. (1993) 'Excessive Deficits: Sense and Nonsense in the Treaty of Maastricht', *Economic Policy*, 16, 58–100.

Buiter, W. and Grafe, C. (2004) 'Patching up the Pact: Suggestions for Enhancing Fiscal Sustainability and Macroeconomic Stability in an Enlarged European Union', *Economics of Transition*, 12, 67–102.

Buti, M., Franco, D. and Ongena, H. (1997) *Budgetary Policies during Recessions: Retrospective Application of the 'Stability and Growth Pact' to the Post-War Period* (Brussels: European Commission).

Casella, A. (2001) 'Tradable Deficit Permits', in Brunila, A., Buti, M. and Franco, D., *The Stability and Growth Pact* (Basingstoke: Palgrave Macmillan).

Collignon, S. (2004) 'The End of the Stability and Growth Pact?', *International Economics and Economic Policy*, 1, 15–19.

de Haan, J., Berger, H. and Jansen, D-J. (2003) 'The End of the Stability and Growth Pact?', CESifo Working Paper, No. 1093 (Munich: University of Munich, Centre for Economic Studies).

Eichengreen, B. and Wyplosz, C. (1998) 'The Stability Pact: More than a Minor Nuisance?', *Economic Policy*, 13, 65–113.

European Commission (McDougall Report) (1997) *Report of the Study Group on the Role of Public Finance in European Integration Official Publications of the EC* (Brussels: European Commission).

European Commission (2000) 'Public Finances in EMU – 2000', *European Economy, Reports and Studies*, No. 3 (Brussels: European Commission).

European Commission (2001) *Budgetary Challenges Posed by Ageing Populations: The Impact on Public Spending of Pensions, Health and Long-Term Care for the Elderly and Possible Indicators of the Long-Term Sustainability of Public Finances* (Brussels: European Commission), EPC/ECOFIN/655/01-EN Final.

European Commission (2002) 'Stability and Growth Pact', Communication from the Commission to the Council and European Parliament. COM (2002) 668 final. Strengthening the Co-ordination of Budgetary Policies.

Fatás, A. and Mihov, I. (2002) 'On Constraining Fiscal Policy Discretion in the EMU', *Oxford Review of Economic Policy*, 19, 100–12.

Geraats, P. (2002) 'Central Bank Transparency', *Economic Journal*, 112, F532–F565.

Ghosh, A. and Phillips, S. (1998) 'Warning: Inflation May be Harmful to Your Growth', *IMF Staff Papers*, 45, 672–710.

Issing, O. (2004) 'The Stability and Growth Pact: The Appropriate Fiscal Framework for EMU', *International Economics and Economic Policy*, 1, 9–13.

Janssen, R. and Watt, A. (2006) 'Monetary Policy Tightening in a Fragile Recovery: Are the ECB's Concerns about Wage Formation Justified?', *European Economic and Employment Policy Brief*, No. 1 (Brussels: European Trade Union Institute for Research, Education and Health and Safety, or ETUI-REHS).

Kiander, J. and Virén, M. (2000) 'Do Automatic Stabilisers Take care of Asymmetric Shocks in the Euro Area', VATT, Discussion Paper, No. 234 (Finland: Government Institute for Economic Research).

León-Ledesma, M.A. and Thirlwall, A.P. (2002) 'The Endogeneity of the Natural Rate of Growth', *Cambridge Journal of Economics*, 26, 441–59.

McCombie, J.S.L. and Thirlwall, A.P. (2004) *Essays on Balance of Payments Constrained Growth* (London: Routledge).

Munnell, A.H. (1992) 'Policy Watch: Infrastructure Investment and Economic Growth', *Journal of Economic Perspectives*, 6, 189–98.

Prodi, R. (2002) Interview with *Le Monde*, 17 October.

Taylor, J. (ed.) (1999) *Monetary Policy Rules* (Chicago, IL: University of Chicago Press).

Thirlwall, A.P. (1980) 'Regional Problems are "Balance of Payments" Problems', *Regional Studies*, 14, 419–25.

Von Hagen, J. (2003) 'Fiscal Sustainability in EMU from the Stability and Growth Pact to a Sustainability Council for EMU' (mimeo).

Woodford, M. (2001a) 'Fiscal Requirements for Price Stability', National Bureau of Economic Research, Working Paper 8072 (Washington, DC: NBER).

Woodford, M. (2001b) 'The Taylor Rule and Optimal Monetary Policy', *American Economic Review*, 91, 232–7.

Wyplosz, C. (2006) 'European Monetary Union: The Dark Side of a Major Success', *Economic Policy*, 36, 207–61.

4
Does the Maastricht Treaty Matter for Real Convergence?

*Davide Furceri**

Introduction

In December 1991, the heads of the EU states signed a historic treaty in the Dutch city of Maastricht. It came into force in 1992 and represented the first significant step towards the creation of the European Monetary Union (EMU). The strategy in the Treaty, to move towards a creation of a monetary union in Europe, was based mainly on two principles: the necessity to guarantee a gradual process of convergence and the requirement to grant 'membership' only once the applicant countries had satisfied the convergence criteria[1] stated in the Treaty. These criteria, in fact, were established in order to achieve nominal convergence and to reduce the economic differences among the EU countries before joining the EMU in 1999.

Although it is possible to argue that the convergence criteria led to an effective convergence in terms of most of the target variables, it is not clear whether the Maastricht Treaty and the SGP (generally seen as the successor of the Maastricht Treaty) influenced the real convergence process in the EMU. In fact, although the SGP was designed to guarantee simultaneously price stability and sustained growth, the Maastricht criteria and the requirement of balanced budgets in the medium term have imposed constraints that could be unfavorable to growth.

Moreover, before they joined the EMU, the member countries could use domestic monetary and exchange rate policies to expand the economy and to achieve external (balance-of-payments) equilibrium. Since

* I would like to thank Sara Borelli, Georgios Karras and Paul Pieper for the useful comments. I, alone, am responsible for any errors.

1999, these countries have lost these two important economic policy instruments, but they continue to have to deal with the same 'problems' (targets).

Descriptive analysis of the statistical data suggests that in recent years, and especially since 2001, economic growth in the EMU has been very modest, especially when compared with that of the other developed countries.

The aim of this chapter is to evaluate whether the Maastricht Treaty and the SGP matter for the process of real convergence of the EMU member countries. To this end, we use the classical approach of convergence analysis to investigate whether the speed of convergence changed significantly after the Maastricht Treaty and the SGP came into force. Moreover, we provide an accounting decomposition of the convergence process at the aggregate level, estimating the speed of convergence for different production sectors.

The chapter is organized as follows. The next section describes the nominal convergence process regarding the variables related to the convergence criteria. This is followed by an analysis of the impact of the Treaty and of the SGP on the real convergence pattern in the EMU. Next, the convergence process is analysed for different production sectors. Finally, the last section presents the main conclusions.

The Maastricht Treaty and nominal convergence

Inflation rate

The reduction in, and convergence of, the inflation rate was a necessary target as the use of exchange-rate policy gradually disappeared. Moreover, before the birth of the EMU, the candidate countries were asked to provide evidence that they had the same preferences in terms of inflation. This, in fact, was necessary to avoid the danger that some countries could be disadvantaged by a higher *ex post* inflation rate.[2]

Figure 4.1 describes the pattern of the inflation rates from 1980 to 2003 for the EMU member countries. In the figure, we have plotted the difference between the countries inflation rates and the observed average inflation rate of the three best performing countries.

In 1980, the inflation rate was rather high for most of the EMU member countries. Moreover, before the convergence criteria were introduced, countries had already started to converge towards lower levels. However, the difference in the inflation rates remained remarkably high until 1992. After the Maastricht Treaty, the inflation rates started to converge notably, reflecting the strong commitment of the member countries to this target.

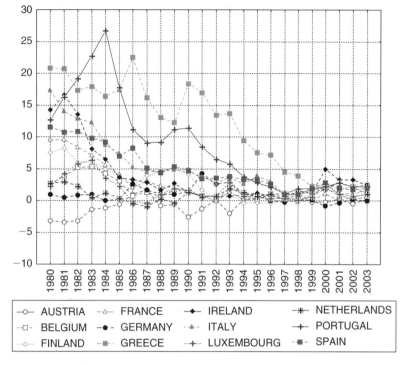

Figure 4.1   Inflation convergence
Sources: Eurostat.

Interest rates

Another important requirement of the Maastricht Treaty was the convergence of interest rates. The main justification for this is that excessively large differences in interest rates before entering the monetary union could lead to large capital gains and losses at the moment of joining the EMU.

Analysing Figure 4.2, we can see that in the 1980s the dispersion of the national interest rates was extremely high. Some countries had interest rates close to 20 per cent and others lower than 10 per cent. In the 1990s the interest rates started to converge considerably. This was mainly due to a greater co-ordination of national monetary policies. The target for interest rates was finally achieved in 1999 by eleven member countries, and by Greece in 2000.

Exchange rate stability

According to the Maastricht Treaty, the candidates had to maintain the fluctuation of their exchange rates within a set band during the two

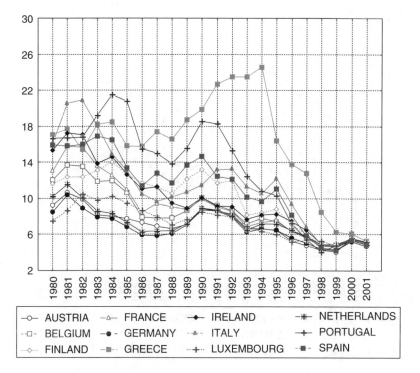

Figure 4.2 Interest rate convergence
Source: Eurostat.

years preceding their accession to the EMU. However, it is important to underline that though the width of these bands was ±2.25 per cent when the Treaty was signed, it became ±15 per cent after August 1993. Thus the stringency of this requirement was notably reduced after the Maastricht Treaty.

The necessity of having no devaluations for the two years preceding admission to the EMU was due to the fact that a country could take advantage of having a more favourable exchange rate (compared to the others) if it devalued its exchange rate immediately before entering the EMU. Thus, in 1999, all the EMU countries fixed their exchange rates irreversibly against the Euro.

National government debt

The main reason for requiring convergence in national government debt is that countries with a higher debt have an incentive to create unanticipated inflation. As a result, this would create problems for the countries with lower debts.

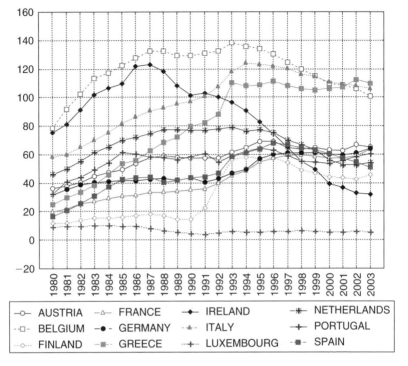

Figure 4.3   Debt convergence
Source: Eurostat.

Figure 4.3 shows that countries started to converge in terms of their debt level only several years after the Maastricht Treaty was signed. This was clearly due to the slow adjustment process intrinsic in changing the stock of debt. However, some candidate countries did not fulfil the debt target in 1999 (and still have not today). In fact, special derogations were allowed for Italy, Belgium and Greece. Thus, it does not seem that both the Maastricht Treaty and the SGP significantly affect the convergence of the government debt.

Budget deficit

Before the Maastricht Treaty, a large majority of countries had budgets that were not balanced and many had incurred large public budget deficits. After the imposition of the convergence criteria, government deficits started to decrease and converge dramatically until 1999 (Figure 4.4). However, after the birth of the EMU, the deficit to GDP ratios increased again. Moreover, it seems that the Maastricht Treaty and the SGP were

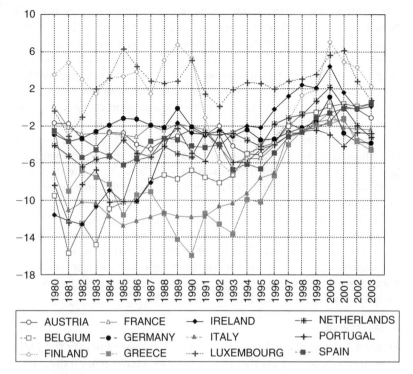

Figure 4.4 Deficit convergence
Source: Eurostat.

more effective and threatening for small and intermediate countries than for large countries. An example of this is the fact that the two largest countries participating in the Union (Germany and France) did not meet the budget deficit target in either 2003 or 2004.

To conclude, it seems that during the 1990s the member countries adopted policies to reduce their deficit, though not dramatically. However, after 1997 (until 2001) there was a period of substantial growth in Europe that certainly contributed to reducing the deficit to GDP ratio.

Real convergence in the European Monetary Union

One of the main rationales for the creation of the EMU is the expected positive effect on economic growth for the member countries. As stated in the Delors Report (1989), 'The creation of the single monetary zone will reinforce the potential advantage of the common market as it will reduce uncertainty related to trade within the Community, diminish the transaction costs, eliminate the variability of the exchange rates and reduce the sensitivity of the Community to external shocks.' Although output growth is expected to increase in the long run for all the member countries, the net impact of the creation of the monetary union, and of the criteria established to determine the accession of the candidate countries to the Eurozone on the *real* convergence process, is not clear.

We use the classical approach of convergence analysis to test whether the Maastricht Treaty and the SGP mattered for real convergence in the EMU. I call this the classical approach because it was the first methodology used in literature and because it uses standard econometric techniques.

OECD data on real GDP per capita in purchasing power parity (PPP) are used to investigate whether the EMU member countries show β and σ conditional convergence from 1980 to 2003. In particular, we will split the sample period to test whether the speed at which the member countries were converging (or diverging) changed significantly before and after the Maastricht Treaty and the Stability Pact.

σ-convergence

Figure 4.5 shows the pattern of the log of GDP per capita for the EMU member countries. We say that the data show σ-convergence if the standard deviation of *logGDP* of the member countries decreases over time. Analysing Figure 4.5, we can derive two main conclusions. First, the EMU (and, more generally, the EU15 countries) displayed an almost stable rate of growth, especially until 2001. An exception is Ireland which displayed remarkably high rates of growth after 1992. However, after 2001, the European aggregate rate of growth was very modest, especially if compared with the growth rates of the other developed countries. The second consideration is that the dispersion of the real per capita GDP levels in 1980 is very close to that in 2003. In particular, if we compare the standard deviations of *logGDP* at the beginning and at the end of period, we can see that in 2003 the income distribution among the EU members is more unequal (Table 4.1).

Furthermore, this process of relative divergence is more remarkable for the EMU than for the EU15 countries. In fact, the standard deviation of *logGDP* for the Euro-zone increased by 17 per cent from 1980 to 2003.

By splitting the entire period of analysis into two sub-periods, before and after the Maastricht Treaty, we can see that this increase is mainly registered during the first sub-period (1980–91). After the Maastricht

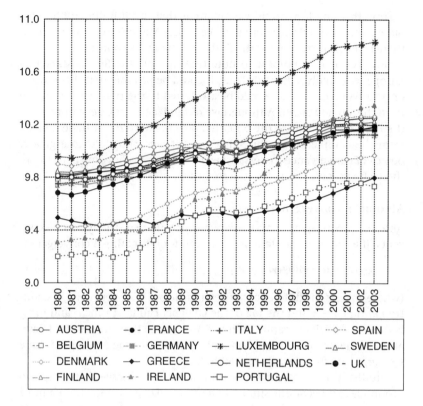

Figure 4.5   GDP per capita

Table 4.1   σ-convergence

Standard deviation of log(*GDP*)

	1980	1991	1992	1997	1998	2003
EMU	0.237	0.260	0.261	0.259	0.262	0.277
EU15	0.223	0.236	0.235	0.234	0.236	0.248

Treaty, in fact, the dispersion of the income per capita of the member countries remained relatively unchanged until 1997, and then it increased from 1997 to 2003. Moreover, this pattern is very similar for the EU15 countries.

From this simple analysis, we can argue that this it is difficult to attribute a period of relative convergence to the Maastricht Treaty; in fact, there is no clear pattern for the EMU and the EU15 countries.

However, it is important to note that in 1992 the Single Market in Europe was finally achieved. Thus, it could be possible that this process of (relative) convergence could be attributed to the trade effects arising from the Single Market. Although we recognize that the development of the EMU could increase the potential benefits in terms of trade derived from the completion of the Single Market, and thus lead to a greater degree of convergence (or less dispersion in terms of income per capita), these effects have not yet manifested themselves.

Absolute β-convergence

Absolute β-convergence and σ-convergence are two strictly related concepts. If we look at the standard equation for estimating β convergence:

$$g_{i,t,t+\tau} = \alpha - \beta \log(y_{i,t}) + \varepsilon_{i,t} \tag{4.1}$$

(where $g_{i,t,t+\tau}$ is the difference between the log of GDP per capita of country i at time $t + \tau$ and the log of the GDP per capita at time t, and $\ln y_{i,t}$ is the log of GDP per capita at time t) we can see that the standard deviation of the log of GDP per capita of country i at time t (σ_t) and at time $t + \tau(\sigma_{t+\tau})$ are functionally related to β.

Intuitively, if we consider two economies and observe that these two economies are becoming similar in terms of GDP per capita, then it must be the case that the relatively poorer economy is growing faster. Thus a necessary condition for the existence of the σ-convergence is the existence of absolute β-convergence.[3]

However, in the previous section we did not find σ-convergence among the EMU and the EU15 countries (actually, we found divergence), and thus we cannot directly infer the presence of absolute β-convergence among these countries. To try to establish this, we estimate the following model:

$$g_{i,t,t+\tau} = \alpha - (1 - e^{-\lambda\tau})\log(y_{i,t}) + \varepsilon_{i,t} \tag{4.2}$$

where β is $(1 - e^{-\lambda\tau})$. To find an estimate of λ (the speed of convergence, or divergence if negative) we use non-linear least squares and panel data estimation with fixed time effects. For the latter, we considered two subsamples for each period of analysis, where all the sub-periods are assumed to have the same λ. In this way, we double the number of observations in the sample and we allow for time effects.

Table 4.2 Absolute β-convergence (λ)

Non-linear least squares[a]

	1980–2003	1980–91	1992–2003	1992–97	1998–2003
EMU	0.325	0.026	0.010	0.009	−0.004
	(0.617)	(0.795)	(0.574)	(0.545)	(−0.249)
EU15	−0.030	0.005	0.011	0.009	−0.002
	(−0.245)	(0.408)	(0.701)	(0.616)	(−0.181)

[a]*t*-statistics in parentheses.

Table 4.3 Absolute β-convergence (λ)

Panel estimation (fixed effects)[a]

	1980–2003	1980–91	1992–2003	1992–97	1998–2003
EMU	0.006	0.001	0.003	0.005	−0.009
	(0.539)	(0.110)	(0.267)	(0.550)	(−1.066)
EU15	0.009	0.006	0.003	0.005	−0.008
	(0.761)	(0.465)	(0.328)	(0.551)	(−0.914)

[a]*t*-statistics in parenthesis, standard errors corrected for heteroscedasticity.

In Table 4.2 and Table 4.3 we report the results for λ for different time periods and for both the EMU and the EU15 countries. In particular, we considered five different periods of analysis: before and after the Maastricht Treaty (1980–91 compared with 1992–2003), before and after the Stability and Growth Pact (1992–97 compared with 1998–2003), and the overall period (1980–2003).

Analysing the results in Table 4.2 and Table 4.3 we can see that for the overall period there is no absolute convergence among the EMU and the EU15 countries. Moreover, it emerges that neither the Maastricht Treaty nor the SGP affect the convergence process. In fact, the speed of convergence for all the sub-periods considered in the analysis is not significantly different from zero.

Furthermore, it does seem that the results are robust to different methods of estimation.

Conditional convergence

The existence of β-convergence relies on the key and unrealistic assumption that countries differ only in their initial capital–labour ratio and GDP per capita. However, countries have different steady-state levels according to differences in such variables as technology, the saving rate, population growth, depreciation and so on. Thus, countries could converge *conditionally* to their steady-state level.

There are two main ways to test for the existence of conditional convergence. The first is to restrict the analysis to those countries that have the same steady-state levels. The second consists of taking into account variables that affect the steady-state level. Regarding the first method, results in the literature have shown that restricting the analysis to homogeneous countries such as the OECD, Europe, and some US states has shown the tendency for relatively poorer countries (regions) to grow faster than rich ones.[4] However, in our chapter, using countries that are generally considered homogeneous, we did not find any convergence for any period and sub-period from 1980 to 2003.

Regarding the second approach, several papers have tried to determine the effect of different variables that affect the level of GDP per capita and the growth rate.[5] In this chapter, we will focus on those variables that could significantly differ among the EMU and the EU15 countries during the last two decades. In particular, we considered: investment (as a share of GDP), population growth, inflation rate, trade openness (defined as the ratio of GDP to exports and imports) and government spending (as a share of GDP). Moreover, some of these variables – such as inflation, government spending and investment – are strictly related to the process of nominal convergence of the EMU (in terms of fulfilment of the Maastricht criteria). In this way, we can directly inspect whether these convergence criteria influenced real convergence as much as nominal convergence.

In Table 4.4 and Table 4.5, we present the results obtained estimating the following model for the EMU and the EU15 countries for the same periods and sub-periods as we analysed in the previous section:

$$g_{i,t,t+\tau} = \alpha - (1 - e^{-\lambda\tau})\log(y_{i,t}) + \gamma\Omega_{i,t} + \varepsilon_{i,t} \tag{4.3}$$

where $\Omega_{i,t}$ contains the variables listed above that hold constant the steady state of economy i.

We use non-linear least squares to estimate equation (4.3), given the fact that the results in previous section are robust to the two different methods of estimation (at least regarding the *t*-statistics) and that the non-linear method provides more accurate estimates for non-large samples.[6]

Inspection of Table 4.4 shows that there is no conditional convergence among the EMU countries for the overall period (1980–2003). The same results emerge if we consider the two sub-periods before and after the

Table 4.4 Conditional convergence

Non-linear least squares

EMU growth rates

	1980–2003	1980–91	1992–2003	1992–97	1998–2003
GDP$_t$	0.257	0.000	0.017	−0.308	−0.010
	(0.285)	(0.154)	(0.835)	(−26.119)*	(−0.712)
Investment	−0.000	0.020	−0.030	−0.252	0.011
	(−0.008)	(0.682)	(−0.894)	(−1.907)***	(0.290)
Trade	0.007	0.005	0.007	0.081	0.006
	(0.467)	(1.151)	(1.672)***	(4.008)*	(1.515)
Government	−0.012	−0.006	−0.003	−0.255	−0.006
	(−0.280)	(−0.212)	(−0.205)	(−3.016)*	(−0.714)
Population	0.008	−0.005	0.008	−0.065	−0.002
	(0.707)	(−1.093)	(1.489)	(−2.733)*	(−0.649)
Inflation	−0.005	−0.001	−0.005	−0.107	0.004
	(−0.399)	(−0.278)	(−0.585)	(−3.512)*	(0.389)

Notes: *t*-statistics in parentheses; *** significant at 10%, * significant at 1%.

Table 4.5 Conditional convergence

Non-linear least squares

EU15 growth rates

	1980–2003	1980–91	1992–2003	1992–97	1998–2003
GDP$_t$	−0.030	0.001	0.018	0.025	−0.007
	(−0.234)	(0.083)	(1.099)	(1.323)	(−0.592)
Investment	−0.082	0.013	−0.025	−0.042	0.017
	(0.166)	(0.628)	(−1.209)	(−1.713)***	(0.711)
Trade	0.009	0.005	0.006	0.008	0.006
	(1.043)	(1.480)	(1.906)***	(1.961)**	(1.896)***
Government	−0.019	−0.009	−0.006	−0.017	−0.003
	(−0.666)	(−0.468)	(−0.591)	(−1.005)	(−0.641)
Population	0.007	−0.004	0.008	−0.005	−0.003
	(0.675)	(−1.077)	(2.073)**	(−0.980)	(−1.326)
Inflation	−0.002	−0.001	−0.005	−0.011	0.007
	(−0.198)	(−0.330)	(−0.678)	(−1.719)***	(1.018)

Notes: *t*-statistics in parentheses; *** significant at 10%; ** significant at 5%.

Maastricht Treaty. Moreover, the only variable that seems to significantly explain GDP growth rate after the Maastricht Treaty is trade openness. However, this could be attributed to the achievement of the Single Market in the EU rather than to the Treaty itself. Nevertheless, analysing the two sub-periods, before and after the SGP, the EMU countries show conditional divergence from 1992 to 1997. Moreover, all the variables included in the analysis seem to significantly explain the variability of growth. Repeating the same analysis for the EU15 countries, we derived almost the same results. An exception is represented by the fact that, from 1992 to 1997, these countries do not show conditional divergence. Thus, it seems that the process of nominal convergence for the EMU countries has led to real conditional divergence among these countries, though this period is too short to attribute to these variables a significant role in explaining long-run growth.

Sectoral convergence

The previous section has shown that there is no convergence among the EMU and the EU15 countries for different periods. However, convergence could emerge at sectoral level.

To test for convergence at sectoral level we continue to use the classical approach, both because we think that it is still useful for our purpose,[7] and because we want to maintain comparability with the analysis conducted in the previous section.

In particular, we analyse empirical convergence of productivity levels for six sectors: (1) agriculture, hunting and forestry, fishing; (2) industry, including energy; (3) construction; (4) wholesale and retail trade, repairs, hotels and restaurants, transport; (5) financial intermediation, real estate, renting and business activities; and (6) other service activities.

We start our analysis by considering σ-convergence. Figure 4.6 describes the standard deviations of the productivity level for the six sectors listed above for the EMU countries from 1992 to 2003. Figure 4.6 shows clearly that there is a different behaviour for the sectors analysed. In fact, while some sectors such as agriculture, industry and construction do not converge (they actually diverge), other sectors show a considerable convergence (in the σ sense). In particular, this convergence process is remarkable in the financial and in the other service activities sectors.

Comparing these results with those presented in Table 4.1, it is possible to see that the relatively small divergence in the Euro area that has occurred since the Maastricht Treaty has been driven by the agriculture, industry and construction sectors. In fact, the dispersion of the productivity levels

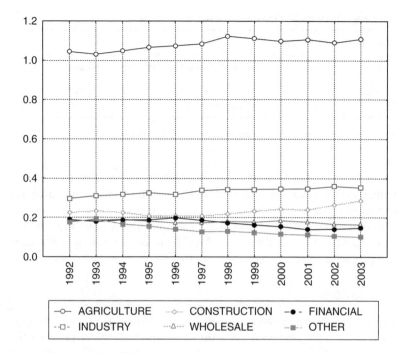

Figure 4.6   Sectoral sigma convergence

for these sectors not only diverges over time but is also much higher than that of the other sectors.

An important feature of this analysis is that it allows us to make direct inferences about β-convergence for those sectors converging in the σ sense. In particular, we should expect that the wholesale, financial services and the other service activities sectors converge. Conversely, we cannot immediately make any inferences about the other sectors.

In Table 4.6, we present the results for β-convergence for each of the six sectors. Analysing the results, we can observe that the sectors behave in a different way in terms of absolute convergence. In particular, while there is no convergence regarding the agriculture and industry sectors, there is absolute divergence in the construction sector, and there is absolute convergence in the other sectors. In particular, analysing the speed of convergence (or divergence), this is particularly high in the construction and in the other service activities sectors.

Again, comparing these results with those obtained in Table 4.3 it does seem that the absence of absolute convergence among the EMU

Table 4.6   Absolute β-convergence (EMU 1992–2003)

Non-linear least squares

	Agriculture	Industry	Construction	Wholesale	Financial	Other
Production	0.000	−0.001	−0.070	0.034	0.043	0.072
1992	(0.016)	(−0.075)	(−1.945)***	(1.667)***	(1.636)***	(3.013)*

Notes: *t*-statistics in parentheses; *** significant at 10%; * significant at 1%.

countries from 1992 to 2003 has been driven by the first two sectors (which do not converge) and by the construction sector which diverges considerably, offsetting the convergence of the other sectors. In fact, the period of investigation is short and it may take longer (much longer) for convergence to be shown in the data. Thus, only future investigation can provide a clear answer to this question.

Conclusions

The Maastricht Treaty represents the first significant step toward the creation of the EMU. Before it came into force in 1992, the economic situation in the EU countries preparing to join the EMU varied greatly and the Maastricht Treaty was designed to create economic convergence between these countries to ensure sustainability of a single currency.

However, although the economic literature and empirical evidence in this chapter suggest that the Maastricht Treaty and the convergence criteria led to an effective convergence for most of the target variables related to the parameters stated in the Treaty (such as inflation, interest rate, and budget deficits), it is not clear whether the Treaty influenced the real convergence process for the EMU (and more generally the EU) countries.

Using OECD data on real GDP per-capita for the period 1980–2003, the empirical evidence on absolute β and σ-convergence found in this chapter suggests that the Maastricht Treaty and the Stability and Growth Pact (introduced to guarantee simultaneously price stability and sustained growth) have not mattered for real convergence in the Euro area, at least until now. In fact, empirical evidence suggests that the dispersion of income among the EMU (and the EU) countries has continuously increased over time, and it seems that there is no particular difference between the sub-periods before and after the Maastricht Treaty, or the SGP.

The same conclusion is reached when considering conditional convergence. Regarding this analysis, in fact, the chapter did not find any convergence or divergence except for the period from 1992 to 1997. In this sub-period all the variables related to the convergence criteria and included in the analysis are highly significant, and there is conditional divergence for the EMU countries (but not for the EU15 countries). Thus, it seems that the Maastricht criteria (negatively) affected the convergence process, at least for the EMU countries.

The conclusions derived so far, however do not exclude the fact that at industry level there has been real convergence. In fact, considering six different production sectors, and analysing β and σ-convergence for the sectoral productivity levels, this chapter found empirical convergence for some of these sectors (namely, wholesale and retail trade, repairs, hotels and restaurants, transport; financial intermediation, real estate, renting and business activities; and other service activities), absence of convergence for other sectors (agriculture, hunting and forestry, fishing; and industry, including energy), and significant divergence for the construction sector.

Analysing together the results obtained for the aggregate levels of GDP per capita and for the sectoral levels of productivity, it does seem that the results obtained at aggregate level have been driven by those sectors with no convergence or absolute divergence. In fact, these sectors are also characterized by a considerably higher standard deviation of the log of the per capita GDP, implying a bigger weight in the sectoral aggregation.

To conclude, it is important to remark that the analysis presented in this chapter is only a first attempt to establish whether the Maastricht Treaty and its convergence criteria will matter for real convergence in the Euro area, and that only future investigation will provide a clear answer to this question. In fact, the period of investigation is too short and it may take much longer for convergence to be shown in the data.

Notes

1   The Maastricht criteria are: (1) price stability: inflation is not more than 1.5% higher than the average of the three lowest inflation rate of member states; (2) convergence of the interest rates: the long-term interest rate is not more than 2% higher than the average observed in the three low-inflation countries; (3) exchange rate stability: participation in the exchange rate mechanism for at least two years of the EMS without any devaluation; (4) government deficit not higher than 3% of the GDP; (5) government national debt not higher than 60% of the GDP.
2   One of the main advantages (or disadvantages) of joining a monetary union is the reduction (or the increase) in the inflation rate. Since the strategy of the common monetary policy is jointly designed, countries that had an *ex ante*

lower inflation rate would have been disadvantaged, while conversely countries with an *ex ante* higher inflation rate would have greater benefits.
3   This result has been informally pointed out by Sala-i-Martin (1996), and formally proved by Furceri (2005).
4   Dowrick and Duc-To Nguyen (1989); Sala-i-Martin (1996).
5   Ashauer (1989), Barro (1995), Bloom and Sachs (1998), Dasgupta (1995), De Long and Summers (1991), Eisner (1991), Frankel and Romer (1999), Karras (1993), Evans and Karras (1994a, 1994b, 1996), Mauro (1995), Munnel (1992), Przeworski and Limongi (1993).
6   Remember, in fact, that the proprieties of the Ordinary Least Squares (Maximum Likelihood) are only asymptotically invariant to monotonic transformations, and thus should be used only for very large samples.
7   Krugman (1987) pointed out that to test for empirical convergence of productivity at industry level, the new growth theory could be useful. In particular, he suggests that new growth theory models could best describe the manufacturing sector, while the other sectors can be better analysed by using the classical growth models.

References

Ashauer, D.A. (1989) 'Is Public Expenditure Productive?', *Journal of Monetary Economics*, 23, 51–63.
Barro, R.J. (1995) 'Inflation and Economic Growth', *Bank of England Quarterly Bulletin*, 35, 166–76.
Bloom, D. and Sachs, J. (1998) 'Geography, Demography and Economic Growth in Africa', *Brookings on Economic Activity*, 2, 207–95.
Dasgupta, P. (1995) 'The Population Problem: Theory and Evidence', *Journal of Economic Literature*, 33, 1879–902.
De Long, B. and Summers, L. (1998) 'Equipment Investments and Economic Growth', *The Quarterly Journal of Economics*, 106, 445–502.
Delors Report (1989), *Report on Economic and Monetary Union in the European Community* (Luxembourg: Office for Official Publications of the European Communities).
Dowrick, S. and Nguyen, D. T. (1989) 'OECD Comparative Economic Growth 1950–85: Catch-up and Convergence', *American Economic Review*, 79, 1010–30.
Eisner, R. (1991) 'Infrastructure and Regional Economic Performance', *Federal Reserve Bank of Boston*, Sept.–Oct., 47–58.
Evans, P. and Karras, G. (1994a) 'Are Government Activities Productive? Evidence from a Panel of U.S. States', *Review of Economics and Statistics*, LXXVI, 1–11.
Evans, P. and Karras, G. (1994b) 'Is Government Capital Productive? Evidence from a Panel of Seven Countries', *Journal of Macroeconomics*, 1, 271–80.
Evans, P. and Karras, G. (1996) 'Do Economies Converge? Evidence from a Panel of U.S. States', *Review of Economics and Statistics*, LXXVIII, 384–88.
Frankel, J.and Romer, D. (1999) 'Does Trade Cause Growth?', *American Economic Review*, 89, 379–99.
Furceri, D. (2005) 'β and σ-convergence. A Mathematical Relation of Causality', *Economics Letters*, 89, 212–15.

Karras, G. (1993) 'Money, Inflation, and Output Growth: Does the Aggregate Demand – Aggregate Supply Model Explain the International Evidence?', *Weltwirtschaftliches Archiv*, 29, 662–74.

Krugman, P. (1987) 'The Narrow Moving Band, the Dutch Disease, and the Competitive Consequences of Mrs. Thatcher', *Journal of Development Economics*, 27, 41–55.

Mauro, P. (1995) 'Corruption and Growth', *Quarterly Journal of Economics*, 110, 681–712.

Munnel, A. (1992) 'Why Has Productivity Growth Declined? Productivity and Public Investment', *New England Economic Review*, Jan.–Feb., 3–22.

Przeworski, A. and Limongi, F. (1993) 'Political Regimes and Economic Growth', *Journal of Economic Perspectives*, 7, 51–69.

Sala-i-Martin, X. (1996) 'The Classical Approach to Convergence Analysis', *Economic Journal*, 106, 1019–36.

5
Is the Transatlantic Gap in Economic Growth Really Widening?*

Jochen Hartwig

Introduction

Over the past ten years, public interest in international comparisons of the economic performance of nations seems to have risen significantly. Today, a plethora of international comparisons is performed by organizations such as the OECD, the International Monetary Fund (IMF), and the World Trade Organization (WTO). While these international organizations are not much devoted to compiling country rankings, other public and private research institutions are less hesitant. One regular outcome of such rankings – regardless of whether they refer to international competitiveness or macroeconomic performance – is that they assign high marks to the US economy. Table 5.1 illustrates that the US has outperformed 'Old Europe' with respect to economic growth since

Table 5.1 Difference in growth rates of real GDP between the USA and the European Union (EU15)

	GDP growth rate, USA	GDP growth rate, EU15	Difference (% p.a.)
1980–97	2.6% p.a.	2.3% p.a.	0.3
1997–2004	3.2% p.a.	2.3% p.a.	0.9

Source: OECD Quarterly National Accounts.

---

* An abbreviated and simplified version of this chapter is a section of my paper 'On Spurious Differences in Growth Performance and on the Misuse of National Accounts Data for Governance Purposes', which appeared in the *Review of International Political Economy* (2006), 13(4), 535–58.

the mid-1990s. National accounts data show this clearly. The gap between the growth rates of real GDP in the two continents has widened by more than half a percentage point (PP) per year.

Europeans will be familiar with the conclusions that have been drawn from such findings in national policy debates. Many feel that European countries could also grow faster if only their institutions were adequately designed. In several European countries public debate centres on the question of how to devise 'structural reforms' in order to make the set-up of the respective economy more similar to that of the United States. Tax-cutting, reducing the size of the public sector, and 'labour market reforms' (e.g., introducing a low-wage sector, curtailing the influence of trade unions, and increasing either weekly or lifetime working hours) are typical ingredients of this kind of debate, which is also promoted by the above-mentioned international organizations. Arguably, the main impact of national accounts on governance can be found here.

We shall not discuss the theoretical validity of the arguments behind the debate just sketched out. Of course, the better growth performance of the US could be due to reasons other than a more flexible labour market, and so on. Our point here will be that a careful analysis of the relevant national accounts data reveals part of the US lead in growth to be a statistical artefact. To show this, we will calculate the portion of the gap between transatlantic growth rates of real GDP that is solely attributable to differing methods to construct deflators on both sides of the Atlantic. As we will see, this portion is substantial.

The influence of differing deflation methods on the transatlantic growth gap

In 1996, a commission headed by Michael Boskin concluded that the US Consumer Price Index (CPI) was biased upwards by as much as 1.1 per cent per year (Boskin *et al.*, 1996). In the aftermath of the Boskin report, the US Bureau of Labor Statistics (BLS) implemented several reforms in the calculation of the CPI[1] which prompted the published rate of consumer price inflation to go down. Since, in the US, approximately 50 per cent of all expenditures that make up nominal GDP are deflated using CPI components, the elimination of an upward bias of 1.1 PP – if this was a proper estimate – would translate into an annual growth rate of real GDP that is higher by 0.6 PP (cf. Eldridge, 1999, p. 43).

The Boskin Commission identified four sources of upward bias in the CPI: the *lower level substitution bias*, the *upper level substitution bias*, the *outlet substitution bias*, and the *quality change and new product bias*.

In what follows, these biases – except for the outlet substitution bias because the BLS has done nothing to eliminate it – will be explained; and the impact of their removal (or moderation, respectively) by the BLS on the rate of inflation and on the growth rate of real GDP will be quantified.

No reproach is implicit in these calculations. We do not share the opinion of, say, Grant (2000) that the BLS is guilty of 'book-cooking'. However, one has to make clear that most European countries have not yet implemented reforms in the calculation of deflators comparable to those in the US, and probably never will. The main reason for differing calculation methods is a different 'philosophy' on what the CPI should measure. In most European countries – the Netherlands and Sweden being exceptions – the statistical offices maintain the 'traditional' view that a price index should track the price of a certain basket of goods. It should be a 'cost-of-goods index' (COGI). In the US, however, the majority of statisticians are convinced that the consumer price index should reflect the development of the cost of living ('cost-of-living index' or COLI: cf. Triplett, 2001a). In COGIs, the 'substitution biases' that occupy much space in the Boskin report are not at issue. Comparability is impaired by differing methods reflecting differing 'philosophies'; and it is unlikely that this problem will ever vanish.

It is tempting to ask: 'How much higher would growth in Europe be if the European statistical offices used US deflation methods?' However, the 'Balkanization' of European statistics (every national office has its own conventions: cf., for instance, Ahnert and Kenny, 2004), in conjunction with the fact that comparative research on European price indexes has just begun (cf. Wynne and Rodriguez-Palenzuela, 2004), renders this question intractable for the time being. Alternatively, we could ask: 'By how much have the reforms increased real growth in the US?' Or, in other words: 'By how much would economic growth in the US be lower if the same deflation methods that are common in Europe were used?' If we can answer this question, we will obtain growth rates for the US that can be compared with European rates on an equal footing.

Removal of the lower level substitution bias

Impact on the rate of consumer price inflation

A cost-of-living index must be able to display the fact that consumers tend to substitute goods and services that become relatively more expensive for others that become cheaper. If it cannot, then the index is 'upward-biased': that is, it indicates more inflation than there actually is.

Substitution can take place within the same basic spending category of the CPI, known as *entry level items* (ELIs: e.g., apples), or across ELIs. If a 'Granny Smith' becomes more expensive, you can substitute it for a 'Golden Delicious', or you choose a fruit from another ELI, such as bananas or citrus fruits. Substitution of an apple for an apple would be a lower level substitution; the switch from an apple to a banana is an example of an upper level substitution.

The Boskin Commission's estimate for the lower level substitution bias in the published rate of inflation was 0.25 PP per year. To remove it, the Commission proposed to change the way the mean price is calculated for each ELI.[2] Instead of the arithmetic mean, the geometric mean should be computed. It is possible to show that, if the elasticity of substitution between goods is one, then a geometric mean captures exactly the change in the cost of living (cf. Moulton and Smedley, 1995). Moreover, explorations at the BLS had shown that the use of the geometric mean leads to an attenuation in the rise of the index, and the difference was more or less arbitrarily interpreted as lower level substitution bias (cf. Triplett, 2001a, pp. 124–5, for a critique).

Since 1 January 1999, the BLS has used the geometric mean formula for the purpose of elementary aggregation for 61 per cent of the ELIs. The geometric mean under-states the rise in the cost of living when substitution between goods or services does not occur and thus would introduce a downward bias into the CPI in these cases. BLS doubts the existence of substitution behaviour for 39 per cent of the ELIs, including shelter, public utilities, and health care. The removal of the lower level substitution bias led to a 0.21 PP drop in the annual rate of inflation (cf. Eldridge, 1999, p. 41). This roughly conforms to the estimate of the Boskin Commission.

Impact on the growth rate of real GDP

Seskin (1999) reports the results of the 1999 revision of the US National Income and Product Accounts (NIPAs) in the official journal of the Bureau of Economic Analysis (BEA).[3] Every 3–4 years, the BEA carries out comprehensive revisions of the NIPAs; and it uses these opportunities to introduce new methodologies, definitions or improved data. The NIPA time series are then calculated backwards to 1959 (or even to 1929) on the new basis so that every comprehensive revision changes US economic history to some extent. A comparison of the old and new time series reveals the effects of the statistical revisions on levels and growth rates. The year 1999 marked the introduction of the geometric mean formula for the purpose of elementary aggregation not only to the CPI, but also to the NIPA deflators. As a result of the 1999 Comprehensive Revision, the growth rate of real GDP was revised upward by 0.4 PP per annum over the period 1995–98 (cf. Seskin, 1999, p. 17).

However, the switch to the geometric mean formula was not the only reform BEA introduced in 1999. Also, and equally important, the expenses of enterprises and the government for software were reclassified. These no longer counted as intermediate inputs, but as capital formation instead. Since intermediate inputs do not increase GDP, but investments do, this reclassification had an impact on the GDP level. And because software production is a business that currently grows faster than the overall economy, the growth rate of GDP was also pulled up for recent years. Jorgenson and Stiroh (2000, Table 2) estimate that software investment contributed 0.2 PP to real annual growth in the US over the period 1995–98. Taking this estimate for granted, we can attribute the other half of the 0.4 PP increase of the GDP growth rate after the 1999 comprehensive revision to the removal of the lower level substitution bias.

Here, we are only interested in the effects of statistical *differences* between the US and European countries on published growth rates. The reclassification of software (outside the household sector) as a capital good is not a statistical difference. In the meantime, all OECD countries (except Turkey) count the respective software expenses as investment. But note that not all countries follow the US practice of calculating their time series (so far) backwards after switching to new methodologies or definitions. If they don't, then their historical GDP levels and recent growth rates are biased downwards *vis-à-vis* the US.

Table 5.2 summarizes the estimates of the quantitative impact of US reforms to deflation methods on inflation and real growth along with the sources of these estimates and a 'period'. The 'period' is the year for

Table 5.2   Impact of statistical changes on the rates of inflation of real GDP growth in the US

Bias removed	Rate of inflation (% p.a.)	GDP growth (% p.a.)
Lower level substitution bias	−0.21[a]	0.20[b]
Upper level substitution bias	−0.15[c]	0.10[d]
Quality change and new product bias	−0.06[e]	0.19[f]–0.29[g]

Sources:
[a] Eldridge (1999), period: 1997;
[b] Seskin (1999), Jorgenson and Stiroh (2000), period: 1995–8;
[c] *Economic Report of the President* (1999), Hartwig and Schips (2005), period: since 2002;
[d] Landefeld, Parker and Triplett (1995), period: 1973–94;
[e] *Economic Report of the President* (1999), Hartwig and Schips (2005), period: 1983–2003;
[f] Vanhoudt and Onorante (2001), period: 1995–8;
[g] Schreyer (2001), period: 1987–93, based on a fixed 1987-weights Laspeyres volume index of final expenditure.

which the estimate has been calculated or the period of time over which annual growth rates have been averaged in the sources. As can be seen from the table, the periods do not always overlap; but that doesn't matter as long as we assume that the effect within the respective periods can be extrapolated. In other words, we assume that, were the reforms revoked, the respective growth rates would fall back to their *status quo ante*. This seems to be a plausible assumption for most cases except, perhaps, for the impact of the removal of the upper level substitution bias on real growth (see below).

Removal of the upper level substitution bias

Impact on the rate of consumer price inflation

The Boskin Commission also criticized the CPI for not taking account of the possibility that consumers reduced their cost of living by substituting goods and services across ELIs. The Commission estimated that this default would introduce an upward bias of 0.15 PP per year into the published rate of inflation.

The upper level substitution bias is in fact a problem of outdated weights. The CPI is a hierarchical construct, with the ELI being its basic category. A sequence of aggregations leads up to the top-level 'major groups', such as 'food and beverages', which are then aggregated to obtain the CPI. Each category in the CPI carries a certain weight; only the goods or services entering the ELIs (e.g., different apple brands) are not weighted.[4] But for all component indexes from ELI up, weights have to be chosen. It is straightforward to take the share of spending for, say, apples in all consumers' spending as the weight of the ELI 'apples' in the index.

Upper level substitution leads to a rearrangement of the consumer basket and to new de facto weights for the components. So, frequent updating of the index weights to adapt them to the new de facto weights would remove the upper level substitution bias. This is exactly what the Boskin Commission recommended.

Beginning with 2002, BLS updates CPI weights every second year based on the BLS Consumer Expenditure Survey. This should have eliminated the upper level substitution bias.[5]

A solution to the problem of outdated weights other than updating them every second year on the basis of the Consumer Expenditure Survey would be to calculate a 'chain index'. The Consumer Price Index – all urban consumers (CPI-U) is no chain index, but BLS also computes such a chain index, the C-CPI-U. In a chain index, weights are updated every period by taking either the share of spending for, say, apples in all consumers' spending in the (at any one time) previous period as a weight – as in the (chained) Laspeyres index – or the mean of this share over two adjacent periods (as in the Fisher and Törnqvist indexes).

Impact on the growth rate of real GDP

The weighting issue is also crucial for the calculation of real growth. GDP growth is a weighted average of the growth of the components of GDP (consumption, investment, etc.), with the growth of each component on its part being a weighted average of the growth of the various sub-components. The EU member states resolve the weighting problem by taking the share of each component in the previous year's nominal GDP as a weight (respectively the share of each sub-component in the previous year's nominal value of the higher level component). This is tantamount to calculating 'real' GDP as a chained Laspeyres volume index.[6] In the US, the BEA has chosen to use a chained Fisher index instead and has implemented chaining in the course of the 1995/96 comprehensive NIPA revision. While the choice of the index formula – Laspeyres or Fisher – has no substantial impact on international comparisons, the switch to chaining has. The former practice was to use the component shares in nominal GDP not in the previous year but in a fixed 'base year' as weights, and to update the base year every ten years. (The last base year in the US was 1987.) Obviously, the switch to chaining was a reform of deflation methods. It was a new choice of relative prices deemed relevant to weighting. Components that increased their share in total GDP recently get a higher weight. Here we can see the analogy to the removal of the upper level substitution bias in the CPI most clearly (cf. also Triplett, 1997, p. 22).

Under the old regime, when an economic sector or GDP component was growing fast, and with falling prices, its weight in the total economy was still evaluated at the old prices of the base year, which were still 'high'. So, overall growth was reported higher than under the new regime. BEA believes this to be the typical case and, therefore, maintains that the switch to chaining would *lower* 'real' GDP growth (cf. Landefeld and Grimm, 2000, pp. 18–19). On the other hand, there are also sectors and GDP components that exhibit fast growth at rising prices, such as the production/consumption of health care services. Here, chained volume indexes show higher growth rates than fixed-weight indexes. Which tendency is predominant is an empirical question. In the US, the switch to chaining – as opposed to fixed 1987 weights – *raised* the growth rate of 'real' GDP by 0.4 PP per annum on average over the period 1959–72 and by 0.1 PP per annum between 1973 and 1994 (cf. Landefeld, Parker and Triplett, 1995, p. 35).

There may be doubts, however, whether this value of 0.1 PP per annum can be extrapolated into the future. If the Landefeld and Grimm (2000) argument is valid, then chained indexes would exhibit higher growth rates than fixed-weight indexes before the base year of the fixed-weight index, and lower growth rates afterwards (cf. Scarpetta *et al.*, 2000, p. 86). Schreyer (2001, pp. 354–6) presents evidence for five countries that Fisher volume indexes of final expenditure that combine weights from the base year and the final year, grow slower than the corresponding fixed-weight Laspeyres indexes subsequent to base years. Kohli (2004, p. 349), on the other hand, shows that the chained Törnqvist volume index of 'real' GDP displays higher growth than the Laspeyres volume index with fixed 1960 weights for 20 OECD countries out of 26 over the period 1960–96. Since the US is included in both samples, the empirical evidence is mixed.

If we suspect that the removal of the upper level substitution bias has raised the growth rate of 'real' GDP in the US after 1996 by 0.1 PP or so, we have to concede that the transatlantic comparability of growth rates is thereby impaired since, when the first version of this chapter was written, half of the EU countries (including the 'heavy weight' Germany) had not yet changed their national accounts to a chained, annually re-based Laspeyres method (cf. Ahmad *et al.*, 2003, p. 28). On 30 November, 2005, Eurostat announced that most EU countries had completed the introduction of chaining into their national accounts.[7] At the same time, the so-called financial intermediation services indirectly measured (FISIM) have been reallocated between final and intermediate consumption, which is something that the US had introduced earlier (cf. Moulton and Seskin, 2003) but which did not have a great impact on the growth rate of 'real' GDP (cf. Hartwig, 2006, pp. 427–8). The effect of these two statistical changes on quarterly EU growth rates of 'real' GDP was negligible, ranging from −0.1 to +0.1 per cent in recent years. It appears that, overall, the annual GDP growth rate might be revised slightly upwards just as in the US. In this case, the transatlantic gap in economic growth shown above in Table 5.1 would be slightly reduced. We will have to wait for the OECD to take account of the latest statistical changes in Europe in their database to validate this hypothesis.

Removal of the quality change and new product bias

Impact on the rate of consumer price inflation

The Boskin Commission allocated more than half of the upward bias that it perceived to the quality change and new product bias. If this bias were completely eliminated, the annual rate of consumer price inflation would be 0.6 PP lower, according to the Commission.

Surprisingly, given the presumed magnitude of this bias, the Commission made no concrete proposals how to remove it. The BLS took action itself and in 1998 adopted the so-called hedonic method for deflating expenses for certain goods whose quality improves quickly. The hedonic method constitutes one of several means of coping with the fact that goods and services whose price development one wishes to measure may change in quality. The basic idea is to estimate the money value of certain product characteristics by performing statistical regression analysis on cross-section or pooled data. The hedonic method seems to lend itself especially well to computer hardware. On the one hand, hardware quality (computing speed) improves quickly, whereas the price for a desktop computer remains rather stable. This means that there is a large difference between a quality-adjusted and a non-quality-adjusted price index for computers. On the other hand, all relevant product characteristics, such as computing speed or memory size, can be easily quantified (which is necessary for the regression analysis). The estimated coefficients are used to deduce the estimated money value of quality improvements from price increases. If prices, say, for desktop computers remain stable, then the quality-adjusted price index will show a decline in desktop prices.

In the meantime, BLS uses the hedonic method not only for calculating quality-adjusted prices for desktop computers, but also for television sets, DVD players, video recorders, camcorders, audio systems, microwave ovens, refrigerators, freezers, washing machines, tumble-dryers, college textbooks, non-residential structures, photocopying equipment and possibly other goods; their number increases continuously. Some time ago, Moulton (2001) noted that 18 per cent of all expenditures that make up nominal US GDP were deflated using price indexes which use hedonic methods. It has to be emphasized, however, that the switch to hedonic techniques has not always lowered the rate of price increase; for some goods and services the latter has increased (cf. Hartwig and Schips, 2005, for further detail).

The removal of the upward 'quality change bias' in the CPI with the help of hedonic techniques had no great impact on the rate of consumer price inflation, though. This is revealed by a comparison of the CPI-U with another index published by BLS, the Consumer Price Index research series using current methods (CPI-U-RS). The CPI-U-RS answers the question of how the CPI would have developed if the current up-to-date definitions and methodologies had been in use in December 1977 (the starting point of that series). The CPI-U itself is never revised since it forms the basis for numerous indexed contracts and also for adaptations of social benefits. Hence, the difference between the two series is a measure of the impact of

CPI revisions on the index level. If a revision was introduced in, say, January 1999, we can evaluate its impact on the index level over the *earlier* period, December 1977–December 1998 because the CPI-U-RS calculates the revision backwards. We can then extrapolate the difference between the two series by assuming that, from January 1999 onwards, the revision lowers the CPI-U by the amount of the difference.

Stewart and Reed (1999) examine the magnitude of the difference between the CPI-U and the CPI-U-RS as well as its sources. Over the period 1978–98, the CPI-U-RS grew at an average annual rate of 4.28 per cent while growth in the CPI-U amounted to 4.73 per cent. But we cannot attribute the difference of 0.45 PP per year entirely to the CPI revisions in the aftermath of the Boskin report.[8] A closer inspection shows that the gap between the two series opens up in the late 1970s and early 1980s as a consequence of a revision to the calculation of homeowners' implicit rent in 1983. Before 1983, real estate prices and capital costs were used to approximate homeowners' implicit rent. These rose quickly at that time. Since 1983, BLS has taken rent equivalents as a proxy for homeowners' implicit rent. This revision was the only significant action taken to remove any upward bias from the CPI before 1998 (cf. Stewart and Reed, 1999, p. 31). So, if we concentrate on the period from 1983 onwards, we get an accurate estimate of the impact of the 'Boskin revisions'.

Carrying Stewart and Reed's analysis forward to December 2003 – the current end point of the CPI-U-RS – and focusing on the period December 1982–December 2003, we find that the CPI-U grows on average 0.25 PP faster than the CPI-U-RS each year (see Figure 5.1). Of these 0.25 PP we

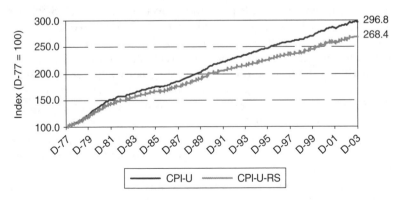

Figure 5.1 Consumer Price Index: all urban consumers (CPI-U) and Consumer Price Index research series using current methods (CPI-U-RS), 1977–2003
Source: BLS homepage (http://www.bls.gov).

know 0.21 PP to be attributable to the removal of the lower level substitution bias (see above). The upper level substitution bias and the new product bias are not removed from the CPI-U-RS because component weights are not updated in this index (cf. Stewart and Reed, 1999, p. 34). So we can conclude that the difference between 0.25 PP and 0.21 PP (i.e., 0.04 PP) must be attributable to the removal of 'quality change bias' through the use of hedonic techniques.[9] Objectively speaking, 0.04 per cent is not much; but such a low value is coherent with the fact that the lion's share of the removed upward bias falls on computers (cf. Landefeld and Grimm, 2000, p. 18) which, together with peripheral equipment, merely carry a weight of 0.23 per cent in the CPI (cf. BLS, 2004, Appendix 4).[10]

Impact on the growth rate of real GDP

Computers are not only consumption goods, but also – and more prominently – capital goods for business firms and the government. Hedonic quality adjustment of computer prices in the US goes beyond making adjustments to the Consumer Price Index. As early as 1985, the Bureau of Economic Analysis adopted the hedonic method for the quality adjustment of the GDP deflator, especially for the capital goods deflator that enters it (cf. Moulton, 2001, p. 4). According to BEA's hedonic deflator, computer prices dropped by 88 per cent between 1986 and 1998 (cf. Triplett, 2001b). This huge decline in quality-adjusted computer prices was fully reflected in the US GDP deflator and increased 'real' spending on computers – and thus 'real' GDP – since before the beginning of the genuine computer boom. Now it becomes clear why, in the comprehensive NIPA revision of 1999, the growth rate of 'real' GDP was revised upwards 'merely' by 0.4 PP per annum over the period 1995–98 (see above). The quality change bias had already been addressed since 1985; and the upper level substitution bias had been removed in 1995/96. Only the lower level substitution bias was eliminated in 1999.

The US was the first nation to introduce a quality-adjusted price index for computers into their national accounts. Seven EU15 countries still don't apply hedonic methods at all; in the other eight countries, the use of hedonics is very limited compared to the US (cf. Ahnert and Kenny 2004, pp. 27–8). So, to establish better comparability, we might ask how much lower US growth would have been if computer prices had not been quality-adjusted.

Vanhoudt and Onorante (2001) try to answer this question on the basis of the traditional 'growth accounting' approach.[11] They contrast the official deflator of the US fixed capital stock (which has quality-adjusted computer prices) with a 'traditional' deflator that does not adjust computer prices for quality changes. They construct the latter using data from Jorgenson and Stiroh (2000). Since computer prices are higher in the 'traditional' deflator, the whole index is pulled up *vis-à-vis* the official deflator. Hence the 'real' capital stock, which enters into the growth accounting, is smaller. Vanhoudt and Onorante calculate the growth rate of US labour productivity using their alternative estimates for the 'real' capital stock and compare it with the official data. They find that, without hedonic adjustment of computer prices, labour productivity growth was 0.19 PP per annum slower over the period 1995–98 than with such an adjustment made.[12] This means that the removal of the upward 'quality change bias' in the GDP deflator through hedonic quality adjustment of computer prices has also increased the growth rate of 'real' GDP by 0.19 PP per annum (cf. Table 5.2).

Schreyer (2001) adds communication technology as well as a range of electronic appliances to the picture. His approach is to calculate two different price indexes for each of the information and communication technology (ICT) products: one with full quality-adjustment of the prices in question, the other without any quality-adjustment at all. For each product, Schreyer takes 'lower bound' estimates of the difference in growth rates between the two indexes from the literature. These are 10 PP per annum for computers and 2 PP per annum for most other products. Schreyer deflates current ICT expenditures with both the adjusted and the unadjusted price indexes and then aggregates over all goods and services. He thus arrives at two different fixed-weight Laspeyres volume indexes for total final expenditure. With quality-adjusted ICT prices, 'real' US final expenditure grew 0.29 PP per annum faster over the period 1987–93. (Remember that this has to be interpreted as a lower bound, according to Schreyer.[13]) Admittedly, final expenditure differs from GDP, with the difference consisting in 'changes in stocks'. Schreyer (2001, p. 353) claims, however, that the bias generated by this omission is small.

There is an additional positive effect of hedonic deflation on 'real' growth which is not related to the capital or ICT deflators. Though probably important, this effect is absent from Table 5.2 since no evidence exists to date on how to quantify it.

This additional effect concerns the value added of the wholesale and retail trade sectors, which are among the largest service industries. Value added in each sector is measured by the value that it literally 'adds' to purchased 'intermediate inputs'. In wholesale and retail trade, value added is defined as the trade margin. To arrive at the 'real' value added, the trade margin has to be deflated. In the US, a sales price index is used to deflate the trade margin while in Europe it is normally assumed that trade services grow in proportion with the volume of sales. The BEA's use of a sales price index that is adjusted for quality change as a deflator in fact implies that the sale of higher quality goods requires more effort on the part of the trade industries than the sale of goods of lower quality. While this might be a defensible proposition in some cases,[14] transatlantic comparability of 'real' growth rates is nevertheless impaired since the European countries use different deflation methods. Ahmad *et al.* (2003, p. 25) show that the US trade deflator did not rise at all between 1993 and 2001 while, over the same period, the German deflator rose by 30 per cent, and the Italian by 20 per cent. Concomitantly, 'real' value added per employed person in the wholesale and retail industry has increased by 40 per cent in the US, but only by 10 per cent in Italy, and not at all in Germany.

As already stated, it is hard to distinguish 'really real' productivity increases in US trade from statistical artefacts; but the fact that the distribution industry – together with residential construction – has been considered as the motor of US expansion since the second half of the 1990s should keep us vigilant with regard to measurement biases in the context of international comparisons of economic performance. Further research is needed in this area.

Conclusion

Useful as they are as a source of information for anybody in charge of macroeconomic governance tasks, national accounts can also be misused in the context of governance. The current debate over economic growth that comes along with a plethora of international comparisons performed, rankings compiled, and far-reaching policy conclusions drawn can serve as an example of such a misuse. In many European countries, the seemingly better US growth performance has spawned plans for 'reforms' that would make the set-up of the respective economy more similar to that of the United States. Tax-cutting, reducing the size of the public sector, and 'labour market reforms' (e.g., introducing a low-wage sector, curtailing the influence of trade unions, and increasing either weekly or lifetime working hours) are typical ingredients of such reform plans, which are also promoted by international organizations such as the OECD, the IMF and the WTO. Yet a comparison of Tables 5.1 and 5.2 shows that the divergence in growth rates between the US and the EU since 1997 can basically be explained in terms of changes to deflation methods which were introduced in the US after 1997, but not – or only to a very limited extent – in Europe.[15] It is hoped that this finding will inform forthcoming reform debates.

Notes

1 BLS publishes several CPIs. We focus on the CPI-U, the Consumer Price Index – All Urban Consumers.
2 This procedure is called 'elementary aggregation'.
3 The BEA, not the BLS, is the statistical office in charge of the US National Accounts.
4 The average price for apples is calculated by applying the geometric mean formula to all apple sales (see above).
5 This conclusion is in accordance with the *Economic Report of the President* (1999, p. 94), which forecasts a reduction of 0.17 PP in the rate of inflation thanks to the regular updating of the CPI weights. These 0.17 PP can be split into 0.15 PP due to the removal of the upper level substitution bias and 0.02 PP as a result of the moderation of the new product bias, which is a part of the quality change and new product bias. Cf. Hartwig and Schips (2005) for greater detail.
6 Henceforth, 'real' is put in inverted commas in 'real GDP' to make clear that 'real' GDP is no bulk of things. 'Real' GDP is nothing but a volume index.
7 Cf. http://epp.eurostat.cec.eu.int/cache/ITY_PUBLIC/NATIONAL_ACCOUNTS_2005/EN/NATIONAL_ ACCOUNTS_2005-EN.PDF.
8 At the time Stewart and Reed wrote their contribution, two of these revisions were already in effect: (1) the hedonic quality adjustment of prices for computers and television sets, and (2) the switch to the calculation of geometric means in the process of elementary aggregation.
9 In Table 5.2, these 0.04 PP are added to our estimate of 0.02 PP for the new product bias (see above) to yield an estimate for the removal of the quality change and new product bias of 0.06 PP.
10 Our estimate for the removed quality change and new product bias of 0.06 PP deviates from the Boskin Commission's estimate of 0.6 PP by a factor of ten. This is explained by the fact that the Commission defined the upward quality change bias very broadly to include such things as the improved safety of air travel, higher freshness of fish thanks to better transport facilities or the reduction of pain thanks to minimally invasive surgery (cf. Gordon, 2000, p. 29). Obviously, hedonic techniques are incapable of removing these kinds of biases.
11 'Growth accounting' was introduced by Solow (1957).
12 Cf. Vanhoudt and Onorante (2001), p. 77. An error has sneaked into their Table 6, but the correct figures are in the text.
13 'Real' final expenditure grows faster based on the quality adjusted price index for ICT products in all five countries examined by Schreyer. The difference in growth rates ranges from 0.03 PP per annum (Canada) to 0.73 PP per annum (Japan); cf. Schreyer (2001, pp. 354–6).
14 Triplett and Bosworth (2004, p. 240) remain sceptical, though, with respect to computers. Electronic stores sell boxes filled with computers. The salesperson's effort is hardly associated with the technical characteristics of the machine inside the box. Even so, electronic stores have witnessed the strongest productivity growth of all outlet categories in the US between 1987 and 2001, according to official statistics (cf. Triplett and Bosworth, 2004, Table 8-1).

15 There are known issues other than differing deflation methods that impair transatlantic comparability of National Accounts data, such as the treatment of FISIM or the expenditures for military equipment in the respective accounts. But evidence exists that, although these differences bias the comparison of GDP levels, their influence on GDP growth rates is negligible (cf. Hartwig, 2006, for more detail).

References

Ahmad, N., Lequiller, F., Marianna, P., Pilat, D., Schreyer, P. and Wölfl, A. (2003) 'Comparing Labour Productivity Growth in the OECD Area: The Role of Measurement', OECD Directorate for Science, Technology and Industry Working Paper, No. 14/2003.

Ahnert, H. and Kenny, G. (2004) 'Quality Adjustment of European Price Statistics and the Role for Hedonics', European Central Bank Occasional Paper, No. 15.

BLS (2004) *BLS Handbook of Methods*, ch. 17, 'The Consumer Price Index' (http://www.bls.gov/opub/hom/pdf/homch17.pdf).

Boskin, M. J., Dulberger, E. R., Gordon, R. J., Griliches, Z. and Jorgenson, D. W. (1996) *Toward a More Accurate Measure of the Cost of Living: Final Report to the Senate Finance Committee* (Washington, DC).

Economic Report of the President (1999) (Washington, DC).

Eldridge, L. P. (1999) 'How Price Indexes Affect BLS Productivity Measures', *Monthly Labor Review*, February, 35–46.

Gordon, R. J. (2000) 'The Boskin Commission and its Aftermath', NBER Working Paper, No. 7759 (Washington, DC: NBER).

Grant, J. (2000) 'Bundesbank Mocks US IT Book-cooking', *Financial Times*, 4 September.

Hartwig, J. (2006) 'Messprobleme bei der Ermittlung des Wachstums der Arbeitsproduktivität – dargestellt anhand eines Vergleichs der Schweiz mit den USA', *Jahrbücher für Nationalökonomie und Statistik*, 226(4), 418–35.

Hartwig, J. and Schips, B. (2006) 'Verzerrungen von Konsumentenpreisindices und ihr Einfluss auf das "reale" Wirtschaftswachstum – Dargestellt am Beispiel der USA', *Jahrbücher für Nationalökonomie und Statistik*, 225(4), 394–412.

Hulten, C. R. (2003) 'Price Hedonics: A Critical Review', *Federal Reserve Bank of New York Economic Policy Review*, September, 5–15.

Jorgenson, D. W. and Stiroh, K. J. (2000) 'Raising the Speed Limit: U.S. Economic Growth in the Information Age', *Brookings Papers on Economic Activity*, No. 1, 125–211.

Kohli, U. (2004) 'An Implicit Törnqvist Index of Real GDP', *Journal of Productivity Analysis*, 21(3), 337–53.

Landefeld, J. S., Parker, R. P. and Triplett, J. E. (1995) 'Preview of the Comprehensive Revision of the National Income and Product Accounts: BEA's New Featured Measures of Output and Prices', *Survey of Current Business*, July, 31–8.

Landefeld, J. S. and Grimm, B. T. (2000) 'A Note on the Impact of Hedonics and Computers on Real GDP', *Survey of Current Business*, December, 17–22.

Moulton, B. R. (2001) 'The Expanding Role of Hedonic Methods in the Official Statistics of the United States', mimeo, Bureau of Economic Analysis.

Moulton, B. R. and Seskin, E. P. (2003) 'Preview of the 2003 Comprehensive Revision of the National Income and Product Accounts. Changes in Definitions and Classifications', *Survey of Current Business*, June, 17–34.

Moulton, B. R. and Smedley, K. E. (1995) 'A Comparison of Estimators for Elementary Aggregates in the CPI', Paper presented at the Western Economic Association International Conference, San Diego, CA, 7 July.

Scarpetta, S., Bassanini, A., Pilat, D. and Schreyer, P. (2000) 'Economic Growth in the OECD Area: Recent Trends at the Aggregate and Sectoral Level', OECD Economics Department Working Paper, No. 248.

Schreyer, P. (2001) 'Information and Communication Technology and the Measurement of Volume Output and Final Demand – A Five-Country Study', *Economics of Innovation and New Technology*, 10(5), 339–76.

Seskin, E. P. (1999) 'Improved Estimates of the National Income and Product Accounts for 1959–98: Results of the Comprehensive Revision', *Survey of Current Business*, December, 15–43.

Solow, R. M. (1957) 'Technical Change and the Aggregate Production Function', *Review of Economics and Statistics*, 39(3), 312–20.

Stewart, K. J. and Reed, S. B. (1999) 'Consumer Price Index Research Series Using Current Methods, 1978–98', *Monthly Labor Review*, June, 29–38.

Triplett, J. E. (1997) 'Measuring Consumption: The Post-1973 Slowdown and the Research Issues', *Federal Reserve Bank of St. Louis Review*, 97(3), 9–42.

Triplett, J. E. (2001a) 'Research on Price Index Measurement: Agendas for the Next Twenty Years. Comment', *Journal of Economic and Social Measurement*, 27 (3+4), 120–30.

Triplett, J. E. (2001b) 'Hedonic Indexes and Statistical Agencies, Revisited', *Journal of Economic and Social Measurement*, 27(3+4), 131–53.

Triplett, J. E. and Bosworth, B. P. (2004) *Productivity in the U.S. Services Sector. New Sources of Economic Growth* (Washington, DC: Brookings Institution Press).

Vanhoudt, P. and Onorante, L. (2001) 'Measuring Economic Growth and the New Economy', *EIB Papers*, 6(1), 63–83.

Wynne, M. A. and Rodriguez-Palenzuela, D. (2004) 'Measurement Bias in the HICP: What do We Know and What do We Need to Know?', *Journal of Economic Surveys*, 18(1), 79–112.

6
Company Tax Competition and Co-ordination in an Enlarged European Union

Margit Schratzenstaller

Introduction

The growing integration of national economies is intensifying competition between nation states for internationally mobile tax subjects and tax bases. Company taxes are one of the most obvious and debated competition instruments employed by national governments competing for mobile firms, investment and profits. Several recent empirical studies estimating tax reaction functions between countries (e.g., Devereux, Lockwood and Redoano, 2002; Devereux and Griffith, 2003) support the hypothesis of a strategic interaction of national tax policies. In the EU – as the largest integrated economic area worldwide in which formal barriers to the mobility of tax subjects and tax bases are increasingly removed – this phenomenon can be expected to become even more pronounced in the future.

On the eve of the eastern enlargement of the European Union in May 2004, the majority of the new member states (NMS) reduced their (in comparison to the old member states, OMS) on average already low corporate tax rates further. It is often anticipated that the still considerable tax rate differential between OMS and NMS will trigger further rounds of company tax rate reductions in all member countries of the enlarged EU, and will thus aggravate company tax competition between EU member states. Moreover, European Court of Justice (ECJ) litigation, the guiding principle of which is to rule out (tax-related) obstacles to the four fundamental freedoms laid down in the EC Treaty (free movement of goods, services, persons and capital), is putting pressure on national company tax provisions which may act as obstacles to capital mobility within the internal market; their enforced elimination should also intensify tax rate competition. Furthermore, the commitment of NMS to comply with the

Code of Conduct for Business Taxation (European Communities, 1998), which requires them to eliminate 'unfair' tax provisions after a transitional period, should increase the pressure on company tax rates to compensate for the loss of special tax incentives as a competition instrument.[1]

This chapter starts with some considerations on the future of company taxation that may be expected in the enlarged EU, which consists of two heterogeneous country clubs – OMS and NMS – characterized by considerable economic divergence. Then some empirical results of selected studies on the development of the company taxation in the EU are presented, and various problems associated with company taxation in the EU are discussed. The chapter concludes with a survey and a critical discussion of the proposals and current initiatives pursued at the EU level to harmonize or co-ordinate company taxes in the EU. Particular attention will be given to the question of whether the proposals and initiatives launched at the EU level are appropriate to deal with the problems associated with company taxation in the EU.

The future of company taxation in the European Union: the theory

In the tax competition literature of the 1990s, two hypotheses concerning the long-term effects of international company tax competition emerged. According to the 'race to the bottom' hypothesis (e.g., Frey, 1990; Sinn, 1997), capital and company taxes should vanish completely in the long run. Another hypothesis, which could be labelled the 'convergence' hypothesis (Pluemper and Schulze, 1999), qualified this rather extreme expectation by suggesting that capital and therefore also company taxes won't disappear completely, but should gradually converge downwards to similar levels. In fact, both hypotheses imply the long-run alignment of corporate taxes across countries at a zero (or at least at a low and decreasing) level and therefore the elimination of cross-country tax rate differentials.

The basic tax competition model

Both hypotheses rest on the so-called basic tax competition model,[2] which models tax competition for perfectly mobile capital between a large number of regions within one country (Zodrow and Mieszkowski, 1983, 1986). Ensuing theoretical work has applied the results of this model to country groups or unions formed by independent jurisdictions (i.e., individual countries). To finance public services, governments can levy two kinds of taxes in this model: a source-based property tax on capital income, and a lump-sum tax on immobile production factors (land or labour). Within this theoretical framework, interregional or international tax competition triggers a 'race to the bottom': governments cannot uphold the taxation of capital in the long run, but are forced to shift the tax burden onto the immobile factors. Under the assumption that governments may raise a limited amount of lump-sum taxes only, so that they also depend on capital tax revenues, capital tax rates will be set at inefficiently low levels to prevent tax-induced capital flight; as a consequence, public services will be under-provided (Janeba and Schjelderup, 2002). The more competing jurisdictions are involved, the higher is the downward pressure on tax rates and levels of public goods (Hoyt, 1991). Applied to the EU, the recent accession of ten new member states can be expected to aggravate tax competition and therefore cause a potential 'race to the bottom', or downward convergence of company tax rates in the EU.

Tax competition between heterogeneous country clubs

The basic tax competition model rests on rather strong assumptions. For the case of the enlarged EU, three extensions of this model, suggested by Zodrow (2001, 2003), are of particular relevance. Their starting point is that several of the model's assumptions do not hold for an economic area consisting of two heterogeneous country clubs, which may lead to different conclusions with regard to the working of company tax competition itself and its effects on the levels of company taxation and public service provision in the enlarged EU: these assumptions are, first, jurisdictions of different size; second, the existence of agglomeration economies; and third, imperfectly mobile capital.

Country size differentials

While the basic tax competition model assumes a large number of small jurisdictions of identical size, the reality in the enlarged EU is characterized by a twofold asymmetry with respect to the size of the competing jurisdictions. On the one hand, there is 'asymmetrical tax competition' between OMS and NMS, which in terms of GDP and population differ considerably in size;[3] on the other hand, the sizes of the individual countries forming the two country clubs differ markedly.

Large countries, in contrast to small ones, do not have to take the worldwide after-tax rate of capital as given, but may influence it via their corporate taxes. Therefore their tax bases are less elastic compared to small countries. A taxed-induced reduction of the domestic after-tax rate of return demands a compensatory increase of the before-tax rate of return, effected by capital outflows (Krogstrup, 2002), which are comparatively smaller in large countries as they impact on the international before-tax rate of return. This implies that large countries, as they face relatively smaller capital outflows induced by company taxation, can set higher tax rates. All other things being equal, this would also imply higher levels of public services in large countries.

In turn, tax rate reductions cause a larger inflow of capital in small countries, due to the prevailing higher tax base elasticity. From this perspective, under-cutting the large countries' company tax rate can be an effective instrument to attract internationally mobile capital. Interesting in this respect is recent empirical work done by Grubert (2001), who studies the development of effective tax rates on US foreign direct investment (FDI) for 60 countries between 1984 and 1992 and finds that effective tax rates in small, open and poor countries declined to a larger extent compared to developed countries. Moreover, Slemrod (2004) finds a positive correlation between tax ratios (corporate tax revenues as a percentage of GDP) and country size.

The different overall size of the two country clubs forming the enlarged EU may be one factor to prevent the complete elimination of the existing tax rate differential between OMS and NMS,[4] which simultaneously might result in lower levels of public services in NMS. However, these conclusions apply only to a limited degree, as the size differential between old and new member countries certainly is not large enough to correspond to the standard theoretical distinction of small and large countries. Country size differentials within the two country clubs seem of greater relevance. Thus existing company tax rate differentials within each country club may be even more stable than the tax rate differential between them.

Agglomeration economies

In the last few years, several papers have analysed tax competition from a different theoretical perspective building on the framework of new economic geography.[5] Incorporating trade costs in a model of international tax competition between countries of different size for FDI that captures agglomeration effects, Haufler and Wooton (1999) show that although the large country sets a higher tax rate, it wins the competition for FDI as agglomeration economies give firms an incentive to choose the larger market as location.

Baldwin and Krugman (2004) set out to explore the persistence of international corporate tax rate differentials in the EU. In their model, the competing jurisdictions differ with respect to the degree of industrialization. Simply put, there is a core country or group of countries where agglomeration economies exist, and a peripheral country or group of countries offering no (or lower) agglomeration rents. Agglomeration rents allow the core (within certain limits) to raise higher corporate taxes than the periphery without the risk of driving capital abroad, as capital becomes a quasi-fixed factor. Borck and Pflueger (2004) show that this result does not only hold for the extreme case in which industry completely concentrates in the core, but also for partial agglomeration.

Applied to the enlarged EU in which OMS can be viewed as the core and NMS as the periphery, this implies the sustainability of a certain tax rate differential as long as the peripheral accession countries have not caught up with the established member states (i.e., they cannot offer agglomeration rents of the same size to investors). Furthermore, agglomeration effects decrease the effectiveness of international company tax competition as they restrict the cross-border mobility of capital.

Imperfectly mobile capital

The effectiveness of international company tax competition requires the absence of political and technical restrictions for cross-border movements of capital and a certain responsiveness of investment to company taxes and cross-country tax rate differentials (Krogstrup, 2004). The first condition is fulfilled in the enlarged EU in which free movement of capital is given. Nevertheless it can be assumed that the mobility of FDI between OMS and NMS in effect is limited. One explanatory factor can be the agglomeration forces already mentioned. Location-specific rents, particularly rents created by public inputs provided for firms (e.g., Haufler, 1998), are another factor that allow the taxation of mobile investment and the sustainability of international company tax rate differentials and in turn limit the options of countries with no or lower location-specific rents to attract FDI by lowering tax rates. Given the prevailing deficits in public infrastructure in NMS and other locational advantages in OMS (as, for example, the qualification of the workforce), location-specific rents based on public services should be higher in OMS, allowing for higher company taxation.

Empirical evidence on the sensitivity of FDI towards tax rates and international tax rate differentials is mixed (Blonigen, 2005). The results obtained in empirical studies lie within a broad range (e.g., Hines, 1999; Desai and Hines, 2001; de Mooij and Ederveen, 2003; Gorter and Parikh, 2003; Mutti and Grubert, 2004). Several empirical studies show that FDI is rather insensitive to company taxation in transformation countries and in NMS, respectively (e.g., Carstensen and Toubal, 2004; Smarcynska Javorcik, 2004; Bénassy-Quéré and Lahrèche-Révil, 2005; Jakubiak and Markiewicz, 2005), whereas company taxation plays a more important role for the attraction of FDI in OMS.

Conclusions

To conclude, two hypotheses may be formulated with respect to the future development of company taxation in the enlarged EU: first, a 'convergence hypothesis' concerning the development of company taxation within the two country clubs, involving downward convergence of tax rates which may be expected within each of the two clubs consisting of rather homogeneous, integrated and geographically close countries offering similar agglomeration and location-specific rents, so that FDI should be rather mobile across countries; and second, a 'tax-rate-differential-persistence hypothesis' concerning the relationship between the two country clubs (i.e., substantial and sustained tax rate differentials between old and new member countries).

Is corporate tax an 'endangered species' within national tax systems? Some empirical evidence

Various company tax burden indicators have been proposed in the theoretical and empirical literature of the last two decades.[6] These tax burden indicators have been developed to tackle different questions. Backward-looking indicators use actual data on tax payments and tax bases to measure the actual tax burden firms carried in the past; they are measures for the distribution of the tax burden. Forward-looking indicators are based on current company tax codes and try to determine the tax burden which is to be expected for hypothetical investment projects or model firms. As they influence location and investment decisions, they are important in determining the allocative effects of company tax systems. Both groups of tax burden measures can be used for international tax burden comparisons and to gauge the development of the company tax burden in individual countries over time, respectively. Therefore they may also be applied as indicators for international tax differentials and the development of the quantitative importance of company taxation over time.

This section reviews some company tax burden indicators and their empirical results for OMS and NMS to identify current trends underlying the (long-term) development of company taxation in the EU. In particular, we will try to find empirical evidence for the two hypotheses stated above: the convergence hypothesis that expects tax rate differentials within homogenous country clubs to narrow, and the tax-rate-differential-persistence hypothesis that expects tax rate differentials between heterogenous countries to persist.

Statutory company tax rates

Statutory corporate tax rates are a simple and therefore popular and often-used measure of the corporate tax burden. They have been on the decline in OMS as well as in NMS (excluding Malta and Cyprus) since 1995 (see Tables 6.1 and 6.2). Between 1995 and 2005, the average company tax rate fell by 8.5 percentage points in the OMS and by 10.7 percentage points in the NMS, thus increasing the average tax rate differential between the two country clubs from 7.3 percentage points to 9.3 percentage points. The median tax rate went down by 6.3 percentage points in the OMS and by 8.5 percentage points in the NMS; accordingly, the tax rate differential between OMS and NMS measured by the median tax rate went up from 9.2 percentage points to 11.4 percentage points. Thus the development of statutory tax rates during the last decade clearly supports the tax-rate-differential-persistence hypothesis.

Judging by most of the dispersion measures applied (standard deviation, variation coefficient, and the spread between the highest and the lowest statutory tax rate), some convergence has taken place in both country clubs within the past ten years (see Table 6.1).

The gradual decline of statutory company tax rates in the EU is certainly a direct consequence of the intensifying tax competition between member states. Even if statutory tax rates are not a good proxy for the effective tax burden, as they do not take into account the rules to determine the tax base, they seem to have an important 'psychological' function insofar as they are perceived as signals concerning a country's general tax environment for international investors. Moreover, it has been shown empirically that governments also use statutory tax rates as instruments to compete for FDI (e.g., Devereux, Lockwood and Redoano, 2002).

Forward-looking effective tax rates

Forward-looking indicators measure the tax burden of a model investment project or of a model firm based on the existing tax code.[7] Unfortunately, with the exception of the Devereux, Griffith and Klemm (2002) study, there are no calculations on the long-term development of hypothetical effective tax rates in OMS. Furthermore, there are only a few comparable results for NMS.

EATR as well as effective marginal tax rates (EMTR) have declined over time in most of the OMS, although cross-country differences are still remarkable. According to the calculations done by the Institute for Fiscal Studies (IFS), EATR and EMTR went down in almost all countries between 1982 and 2005, so that the average as well as the median EATR and EMTR across OMS fell markedly (see Table 6.2). The various dispersion

Table 6.1 Statutory company tax rates[a] in the EU23, 1995–2006 (%)

	1995	1996	1997	1998	1999	2000	2001	2002	2003	2004	2005	2006	1995–2006
Belgium	40.2	40.2	40.2	40.2	40.2	40.2	40.2	40.2	34	34	34	34.0	−6.2
Denmark	34	34	34	34	32	32	30	30	30	30	28	28.0	−6.0
Finland	25	28	28	28	28	29	29	29	29	29	26	26.0	1.0
Germany	56.8	56.7	56.7	56	51.6	51.6	38.3	38.3	39.6	38.3	38.3	38.3	−18.5
Greece	40	40	40	40	40	40	37.5	35	35	35	32	29.0	−11.0
Spain	35	35	35	35	35	35	35	35	35	35	35	35.0	0.0
France	36.7	36.7	36.7	41.7	40	36.7	36.4	35.4	35.4	35.4	35	34.4	−2.3
Ireland	40	38	36	32	28	24	20	16	12.5	12.5	12.5	12.5	−27.5
Italy	52.2	53.2	53.2	41.3	41.3	41.3	40.3	40.3	38.3	37.3	37.3	37.3	−14.9
Luxembourg	40.9	40.9	39.3	37.5	37.5	37.5	37.5	30.4	30.4	30.4	30.4	29.6	−11.3
Netherlands	35	35	35	35	35	35	35	34.5	34.5	34.5	31.5	29.6	−5.4
Austria	34	34	34	34	34	34	34	34	34	34	25	25.0	−9.0
Portugal	39.6	39.6	39.6	37.4	37.4	35.2	35.2	33	33	27.5	27.5	27.5	−12.1
Sweden	28	28	28	28	28	28	28	28	28	28	28	28.0	0.0
UK	33	33	31	31	30	30	30	30	28	30	30	30.0	−3.0
Average	*38.0*	*38.2*	*37.8*	*36.7*	*35.9*	*35.3*	*33.8*	*32.6*	*31.9*	*31.4*	*30.0*	*29.6*	*−8.4*
Median	*36.7*	*36.7*	*36*	*35*	*35*	*35*	*35*	*34*	*34*	*34*	*30.4*	*29.6*	*−7.1*
Standard deviation	*7.9*	*7.6*	*7.7*	*6.7*	*6.2*	*6.4*	*5.3*	*5.8*	*6.1*	*6.0*	*6.1*	*6.0*	*−1.8*
Variation coefficient	*0.2*	*0.2*	*0.2*	*0.2*	*0.2*	*0.2*	*0.2*	*0.2*	*0.2*	*0.2*	*0.2*	*0.2*	*0.0*
Spread	*31.8*	*28.7*	*28.7*	*28*	*23.6*	*27.6*	*20.3*	*24.3*	*27.1*	*25.8*	*25.8*	*25.8*	*−6.0*

(*Continued*)

Table 6.1 Continued

	1995	1996	1997	1998	1999	2000	2001	2002	2003	2004	2005	2006	1995–2006
Czech Republic	41	39	39	35	35	31	31	31	31	28	26	24.0	−17.0
Estonia	26	26	26	26	26	26	26	26	26	26	24	23.0	−3.0
Latvia	25	25	25	25	25	25	25	22	19	15	15	15.0	−10.0
Lithuania	29	29	29	29	29	24	24	15	15	15	15	19.0	−10.0
Hungary	19.6	19.6	19.6	19.6	19.6	19.6	19.6	19.6	19.6	17.7	16	16.0	−3.6
Slovenia	25	25	25	25	25	25	25	25	25	25	25	25.0	0.0
Slovak Republic	40	40	40	40	40	29	29	25	25	19	19	19.0	−21.0
Poland	40	40	38	36	34	30	28	28	27	19	19	19.0	−21.0
Average	*30.7*	*30.5*	*30.2*	*29.5*	*29.2*	*26.2*	*26.0*	*24.0*	*23.5*	*20.6*	*19.9*	*20.0*	*−10.7*
Median	*27.5*	*27.5*	*27.5*	*27.5*	*27.5*	*25.5*	*25.5*	*25*	*25*	*19*	*19*	*19.0*	*−8.5*
Standard deviation	*7.8*	*7.5*	*7.2*	*6.5*	*6.2*	*3.5*	*3.3*	*4.7*	*4.8*	*4.7*	*4.3*	*3.4*	*−4.4*
Variation coefficient	*0.3*	*0.2*	*0.2*	*0.2*	*0.2*	*0.1*	*0.1*	*0.2*	*0.2*	*0.2*	*0.2*	*0.2*	*−0.1*
Spread	*21.4*	*20.4*	*20.4*	*20.4*	*20.4*	*11.4*	*11.4*	*16.0*	*16.0*	*13.0*	*11.0*	*10.0*	*−11.4*
Average EU23	*35.5*	*35.5*	*35.1*	*34.2*	*33.5*	*32.1*	*31.0*	*29.6*	*29.0*	*27.6*	*26.5*	*26.3*	*−9.2*
Difference between EU15/EU8	*7.3*	*7.7*	*7.6*	*7.2*	*6.7*	*9.1*	*7.8*	*8.6*	*8.4*	*10.8*	*10.1*	*9.6*	*2.3*

[a] Including surcharges and local business taxes.

Sources: Institute for Fiscal Studies; Office of Tax Policy Research, University of Michigan; national tax laws.

Table 6.2 Development of corporate tax burden indicators in the enlarged European Union (changes in percentage points)

	Statutory corporate income tax rate[a]	EATR (IFS)[b]	EMTR (IFS)[b]	EATR (ZEW)[c]	Corporate tax ratio (OECD)[d]	Implicit corporate income tax rate (European Comm.)[e]	ETR[f]
Belgium	−6.2	−9.0	−9.0	−10.8	+1.3	+4.2	0.0
Denmark	−6.0	–	–	−8.4	+1.8	−6.3	−2.0
Germany	−18.5	−16.0	−29.0	−11.9	−0.2	–	−7.0
Finland	+1.0	−24.0	−26.0	−20.6	+2.4	+2.5	−17.0
France	−2.3	−9.0	−6.0	−12.2	+0.6	+7.7	+5.0
Greece	−11.0	−15.0	−21.0	–	+2.4[f]	+5.0	+24.0
Ireland	−27.5	+6.0	+10.0	+0.6	+2.2	–	+2.0
Italy	−14.9	−5.0	+1.0	−8.0	+0.5	+4.3	2.0
Luxembourg	−11.3	–	–	−16.8	−0.4	–	–
Netherlands	−5.4	−13.0	−14.0	−11.9	+0.3	+1.2	−1.0
Austria	−9.0	−15.0	−5.0	−14.6	+0.9	+0.4	+6.0
Portugal	−12.1	−28.0	−33.0	–	–	+4.1	+8.0
Sweden	0.0	−24.0	−27.0	−32.5	+2.2	+3.8	−3.0
Spain	0.0	0.0	−2.0	–	+1.2	+13.0	+2.0
UK	−3.0	−2.0	+20.0	−16.1	−0.1	+4.3	−4.0
Average	*−8.4*	*−11.8*	*−10.0*	*−13.6*	*+1.1*	*+3.7*	*+1.1*
Median	*−7.1*	*−12.0*	*−11.0*	*−15.4*	*+1.6*	*+2.9*	*0.0*
Standard deviation	*−1.8*	*−6.7*	*−11.0*	*−4.2*	*−0.4*	*+1.0*	*−13.0*
Variation coefficient	*0.0*	*−0.1*	*−0.2*	*0.0*	*−0.4*	*+0.1*	*−4.0*
Spread	*−6.0*	*−23.0*	*−29.0*	*−19.2*	*−1.1*	*+1.9*	*−0.1*

(Continued)

Table 6.2 Continued

	Statutory corporate income tax rate[a]		EATR (IHS)[g]		EATR (ZEW)[c]		Corporate tax ratio (OECD)[d]		
Estonia	−3.0	–	–	–	0.0	–	–	–	–
Latvia	−10.0	–	–	–	−3.4	–	–	–	–
Lithuania	−10.0	–	–	–	−0.3	–	–	–	–
Poland	−21.0	–	+1.4	–	−6.7	–	−1.0[h]	–	–
Slovak Republic	−21.0	–	+1.7	–	−5.4	–	−1.2[i]	–	–
Slovenia	0.0	–	+1.4	–	0.0	–	–	–	–
Czech Republic	−17.0	–	−4.7	–	+0.5	–	−0.3	–	–
Hungary	−3.6	–	+3.1	–	−1.3	–	+0.3	–	–
Average	*−10.7*	–	*+0.6*	–	*−2.1*	–	*−0.6*	–	–
Median	*−8.5*	–	*+2.5*	–	*−3.8*	–	*−0.9*	–	–
Standard deviation	*−4.4*	–	*−2.4*	–	*+0.3*	–	*0.0*	–	–
Variation coefficient	*−0.1*	–	*−0.1*	–	*0.0*	–	*+0.1*	–	–
Spread	*−11.4*	–	*−6.5*	–	*+0.3*	–	*−0.2*	–	–

Notes:

[a] Including surcharges and local business taxes, 1995–2006.

[b] Institute for Fiscal Studies, 1982–2005.

[c] Zentrum für Europäische Wirtschaftsforschung; OMS: 1984–2003; NMS: 2003–4.

[d] OMS: 1980–2004; NMS: 1995–2004.

[e] 1995–2003.

[f] Gorter and de Mooij (2001), 1990–9.

[g] Institut für Höhere Studien, 2004–6.

[h] 1995–2003.

[i] 1998–2004.

measures indicate that effective marginal tax rates have been converging in the long run in OMS. The same conclusions can be drawn based on the EATR determined by the Zentrum für Europäische Wirtschaftsforschung (ZEW) for the period between 1982 and 2003 (see Table 6.2).[8]

Calculations done for the NMS do not yield unambiguous results. ZEW calculations for 2003 and 2004 show that EATR decreased in almost all NMS (with the exception of the Czech Republic) from 2003 to 2004; at the same time, all dispersion measures point to increasing divergence of EATR across NMS. EATR determined by the Institut für Höhere Studien (IHS)[9] for five NMS (excluding the Baltic States) increase for almost all NMS considered from 2004 to 2006 (again with the exception of the Czech Republic); at the same time, all dispersion measures indicate their convergence.

Backward-looking effective tax rates

Due to legal or illegal tax avoidance (i.e., tax evasion, but also profit shifting, etc.), discretionary administrative practices or the restrictive assumptions underlying forward-looking tax burden measures, actual tax payments may deviate markedly from 'hypothetical' ones (Gorter and de Mooij, 2001). The assumptions on which forward-looking measures rest also preclude the consideration of tax rules which in practice may reduce actual company tax payments considerably. For example, neither EMTR nor EATR account for the intertemporal tax treatment of losses (via loss carry-forward or carry-backward). Moreover, microeconomic effective tax rates on model investment projects or model firms are no adequate proxy for the total tax burden falling on the whole enterprise sector and thus for the quantitative importance of corporate taxes as a revenue source of public budgets. Therefore, several tax burden indicators based on actual tax payments by firms and thus capturing the factual tax burden are proposed in the literature.

It has been repeatedly pointed out by several authors arguing with company tax ratios (i.e., company tax revenues as a percentage of GDP or of total tax revenues) that falling statutory tax rates need not necessarily imply a shrinking importance of company taxes for public budgets (e.g., Quinn, 1997). The core of the argument is that many countries compensated for tax losses induced by tax rate reductions by introducing measures to broaden the tax base in many countries ('tax-cuts-cum-base-broadening': e.g., Devereux, Griffith and Klemm, 2002).

As Table 6.2 shows, company tax ratios have remained stable or even increased in most OMS during the last quarter of the century. In three of the four NMS considered, company tax ratios have fallen since the middle of the 1990s. At first sight, this finding may indicate that the reductions in statutory company tax rates obviously triggered by international tax competition did not result in the disappearance of company taxes, at least in OMS. A comparison of the company tax ratios in the two country clubs yields higher levels in OMS, which may suggest that overall the effective company tax burden in OMS is larger than that in NMS.

However, such conclusions would be too short-sighted. Company tax revenues are not only determined by tax legislation, but also by the development of taxable profits and the quantitative weight of incorporated firms. Therefore tax losses caused by company tax reforms could have been disguised by improved profits: more precisely, by an increased share of corporate profits in GDP (Genschel, 2001). In turn, it may be assumed that the decrease of company tax ratios which can be observed in a number of OMS countries after 2000 is the result of weak economic growth and consequently falling corporate profits rather than of intensified tax competition. Besides their sensitivity to the business cycle, company tax ratios are distorted by loss carry-forward and carry-backward. Finally, an upward trend in tax ratios may be caused by an increasing weight of the corporate sector in the whole enterprise sector (Weichenrieder, 2005).

Company tax ratios are not useful measures for cross-country tax burden comparisons, as their absolute levels depend on the structure of the enterprise sector. Countries with a high share of corporations tend to have higher company tax ratios. Thus company tax ratios cannot be used to help to answer the question of whether company taxation is converging or whether there are persisting international tax differentials.

Several studies try to determine factual tax rates by relating company tax payments to the tax base (i.e., company profits). Microeconomic backward-looking measures relate individual firms' tax payments to some measure of firm profit for a sample of firms to calculate effective average tax rates. Macroeconomic backward-looking tax burden indicators use data on total corporate tax payments and total corporate profits from national accounts.[10]

Gorter and de Mooij (2001), who use individual financial statements[11] and calculate average effective tax rates (ETR) for 14 OMS as the ratio of tax payments to pre-tax profits, derive mixed results for the period between 1990 and 1999. In a slight majority of the OMS included, ETR increased in the period considered; overall, the average ETR across countries increased slightly. At the same time, all dispersion measures show converging ETR.

Backward-looking microeconomic effective tax rates (as well as the forward-looking microeconomic effective tax rates presented above) are of limited use for assessing the development of the total tax burden falling on an economy's enterprise sector. Apart from the problem of choosing the tax base to which firms' tax payments should be related (i.e., whether gross operating profits or pre-tax profits are an adequate indicator of a firm's 'true' profits[12]), the results also depend on the sample of firms included and can vary significantly with firm size, number of branches and the taxes included. It must also be pointed out that ETR may be under-estimated due to the fact that the enumerator includes domestic company tax payments only, whereas the numerator includes also worldwide profits (which may be tax-exempt).

Macroeconomic tax burden indicators appear to be more useful in this respect, as they include tax payments and the profits of the whole enterprise sector of an economy. The European Commission (2005b) calculates (based on the methodology proposed by Mendoza *et al.*, 1994) so-called implicit tax rates (ITR) on corporate income (see Table 6.2) by relating taxes on the income or profits of corporations including holding gains[13] to corporate income.[14] Apart from Denmark, ITR on corporate income were higher in 2003 compared to 1995 in all 12 OMS studied; moreover, all dispersion measures indicate increasing divergence. This may partly be explained by tax-base broadening. However, the European Commission points out the sensitivity of ITR to cyclical fluctuations, so that it does not make much sense to compare yearly ITR on corporate income across countries and their development over time for individual countries, respectively.

Conclusions

The data presented show a rather clear picture for the OMS: company taxation seems to be eroded over time. Also in the NMS, for which there are less empirical data, the existing data suggest a decreasing quantitative importance of company taxes. This provides some empirical justification for the recently expressed fears that the ongoing tax competition in the EU may indeed erode company taxation in the long run. There is also some evidence for a quite large tax rate differential between old and new member states; although, due to the lack of long-term data, this does not provide strong evidence to support the tax-rate-differential-persistence hypothesis. Most of the available data also indicate the convergence of company tax rates within the two country clubs.

Problems of company taxation in the European Union

Company taxation in the EU faces several challenges and problems that are located at different levels and comprise different issues, which are addressed in this section.

Complexity of company tax systems in the EU

Despite a common trend of tax-cuts-cum-base-broadening that undoubtedly has influenced the development of national company tax systems in the past two decades, national company tax codes still show remarkable differences, as international comparisons witness (e.g., European Commission, 2001; Jacobs *et al.*, 2003, 2004). This divergence of national company tax codes is associated with considerable transaction, information and compliance costs for transnational companies as well as for tax administrations. Since 2004, companies that are active in the EU have had to deal with up to 25 different company tax systems. Moreover, as the above survey of different studies on the effective tax burden should have made clear, international tax burden comparisons are rather difficult to make and lead to different – and sometimes even contradictory – results, depending on the methodology applied. This carries the danger of transnational companies making wrong decisions on the location of investment or headquarters and therefore may cause inefficiencies in the allocation of investment.

Tax-related obstacles to capital mobility

Several tax provisions, which can be found in a number of national European company tax systems, may limit the international mobility of capital and of companies as well as the freedom of establishment in the EU: for example, the tax treatment of cross-border losses or exit taxation (European Commission, 2001, 2003). Up to now, there has been no co-ordinated and comprehensive approach to remove such tax provisions hampering free mobility of capital. Previous initiatives of the European Commission to tackle these issues have not been successful.[15] Currently the main and most influential actor in this field is the ECJ, which decides on a case-to-case basis (the European Commission calls this a 'peace-meal-approach': European Commission, 2003) about the admissibility of such provisions.

Profit shifting

The existing statutory tax rate differentials between EU member states induce profit-shifting by transnational companies, which cannot only be shown theoretically, but is also confirmed by empirical analyses.[16] Taxable profits are shifted from high- to low-tax countries via transfer pricing or thin capitalization to reduce transnational companies' overall company tax burdens, supported by the weak enforcement of transfer pricing rules which can be observed in a number of member states (Bartelsman and Beetsma, 2000). As a consequence, transnational companies use public inputs in high-tax countries, but escape taxation, which constitutes a violation of the pay-as-you-use principle, erodes the revenue potential of high-tax member countries, and puts tax rates in high-tax countries under pressure. As they are on average high-tax countries, OMS are hurt most by this phenomenon. Moreover, profit-shifting and the minimization of company tax burdens effects a decrease in total EU-wide corporate tax revenues.

Undesirable economic effects of company tax competition

Economists do not agree on the welfare effects of tax competition imposing constraints on national tax and budget policy.[17] One strand of the literature – inspired by the well-known contribution by Brennan and Buchanan (1980) – expects positive efficiency-enhancing effects, particularly with regard to the performance of the public sector. This literature emphasizes the potential of international tax competition to impose budgetary discipline on wasteful governments ('Leviathans'). From this perspective company tax competition (as well as competition within other taxes levied on mobile tax bases) is beneficial: it intensifies the pressure on EU countries to cut wasteful public expenditures and to reduce the overall size of the public sector to compensate for tax losses caused by tax competition. Company tax harmonization, on the other hand, would reduce welfare as it would represent a tax cartel with increased power to exploit taxpayers fiscally.

Another branch in the literature, however, conceiving governments as benevolent dictators rather than as revenue-maximizing Leviathans, focuses on the potentially harmful economic consequences of international company tax competition. One specific concern relates to the potential erosion of the national tax base which may endanger the long-term sustainability of public finances. From this perspective tax competition is harmful as it may necessitate welfare-reducing expenditure cuts (i.e., cause the under-provision of public inputs: Zodrow and Mieskowski, 1986). As, according to empirical studies (see, e.g., Bénassy-Quéré et al., 2006), firms do not base their locational decisions on the level of company taxes only, but also on the level of public inputs, a continued reduction of company tax rates could prove counterproductive.

At the same time, tax rate differentials between the two European country clubs appear to be quite substantial. This may be explained by barriers to the mobility of FDI allowing the OMS to keep up higher company tax rates; there is – as mentioned above – also empirical evidence that FDI are not very sensitive to taxation in the accession countries. From this perspective the lower company tax rates currently offered by

NMS may be viewed as a 'tax rebate' compensating for lower levels of public services and lower levels of location-specific rents, respectively. This is mirrored in a 'tax premium' that may be levied by OMS due to taxable agglomeration or location-specific rents.

However, the continuation of the current strategy pursued by the NMS to undercut OMS's company tax rates may not be successful, due to the existing mobility barriers between the two country clubs. Further reductions of company tax rates may force the NMS to cut public expenditures, which may prevent them from creating their own location-specific rents or entail the reduction of already existing ones. A slowdown of the economic catch-up process might be the result.

Proposed reforms for company taxation in the European Union

Unlike indirect taxes, the EC Treaty provides no direct legitimation and provisions for the alignment of direct taxes in the EU. According to Article 94 (combined with Art. 308) of the EC Treaty, national laws on direct taxation may be approximated if they impact on the functioning of the internal market (i.e., if they affect the four freedoms enshrined in the EC Treaty). Up to now, only a few measures to coordinate company taxation in the EU have been adopted,[18] as tax issues are one of the few policy areas in which unanimous decisions are required. As already mentioned, the most important player besides the European Commission seeking to advance company tax co-ordination in the EU with a view to removing existing tax obstacles to the freedom of establishment and the free movement of capital is the ECJ, whose judicature is increasingly shaping national (company) tax regimes.

The origin of the discussion about whether (and, if so, how) national company tax systems in the EU should be harmonized or co-ordinated dates back to the beginning of the 1960s. Initially, the debate focused on the potential need to harmonize regular company taxation schemes under the condition of increasingly integrating capital markets within the EU. The European Commission repeatedly launched harmonization initiatives that were supported by scientific experts pointing out the danger that liberalized and open capital markets may trigger unbridled tax competition with potentially harmful economic effects (Patterson, 2001): the Neumark Report (1962), the Tempel Report (1970), and the report presented by the Ruding Committee in 1992 (Ruding Committee, 1992). In 1975 the European Commission put forward a proposal for a directive on the harmonization of corporate tax systems. This proposal suggested the introduction of partial imputation systems and statutory corporate income tax rates between 45 per cent and 55 per cent, but was withdrawn in 1990, together with two proposals for cross-border loss compensation issued in 1984 and 1985. The latest suggestion concerning the harmonization of company systems was presented in 1992 by the Ruding Committee, which proposed a minimum statutory tax rate between 30 per cent and 40 per cent, as well as the harmonization of the tax base. However, no consensus on the necessity, extent and mode of harmonization of national corporate tax systems could be reached among member states.

After the rejection of these initiatives by the member states, there were hardly any discussions on a comprehensive harmonization of European company tax systems during the 1990s. Gradually the focus of the debate shifted away from a comprehensive harmonization approach. Instead, 'unfair' tax competition via preferential tax regimes (i.e., tax privileges which are exclusively granted to foreign investors and which often do not require real economic activities) has emerged as one of the primary concerns of the European Commission (European Commission, 1997). Meanwhile, member states have agreed on a Code of Conduct for Business Taxation aiming at the stand-still and the roll-back, respectively, of harmful tax practices, which is commonly regarded as quite successful. In addition, the main objective of the European Commission in the field of company taxation is to remove the tax obstacles to cross-border activities of transnational companies as already mentioned, and to introduce a harmonized consolidated corporate tax base (e.g., European Commission, 2001, 2003, 2005a). In its report of 2001 (European Commission, 2001), the European Commission lists four harmonization concepts for national company tax systems in the EU, two compulsory and two optional. Only one of these concepts, the European Corporate Income Tax (EUCIT), includes a common tax base as well as a single EU-wide corporate tax rate. The other three concepts – the Compulsory Harmonized Tax Base, the optional Home State Taxation (HST) and the optional Common Consolidated Base Taxation (CCBT) – exclusively aim at the harmonization of the tax base.

The theoretical and political discussion following the European Commission's report mainly concentrated on the two optional harmonization concepts (which go under the headline 'Optional European Consolidated Company Tax'), because compulsory harmonization concepts – especially if they include a harmonized corporate tax rate – do not seem to have a realistic chance of implementation, partly due to explicit resistance by a majority of member states and partly because the European

Commission itself does not support the introduction of a harmonized corporate tax rate. After the release of its 2001 report the European Commission explicitly stressed that the right to set statutory corporate tax rates should remain within member states' sovereignty. Therefore, the introduction of a common corporate income tax rate has almost completely vanished from the political agenda in the last few years. Most recently, however, the accession of the NMS inspired demands for the introduction of a minimum corporate tax rate by several old member states (most prominently France and Germany), who fear that the (on average) low tax rates offered by the NMS will put their own corporate tax rates under pressure and who accuse the NMS of 'tax dumping'.

Since the publication of the European Commission's report most progress has been achieved concerning the HST project. The European Commission, together with a group of tax experts, is working on the development of a pilot scheme to introduce HST for small and medium-sized enterprises for a limited period of time (5 years); due to the lack of support by a number of member states this is possibly for a group of eight member states only, using the option of 'enhanced co-operation' (European Commission, 2004). Also a Working Group including representatives of all member states was set up to discuss the option of introducing a uniform tax base and has been working within several sub-groups focusing on various details associated with the development of a common harmonized tax base for some time now.

The next section provides a short discussion of the harmonization proposals suggested by the European Commission in 2001, taking into account the problems associated with European company taxation in the context of an enlarged EU as sketched above.

Compulsory harmonization concepts

European Corporate Income Tax

The most far-reaching harmonization concept proposed in the European Commission's report is the EUCIT. It would provide for a single tax base and a single corporate income tax rate; the proceeds would go to the EU budget. As an alternative to this complete harmonization of corporate taxation, it is suggested that member states retain the right to set the corporate tax rate according to their own preferences and needs.

Taking into account the considerations presented above, a uniform corporate tax rate for all members of an economic union consisting of two heterogeneous country clubs does not appear as an optimal solution. A harmonized corporate tax rate would probably have to be set somewhere between the average tax rate of the two country clubs, therefore forcing a number of OMS to lower their corporate tax rate. These may end up with insufficiently low levels of public services (Zodrow, 2003). For many NMS, on the other hand, a harmonized tax rate would imply an increase of corporate tax rates, which would preclude the option to compensate for existing disadvantages with respect to many other locational factors by offering tax rebates to foreign investors (Wilson and Wildasin, 2004).

If member states were granted the right to set their own corporate tax rate, a race to the bottom and the complete elimination of the corporate income tax seems unavoidable: as corporate tax revenues would be used to finance the EU budget instead of national budgets, there would be an incentive for member states to act as free-riders.

Compulsory harmonized tax base

The second compulsory harmonization concept is the introduction of a compulsory harmonized tax base (i.e., the design of a common tax code which would replace national ones). The tax base of transnational companies would be determined on the basis of these common rules (including the consolidation of profits and losses). This tax base would be allocated to all member states in which transnational companies are active based on a formula which may contain wages, property and turnover ('formula apportionment'), and is taxed at the national tax rate which would be set freely by member states.

There are a number of advantages in this concept. The effective tax burden could be determined easily, and information costs as well as the danger of wrong decisions on the location of investment would be reduced markedly. Company taxation in the EU would be made transparent; and compliance costs for transnational companies and tax administrations could be reduced considerably (Mintz and Smart 2004). Transnational companies would also have the option of cross-border consolidation of profits and losses; thus one of the most criticized tax-related obstacles for the free movement of capital and the freedom of establishment would be eliminated.

The suggested formula apportionment of profits to the member states involved in the operations of transnational companies gains in appeal with eastern enlargement, particularly if the current diversity of statutory tax rates should persist in the future. Formula apportionment would reduce the options to shift taxable profits from high-tax to low-tax countries.[19] At the same time, formula apportionment is an appropriate way to realize the pay-as-you-use principle. Taxable profits are allocated to those jurisdictions in which they are earned by transnational companies using public services, which would benefit both OMS and NMS.

However, some caveats must be pointed out. The transparency of effect-ive tax rates will intensify tax competition via statutory tax rates, which then would be the only competition parameter left for national govern-ments to compete for mobile companies and investment. There would be an incentive for national governments to attract tax base (i.e., the basis for the formula used to allocate the total tax base to member states) via under-cutting the other member states' statutory tax rates. Harmonizing the tax base only would intensify corporate tax rate competition in the EU as a whole; and particularly within the two country clubs.[20]

In practice, the design of the formula used to distribute the consoli-dated tax base among member states may prove difficult,[21] and depend-ing on the factors included in the formula various distortions may result (Weichenrieder, 2002). If wages were used, tax revenues would be redis-tributed from low-wage to high-wage countries. If turnover was included, the transfer-pricing problem could not be eliminated completely. Including property in the formula may distort investment decisions, as firms may shift capital from high-tax to low-tax countries to benefit from lower tax rates. Finally, the definition of the group whose income is to be consolidated may pose further practical problems (Sorensen, 2004).

Optional corporate tax base harmonization: European consolidated company tax

Home state taxation

Under HST, transnational companies could optionally calculate the tax base for all their EU operations according to the tax code of the member state in which their headquarters are located (the home state).[22] For those companies making use of this option, transaction costs would be lowered, and the complexity of company taxation would be reduced considerably. However, as this is an optional system only, national tax codes would not be eliminated so that overall the complexity and lack of transparency of European company taxation would tend to increase. If all countries participated in the HST system, there would still be 25 different tax codes in the EU, and 25 different tax bases could potentially exist within a single EU country (Mintz and Weiner, 2003).

It can also be expected that countries would compete for headquarters by offering attractive rules for the determination of the tax base (Mintz and Weiner, 2003). Thus the tax-cuts-cum-base-broadening trend which was observable in a number of member states over the last two decades and which may well be considered as efficiency-enhancing would be reversed. Also, this reform proposal contains a free-riding incentive (Weichenrieder, 2002). Narrowing the tax base in one country would not only affect its own corporate tax revenues but also those of the other member states which are allocated a portion of the consolidated tax base. Moreover, subsidiaries may carry different tax burdens in one country, depending on the home state of their parent companies, which may distort competition. Finally, this concept can also be expected to increase the pressure on corporate tax rates.

Common consolidated base taxation

Under the CCBT system, common rules for a consolidated tax base would be established that would be adopted by all member states and could be optionally applied by transnational enterprises to determine taxable profits (instead of the rules provided by national company tax codes). Also this concept would – as an optional one – only reduce the complexity of the European company tax system if adopted by all member states (Mintz and Weiner, 2003). It would also suffer from the potential drawbacks already mentioned, particularly concerning an intensifying pressure on tax rates.

Some tentative conclusions

Given the existing economic divergencies between the two European country clubs, current corporate tax rate differentials can be expected to prevail for some time yet, as OMS will be able to maintain their (on average) comparatively high corporate tax rates. At the same time a scenario in which company tax rates continue to converge downwards in both country clubs cannot be excluded. Therefore in OMS as well as NMS the current levels of company taxation and public services may be put under increased pressure. This is particularly bad news for NMS which may not be able to satisfy their spending needs through increasing the tax burden on enterprises, or at least keeping it at the current level. This stresses the necessity of subsidies for NMS to compensate for possible negative effects of too low corporate tax rates on public spending (Wildasin, 1989). Moreover, the considerations presented in this chapter support the current harmonization strategy followed by the European Commission, which is aimed at the harmonization of corporate tax bases.

Since – as argued above – harmonizing the tax base would increase competition via corporate tax rates, it may well be worth considering complementing tax base harmonization by the introduction of minimum tax rates. In contrast to recent suggestions (e.g., de Mooij, 2004), the introduction of a uniform statutory tax rate in both European country clubs does not seem advisable, however. To leave NMS the option to grant tax rebates as a compensation for locational disadvantages, a two-tier approach may make sense. This solution could provide for a higher minimum tax rate for OMS, reflecting the tax premium, and a lower minimum tax rate for NMS, mirroring the tax rebate: at least for a limited period of time, until the existing economic disparities between the two country clubs have been substantially reduced.

Notes

1　The expectation that the ban of preferential tax regimes may aggravate tax competition in the EU has been repeatedly put forward in the literature; see, e.g., Gorter and Moussa Diaw (n.y.); Keen (2001); Bucovetsky and Haufler (2005).
2　For an exposition of the basic tax competition model, see, e.g., Zodrow (2003) and Wilson and Wildasin (2004).
3　For models of asymmetric tax competition see Bucovetsky (1991) or Wilson (1991).
4　See section 3 of the chapter.
5　See Krogstrup (2002) for a review of papers arguing from a new economic geography perspective.
6　For an overview, see Schratzenstaller (2003, 2005).
7　See, e.g., Jacobs and Spengel (2001) for the model firm approach and European Commission (2001) for the methodology to calculate EMTR and EATR for hypothetical investment projects.
8　The author is indebted to Michael Overesch (ZEW) for providing the data.
9　The author is indebted to Ludwig Strohner (IHS) for providing the data.
10　Also the company tax ratios presented above belong to the group of macro-economic backward-looking measures.
11　These data are taken from the Worldscope Database.
12　For a discussion of these problems see Nicodème (2001).
13　In some countries, e.g., Italy, local business taxes are also included.
14　Defined as corporations' net operating surplus, the difference between received and paid interest and rents, and a specific definition of dividends minus property income from insurance companies and pension funds attributed to policy holders.
15　In 1990, the European Commission put forward a proposal for a directive on cross-border losses (European Commission, 1990) which it withdrew in 2001 due to the lack of support by the Council. Currently the European Commission is working on a relaunch of this initiative. In its recent ruling in the case of Marks & Spencer (December 2005), the ECJ outlawed tax provisions which allow the consolidation of profits and losses between associated companies located in the same member state only; they do not allow cross-border losses to be taken into account.
16　See, e.g., Hines (1999) for an overview of studies on the USA; Bartelsman and Beetsma (2003) for the EU; Clausing (2003); Kind, Midelfart and Schjelderup (2005).
17　See, e.g., Wilson (1999), Oates (2001) or Wilson and Wildasin (2004) for a review of the controversial views discussed in the literature.

18 The parent–subsidiary Directive (Council Directive 90/435/EEC of 23 July 1990, amended by Council Directive 2003/123/EC of 23 December 2003); the merger Directive (Council Directive 90/434/EEC of 23 July 1990); the Council Directive concerning payments between associated companies of different Member States (Council Directive 2003/49/EC of 3 June 2003); the Convention concerning the elimination of double taxation (Convention 90/436/EEC of 23 July 1990).

19 Mintz and Smart (2004) empirically show for Canadian firms that formula allocation indeed limits profit-shifting opportunities.

20 Gordon and Wilson (1986) in a formal analysis show that formula apportionment leads to stronger competition via tax rates.

21 Weiner (2002) gives a detailed explanation of formula apportionment. For a critical discussion of formula apportionment see Hellerstein and McLure (2004) and the literature cited therein.

22 For a more detailed exposition of the two optional concepts, see, e.g., Lannoo and Levin (2002).

References

Baldwin, R. and Krugman, P. (2004) 'Agglomeration, Integration and Tax Harmonization', *European Economic Review*, 48, 1–23.

Bartelsman, E.L. and Beetsma, R.M.W.J. (2000) 'Why Pay More? Corporate Income Tax Avoidance through Transfer Pricing in OECD Countries', *Journal of Public Economics*, 87, 225–52.

Bénassy-Quéré, A., Gobalraja, N. and Trannoy, A. (2006) 'Tax and Public Input Competition', Contribution to the 43rd CEPR Economic Policy Panel Meeting, 21–22 April, Vienna.

Bénassy-Quéré, A. and Lahrèche-Révil, A. (2005) 'Corporate Taxation and FDI Within the EU25', Paper presented at the 2nd Euroframe Conference on Economic Policy Issues in the European Union, 3 June, Vienna.

Blonigen, B.A. (2005) 'A Review of the Empirical Literature on FDI Determinants', NBER Working Paper, No. 1299.

Borck, R. and Pflueger, R. (2004) 'Agglomeration and Tax Competition', DIW Discussion Paper, 408.

Brennan, G. and Buchanan, J. (1980) *The Power to Tax: Analytical Foundations of a Fiscal Constitution* (New York: Cambridge University Press).

Bucovetsky, S. (1991) 'Asymmetric Tax Competition', *Journal of Urban Economics*, 30, 67–181.

Bucovetsky, S. and Haufler, A. (2005) 'Tax Competition when Firms Choose their Organisational Form: Should Tax Loopholes for Multinationals Be Closed?', mimeo.

Carstensen, K. and Toubal, F. (2004) 'Foreign Direct Investment in Central and Eastern European Countries: A Dynamic Panel Analysis', *Journal of Comparative Economics*, 32, 3–22.

Clausing, K.A. (2003) 'Tax-motivated Transfer Pricing and US Intrafirm Trade Prices', *Journal of Public Economics*, 87, 207–23.

De Mooij, R. (2004) 'A Minimum Corporate Tax Rate in the EU Combines the Best of Two Worlds', *Intereconomics*, 39, 180–2.

De Mooij, R. and Ederveen, S. (2003) 'Taxation and Foreign Investment: A Synthesis of Empirical Research', *International Tax and Public Finance*, 10, 673–93.

Desai, M. and Hines, J.R. (2001) 'Foreign Direct Investment in a World of Multiple Taxes', NBER Working Paper, 8440.

Devereux, M.P. and Griffith, R. (2003) 'Evaluating Tax Policy for Locational Decisions', *International Tax and Public Finance*, 10, 107–26.

Devereux, M.P., Griffith, R. and Klemm, A. (2002) 'Corporate Income Tax Reforms and International Tax Competition', *Economic Policy*, 17, 451–95.

Devereux, M.P., Lockwood, B. and Redoano, M. (2002) 'Do Countries Compete over Corporate Tax Rates?', CEPR Discussion Paper, 3400.

European Commission (1990) *Proposal for a Council Directive Concerning Arrangements for the Taking into Account by Enterprises of the Losses of their Permanent Establishments and Subsidiaries Situated in Other Member States*, COM(90)595 final (Brussels: European Commission).

European Commission (2001) *Company Taxation in the Internal Market*, COM (2001) 582 final (Brussels: European Commission).

European Commission (2003) *An Internal Market without Company Tax Obstacles. Achievements, Ongoing Initiatives and Remaining Challenges*, COM(2003)726 final (Brussels: European Commission).

European Commission (2004) *Outline of a Possible Experimental Application of Home State Taxation to Small and Medium-sized Enterprises*, TAXUD C.1/DOC(04) 1410 (Brussels: European Commission).

European Commission (2005a), *Activities of the European Commission in the Tax Field in 2004*, Doc(2005)2304 (Brussels: European Commission).

European Commission (2005b) *Structures of the Taxation Systems in the EU 1995–2003* (Brussels: European Commission).

European Communities (1998) 'Conclusions of the ECOFIN Council Meeting on 1 December 1997 Concerning Taxation Policy (Including Code of Conduct For Business Taxation)', *Official Journal of the European Communities*, 98/C2/01.

Frey, B.S. (1990) 'Intergovernmental Tax Competition', in McLure, C., Sinn, H.-W. and Musgrave, P.B. (eds), *Influences of Tax Differentials on International Competitiveness* (Deventer and Boston, MA: Kleiner), 89–98.

Genschel, P. (2001) *Globalization, Tax Competition, and the Fiscal Viability of the Welfare State*, MPIfG Working Paper, 01/1.

Gordon, R. and Wilson, J.D. (1986) 'An Examination of Multijurisdictional Corporate Income Taxation under Formula Apportionment', *Econometrica*, 54, 1,357–73.

Gorter, J. and Parikh, A. (2003) 'How Sensitive is FDI to Differences in Corporate Income Taxation within the EU?', *Economist*, 151, 193–204.

Gorter, J. and de Mooij, R. (2001) *Capital Income Taxation in Europe: Trends and Trade-Offs* (The Hague: Sdu Publishers).

Gorter, J. and Moussa Diaw, K. (n.y.) 'The Remedy may be Worse than the Disease: A Critical Account of the Code of Conduct', CPB (Netherlands Central Planning Agency) Working Paper, 5.

Grubert, H. (2001) 'Tax Planning by Companies and Tax Competition by Governments: Is there Evidence of Changes in Behavior?', in Hines, J.R. (ed.), *International Taxation and Multinational Activity* (Chicago/London: University of Chicago Press), 113–39.

Haufler, A. (1998) 'Perspectives of Corporate Taxation and Taxation of Investment Income', in Austrian Federal Ministry of Finance and the Austrian Institute of

Economic Research (eds), *Conference Proceedings: Tax Competition and Co-ordination of Tax Policy in the European Union* (Vienna), 139–57.

Haufler, A. and Wooton, I. (1999) 'Country Size and Tax Competition for Foreign Direct Investment', *Journal of Public Economics*, 71, 121–39.

Hellerstein, W. and McLure, C.E. (2004) 'The European Commission's Report on Company Income Taxation: What the EU can Learn from the Experience of the US States', *International Tax and Public Finance*, 11, 199–220.

Hines, J.R. (1999) 'Lessons from Behavioral Responses to International Taxation', *National Tax Journal*, 52, 305–22.

Hoyt, W.H. (1991) 'Property Taxation, Nash Equilibrium, and Market Power', *Journal of Urban Economics*, 34, 123–31.

Jacobs, O.H., Spengel, C., Finkenzeller, M. and Roche, M. (2003) *Company Taxation in the New EU Member States* (Frankfurt/Mannheim: Ernst & Young AG).

Jacobs, O.H., Spengel, C., Finkenzeller, M. and Roche, M. (2004) *Company Taxation in the New EU Member States*, 2nd edn (Frankfurt/Mannheim: Ernst & Young AG).

Jakubiak, M. and Markiewicz, M. (2005) 'Capital Mobility and Tax Competition in the EU after Enlargement', Paper presented at the 2nd Euroframe Conference on Economic Policy Issues in the European Union, 3 June, Vienna.

Janeba, E. and Schjelderup, G. (2002) 'Why Europe Should Love Tax Competition – and the U.S. Even More So', National Bureau of Economic Research, Working Paper No. W9334.

Keen, M. (2001) 'Preferential Tax Regimes can make Tax Competition less Harmful', *National Tax Journal*, 54, 757–62.

Kind, H.J., Middelfart, K.H. and Schjelderup, G. (2005) 'Corporate Tax Systems, Multinational Enterprises, and Economic Integration', *Journal of International Economics*, 65, 507–21.

Krogstrup, S. (2002) 'What do Theories of Tax Competition Predict for Capital Taxes in EU Countries?', HEI (Hautes Etudes Internationales) Working Paper, 05/2002.

Krogstrup, S. (2004) 'Are Corporate Tax Burdens Racing to the Bottom in the European Union?', EPRU Working Paper Series, 2004-04.

Lannoo, K. and Levin, M. (2002) 'An EU Company without an EU Tax?', CEPS (Centre for European Policy Studies) Research Report, Brussels.

Mendoza, E.G. *et al.* (1994) 'Effective Tax Rates in Macroeconomics. Cross-Country Comparisons of Tax Rates on Factor Incomes and Consumption', *Journal of Monetary Economics*, 34, 297–323.

Mintz, J.M. and Smart, M. (2004) 'Income Shifting, Investment, and Tax Competition: Theory and Evidence From Provincial Taxation in Canada', *Journal of Public Economics*, 88, 149–68.

Mintz, J.M. and Weiner, J.M. (2003) 'Exploring Formula Allocation for the European Union', *International Tax and Public Finance*, 10(6), 695–711.

Mutti, J. and Grubert, H. (2004) 'Empirical Asymmetries in Foreign Direct Investment and Taxation', *Journal of International Economics*, 62, 337–58.

Nicodème, G. (2001) 'Computing Effective Corporate Tax Rates: Comparisons and Results', Directorate General for Economic and Financial Affairs Working Paper, 153.

Oates, W.E. (2001) 'Fiscal Competition and European Union: Contrasting Perspectives', *Regional Science and Urban Economics*, 31, 133–45.

Patterson, B. (2001) 'Tax Co-ordination in the EU – the latest Position', Directorate-General for Research Working Paper, Economic Affairs Series, ECON 128 EN 12-2001.

Pluemper, T. and Schulze, G.G. (1999) 'Steuerwettbewerb und Steuerreformen', *Politische Vierteljahresschrift*, 39, 445–56.
Quinn, D. (1997) 'The Correlates of Change in International Financial Regulation', *American Political Science Review*, 91, 531–52.
Schratzenstaller, M. (2003) 'Zur Steuerreform 2005', *WIFO Monatsberichte*, 76, 879–900.
Schratzenstaller, M. (2005) 'Effective Company Taxation in Poland – Some Methodological Considerations and Empirical Results', *Intereconomics*, 40, 89–99.
Sinn, H.-W. (1997) 'The Selection Principle and Market Failure in Systems Competition', *Journal of Public Economics*, 66, 247–74.
Slemrod, J. (2004) 'Are Corporate Tax Rates, or Countries, Converging?', *Journal of Public Economics*, 88, 169–86.
Smarcynska Javorcik, B. (2004) 'The Composition of Foreign Direct Investment and Protection of Intellectual Property Rights', *European Economic Review*, 48, 39–62.
Sorensen, P.B. (2004) 'Company Tax Reform in the European Union', *International Tax and Public Finance*, 11, 91–115.
Weichenrieder, A. (2002) 'Das Kommissionsgutachten zur Unternehmensbesteuerung: Mehr Fragen als Antworten', *ifo Schnelldienst*, 55, 9–11.
Weichenrieder, A. (2005) '(Why) Do We Need Corporate Taxation?', in Oesterreichische Nationalbank (ed.), *Capital Taxation after EU Enlargement* (Vienna), 60–72.
Weiner, J.M. (2002) 'Formula Apportionment and the Future of Company Taxation in the European Union', *CESifo Forum*, 3, 10–20.
Wildasin, D.E. (1989) 'Interjurisdictional Capital Mobility: Fiscal Externality and a Corrective Subsidy', *Journal of Urban Economics*, 25, 193–212.
Wilson, J.D. (1991) 'Tax Competition with Interregional Differences in Factor Endowments', *Regional Science and Urban Economics*, 21, 423–51.
Wilson, J.D. (1999) 'Theories of Tax Competition', *National Tax Journal*, 52, 269–304.
Wilson, J.D. and Wildasin, D.E. (2004) 'Capital Tax Competition: Bane or Boon', *Journal of Public Economics*, 88, 65–91.
Zodrow, G.R. (2001) 'Implications of the Tax Competition Literature for Tax Harmonization in the European Union', Paper Prepared for a Conference on Tax Policy in the European Union held at the Research Centre for Financial and Economic Policy, Erasmus University Rotterdam, The Hague, 17–19 October, www.few.eur.nl/few/research/ocfeb/congreseu/papers.htm.
Zodrow, G.R. (2003) 'Tax Competition and Tax Coordination in the European Union', *International Tax and Public Finance*, 10, 651–71.
Zodrow, G.R. and Mieszkowski, P. (1983) 'The Incidence of the Property Tax: The Benefit View versus the New View', in Zodrow, G.R. (ed.), *Local Provision of Public Services: The Piegout-Model after Twenty-Five Years* (New York: Academic Press), 109–30.
Zodrow, G.R. and Mieszkowski, P. (1986) 'Pigou, Tiebout, Property Taxation, and the Underprovision of Local Public Goods', *Journal of Urban Economics*, 19, 356–70.

7
Does an Ageing Population Justify a Radical Reform of Public Pension Systems in the European Union?

Felipe Serrano and Jesús Ferreiro

Introduction

The analysis of the social, economic and political effects of the ageing process that is currently taking place in the developed countries, especially in the European Union countries, is a matter of great importance. It is only recently that economic analysis has faced such a challenge. Special attention has been paid to the different economic effects of ageing. These include the consequences for economic growth generated by the slower growth of the labour force (Bloom, Canning and Sevilla, 2001), the role played by immigration as a policy to offset the fall in the proportion of the working population (Fehr, Jokisch and Kotlikoff, 2004) and the impact of an ageing population on public finances.

With respect to this problem of an ageing population, one of the fields of research most intensively studied is that of the provision of social security, especially, the future of public pension systems.[1] In many cases, economic and political issues are interrelated and, in practice, the problem of an ageing population is simply an excuse to implement reforms for reasons that are not justified by the demographic change. Nonetheless, it is true that the ageing process will have a substantial impact on the future expenditure on pensions. Therefore, an analysis of the best way to adapt the current system to meet this new challenge is clearly justified.

The cornerstone of our analysis is that any pension system must provide what we term a 'sufficient pension' that allows retired people adequately to finance their consumption needs. The criteria used to choose between the two main pension systems – that is, between a pay-as-you-go (PAYG) scheme and a funded scheme[2] – should incorporate this restriction.

The specification of this restriction is not unambiguous. A clearer definition of a sufficient pension requires a more specific explanation of the relationship between the income enjoyed during the retirement period and the desired and planned level of consumption. However, from a theoretical point of view, the problem is easily understood.

In the life-cycle models (when bequests do not exist), people's lifetime consumption is equivalent to their lifetime income and wealth. An optimal intertemporal allocation of someone's lifetime resources involves a constant path of consumption. The level of consumption is constant over that person's life: people save (and borrow) during their working years, and spend the accumulated wealth during their retirement. Although people can modify their consumption path, consuming more or less during their retirement than during their working life, the level of consumption is always determined by each individual's income. Consequently, the notion of a sufficient pension is a meaningless notion, since by definition the level of consumption-income that each person will enjoy during retirement is (pre)determined by that person's life resources; retirement consumption is a meaningless notion.

However, if we accept that consumption is determined by the social environment in which people live, we can identify a sufficient pension as one that guarantees a level of consumption related to a certain socially-determined retirement standard of living. A sufficient pension would be identified with a set of goods (a pattern of consumption) that, obviously, can change with time and that can be different in different societies.

From a more pragmatic perspective, the target could be identified with a certain replacement rate (that is, the ratio of the pension to the last wage that has been earned). In Germany, the pension target is a replacement rate of 67 per cent for a worker with average earnings who has paid social security contributions for 45 years. In Finland, the replacement rate is 60 per cent after paying social security contributions for 40 years. However, most European countries have not set an explicit target for the replacement rate. Nevertheless, the idea that the government has a responsibility to provide a substitution income that allows a socially accepted retirement standard of living is implicit in all cases.[3]

To start, our analysis of the possible social security systems has a twofold objective. The first is to determine whether or not the pension system provides sufficient income for a socially-determined level of retirement consumption. Whether the selected system favours or worsens economic growth is, obviously, also a question that needs to be considered. But it cannot be the key determinant of the choice between a PAYG and a funded system, as is suggested in many cases. Second, there is the need to determine an objective method to facilitate a comparison between both types of insurance methods.[4]

Microeconomic considerations

Financial profitability versus real profitability

Feldstein adopts a similar position when he proposes a privatization of the current PAYG schemes, arguing that 'the funded system can provide any given level of benefits at a lower cost to working-age people than a PAYG system can' (Feldstein, 1997, p. 3). For Feldstein, and for most other authors that argue for a radical reform of the current PAYG schemes (for example, Blake 2000; McMorrow and Roeger, 2002), the advantage of a funded scheme is the higher rate of return it provides.

As Samuelson (1958) shows, the rate of return in a PAYG scheme is equal to the sum of the rate of growth of the labour force and the rate of growth of productivity: that is, the rate of growth of the resources from which social contributions are paid. This profitability is usually proxied by the long-term real GDP rate of growth. In a funded scheme, the rate of return can be identified with the rate of interest or with an index of the evolution of the returns of a portfolio of assets that are representative of the type of investment resulting from the decision to save for retirement. Aaron's paradox (Aaron, 1966) shows that the chosen scheme should be one that provides a higher rate of return. If, in the long run, the real rate of interest turns out to be higher than the rate of economic growth, the funded scheme would be better than the PAYG scheme. But if the expected long-run rate of economic growth turns out to be higher than the expected rate of financial return, the PAYG scheme would provide the retired population with a higher level of welfare.[5]

The use of the expected rate of return as a criterion by which to choose the pension system is not, however, a sound one. Indeed, Aaron's paradox poses a false theoretical problem because of the impossibility of estimating the true future rate of return (in both real and nominal terms) due to the existence of uncertainty (Davidson, 1991).[6] What we are arguing is that to assume empirically that future rates of return will be the same as past rates is very risky because of the high level of uncertainty.

In a recent paper, Shiller (2005), using a model based on the life-cycle portfolio, shows that the median internal rate of return of the baseline personal account is 2.6 per cent. This rate is the outcome of a simulation based on the long-term historical experience (US stock market, bond market and money market data for the period 1871–2004, adjusted for the median stock market return of 15 countries for the period 1900–2000). In his conclusions, Shiller (2005, p. 27) points out that:

> The simulations presented in Tables 3 and 4 showed a disappointing outlook for investors in the personal accounts relative to the rhetoric of their promoters. I think that the disappointment may be even greater than the tables indicate. The simulations depended on the historical experience of either the United States or the rest of the world for over a century. While a century may seem like a long enough sample period to prove any point, in fact even with a century of data we do not know the true probability distribution of future returns. The twenty-first century may differ fundamentally from the twentieth. Moreover, whenever we look at long historical data on stock markets, we are of course looking at survivors, stock markets that made it, and ignoring countries where conditions turned out so badly that we get little or no stock market data. Obviously, Russia and China were not in Dimson *et al.* for their century-long data set. While it is highly unlikely that the particular upheavals that hit Russia and China in the twentieth century will repeat themselves in the U.S. in the twenty-first century, it should be remembered that nobody predicted in 1900 the kind of upheavals that were to follow in Russia or China. Similarly, it is difficult for us to imagine all the different kinds of things that might disrupt stock market performance in the future. Thus, there is additional uncertainty, uncertainty of regime change or model uncertainty or survivorship bias, that should ideally be taken into account. Unfortunately, there does not seem to be any objective way of quantifying this additional uncertainty about the future.

We think that the disappointment (between the rates of return derived from Shiller's simulations and those espoused by the promoters of individual accounts) may be even greater than his tables indicated. Even with a century of data we do not know the true probability distribution of future returns. There is additional uncertainty, uncertainty of regime change or model uncertainty or survivorships bias, that bias that should ideally be taken into account. Unfortunately, there does not seem to be any objective way of quantifying this additional uncertainty about *the* future.

This rate of return is well below that used by the European Commission when it states that there is a need to radically reform the public pension systems in the European Union. In the paper by McMorrow and Roeger, a rate of return of the funded system for the baseline scenario of 5.25 per cent per annum is assumed for the next 50 years. This rate of return was calculated by Miles and Timmermann (1999) over the period 1965–95 for a balanced portfolio of pension fund assets (i.e., 50 per cent equities and 50% bonds). The rate of return estimated for the PAYG system was close to 2 per cent, for the same period. With these assumptions, it is clear that, by definition, the funded systems have more advantages than the current PAYG systems. The authors accept that there is a 'degree of uncertainty surrounding the baseline forecasts' (McMorrow and Roeger, 2002, p. 44), but it does not prevent them from claiming that their results are clear proof that the introduction of individual accounts is the best solution to the ageing population problem in Europe.

However, if we use the rate of return estimated by Shiller to make the same calculations, we come to dramatically different results, compared with those reached by McMorrow and Roeger. Even if we accept the rate of return that the latter authors estimate for the current PAYG systems, the profitability gap would fall. The reduction of the profitability gap would be even greater if we consider, first, the transition costs, and second, the management costs of both systems.[7]

The transition costs would be those faced by the generation that would bear the costs of the change from the current PAYG scheme to the funded scheme. The size of these costs depends on the extent of the reform, and they are unavoidable. The transition generation would bear these extra costs because, in addition to their individual retirement-motivated saving for their own funded pensions, they must also pay the taxes or social contributions needed to finance the current pensions. The problem cannot be solved, or removed, with a time-smoothing of these costs by issuing public debt. In this case, the burden would be merely distributed among a larger number of generations, thus affecting not only to the first generation in which the transition begins, but also subsequent generations.

The second kind of costs are management costs. The simple comparison of the rates of returns implicitly assumes that the management costs are the same for both systems. However, experience shows that this assumption is false. For instance, the administration costs of the social security system in Spain amounts to 0.7 per cent of total expenditure, compared to 27 per cent that, on average, the private systems in Latin America bear (Murro, 2004). The evidence of the private pension funds in the UK also does not support the assumption that management costs are identical for both systems. In any case, notwithstanding any likely fall in the private costs that could arise from the improvements in the management of the funded system, the decentralized system, by its very nature, faces administration costs higher than those of the centralized pension systems.[8]

Therefore, the putative lower costs of funded systems (due to their higher rates of return) is not a good basis on which to choose between systems.

The problem of an ageing population

The problem of an ageing population that most developed countries are now facing has become the main reason to justify the change from the current PAYG systems to funded individual accounts schemes. The basic argument is founded on the implicit assumption that the pension funds are unaffected by the problem of an ageing population. First, we will see how this problem has arisen, and, later, we will analyse whether the implicit assumption is true.

The problem of an ageing population is as follows. During the next 50 years the PAYG schemes will face, first, the retirement of the cohorts born during the baby boom, and, second, an increase in life expectancy. The overall result will be a significant increase in pension expenditure that will have to be paid for by a proportionally smaller working population. The latter will occur because of the lowering of the birth rates. Therefore, the PAYG system will face the dilemma of *either* increasing social security contributions *or* cutting the benefits paid in order to avoid an unsustainable deficit. If the option is for the first solution, it will generate negative incentives for the people's behaviour which will negatively influence economic growth. If, on the other hand, the second solution is implemented, the cuts in benefits will affect the welfare of the retired population (which is something to be avoided). The change from the PAYG system to funded individual accounts is shown as the best answer to avoid these undesirable consequences. The argument for these accounts is also underpinned by the higher returns earned from the presence in the capital markets of retirement-motivated savings.

The pension systems, regardless of whether they are PAYG or funded schemes, are mechanisms to transfer incomes from the active working population to the retired population. In the PAYG systems the income transfer is explicit and visible, because it is made through the payment of compulsory social security contributions. But in the funded systems the transfer is more opaque, because it is made in an indirect way. The retired population owns accumulated rights on real and/or financial assets that allow them to get a share, proportional to the value of their asset holdings, of the current income generated by the working population, through the payment of interest or sale of accumulated assets.

Consequently, in both systems pensions depend on the level of national income at any particular time: that is, ultimately on the rate of economic growth (Barr, 2000). If economic growth slows down, the amount of income available to be distributed will fall and pensions, regardless of the system, will be lower than they otherwise would have been. On the other hand, if economic growth is high, there will be less reason to worry about an ageing population.

Let us assume that the forecasts of future growth are not good, partly because of the effects of an ageing population on the working population and, subsequently, for the growth of GDP.[9] The economic slowdown has the following consequences. Total wages and salaries, from which the resources of both the PAYG and funded systems are obtained, will rise at a slower rate than that of expenditure on pensions. This will lead to a rise in social security contributions if we wish to maintain the level of benefits, or to a need to reduce benefits if we wish to maintain social security contributions at their original levels. Another option would be a mixture of both measures.

In a funded individual accounts system, and under the assumption of a closed economy and a constant functional income distribution, the consequences of an ageing population would be an initially higher rate of growth of the supply of financial or real assets (the retired population sell their assets to finance their consumption) which is higher than the rate of growth of the demand for those assets (that made by working population). This excess supply will reduce the prices of the assets and, consequently, the income of the retired population. Only an increase in the saving rate of the working population (a fall in their current consumption) could warrant the maintenance of the value of the assets accumulated by the retired population.[10]

The question arises of whether one of the two systems would deal with the problem of an ageing population better than the other. Both systems can appeal to foreign transfers: that is, seek the needed income outside domestic borders. Immigration, in the case of PAYG systems, could increase the supply of labour, thus removing the problem of the lack of taxable wage incomes. In the case of the funded scheme, the solution would be a foreign location for domestic saving, mainly in those countries with a demographic pattern opposite to those of developed economies since in these economies it is assumed that the wages would be lower, due to the abundance of labour, and the interest rate would be higher, due to the scarcity of capital.

Both solutions, however, face important problems. In the case of immigration, it is likely that the inflow of foreign workers would not be high enough to solve the lack of labour force that developed countries suffer as a consequence of the ageing of their populations. Besides, the skills of this foreign labour force might be lower than those of domestic workers, and therefore a massive inflow of foreign workers could lead to a fall in labour productivity and in the rate of economic growth. Furthermore, we cannot ignore the problems of social integration that this option can generate. In sum, all these problems do not mean that that we must necessarily give up this kind of solution to the problem. What we wish to stress is that it cannot be the only solution.

The allocation of savings abroad should take place in developing countries with different population profiles (e.g., Africa, Latin America and Asia). However, it is very unlikely that these economies offer a mix of risk and profitability that is high, and safe, enough to attract a substantial share of the retirement savings. Besides, the lack of transparency and the consequent instability of the international financial system do not lead us to be very optimistic about its capacities to manage efficiently the volume of savings generated by a hypothetical privatization of the public pension systems in *all* the developed countries. Even the most ardent supporters of a radical reform of the current systems accept the fact that such a reform should be accompanied by some reform in the international financial system.[11] This source of uncertainty can be added to those mentioned by Shiller, thus reinforcing his opinion about the problem of the uncertainty surrounding any estimation of the rates of return of funded systems.

If the problem that must be solved to ensure that future pensions are adequate is that of increasing economic growth, and not that of the ageing of the population, we can pose the following questions. Can we influence this economic variable? Does either system have advantage of giving a higher rate of growth without giving up the desired objective? The answer to the first question is 'yes'. In respect of the second question, the answer is subject to a substantial theoretical and empirical controversy, as we must still solve the problem concerning the appropriate criterion by which to choose between the two systems.

Management of the costs arising from the lack of information

The main objective of any pension system, as we mentioned above, is to provide the retired population with a pension that allows them to maintain a socially acceptable standard of living. This pension must be provided with the highest security both during the working years in which the rights are accumulated, or generated, and during the years when the benefit is obtained. That is to say, individuals must have, at any moment, the greatest possible degree of certainty about the resources that are required to pay for their consumption during their retirement period.

The challenge of providing a sufficient pension arises from the impossibility of forecasting the future because of the non-stationary nature of the world in which we live. This lack of information about the future must be central to any analysis of the two systems.

Both insurance systems face, first, the need to anticipate the future value of the relevant variables and, second, the need to correct estimation errors which lead to the existence of costs. Both dimensions of the management of the uncertainty are closely related. The smaller the difficulty in obtaining and processing the needed information, the lower will be the estimation errors and, therefore, the lower the adjustment costs needed. The greater the difficulty in obtaining and processing the needed information, the greater will be the probability of making errors in the estimation and, therefore, the higher will be the adjustment costs needed to maintain the path that warrants the maintenance of the pension target. In sum, *the capacity to minimize these costs is what makes one system better than the other one.*

The costs we are talking about can arise both during the period of gestation of the benefit (during people's working life) or during the period of use (retirement). In the first case, the costs arise in the funded system, *ceteris paribus*, when the true rate of return is lower than the expected one. In the PAYG system, the costs arise when there is a change in the conditions required to obtain a pension of a given value. In the second case, there are risks that are the same for both systems, namely those arising from changes in the longevity risk and the risk of unanticipated inflation.

Risks during the retirement period

The traditional way to face these risks has been through insurance. The essence of insurance is the transfer, sharing, and grouping of risks. Insured agents spread their individual risks among the whole insured population, thus sharing the risk from which they wish to be protected. If grouping is the optimal available mechanism to minimize the costs from the future adverse events that must be faced, but cannot be estimated, then the PAYG system has clear advantages over funded individual accounts. The former keeps the essence of classic insurance: the grouping and the (intergeneration) transfer of the risk. The working population covers the different risks faced by the current retired population.

Moreover, the cost of the cover of these risks is very low because of the economies of scale resulting from the large number of people covered. This issue is especially significant in the case of the risk of increasing longevity. In the case of the unanticipated inflation, the current PAYG systems can easily increase pensions because of their method of finance.

Social contributions paid by workers are indexed to the changes in prices, and, consequently, the social security system is automatically taxing increases in incomes.[12]

It could be argued that this advantage of the PAYG system is the direct result of its compulsory nature and not of any specific feature of the PAYG system per se. Would the same results be reached in a world of individual accounts if the state made the insurance compulsory? The answer could be in the affirmative, although the costs of this kind of shelter would be higher than in a public PAYG system, and it would also generate problems that currently do not exist.[13]

The current private markets offer solutions to these risks through annuities. However, their price is very high. It is estimated that, in the US, private annuities are currently 15–25 per cent more expensive than what average mortality would suggest they should be (Congressional Budget Office, 1998). The standard explanation for the limited size of the individual annuity market is the adverse selection problem (Warshawsky, 1988; Friedman and Warshawsky, 1990; Mitchell *et al.*, 1999). Compulsory insurance, by enlarging the market, could partially solve the problem of adverse selection when there are only individual accounts, and hence reduce the price of annuities. However, compulsory insurance does not remove all the problems related to the existence of adverse selection. Moreover, this measure, by imposing compulsory income transfers, could even lead to a regressive transfer from the low-income to high-income population, because of the positive correlation between life expectancy and income.

Risks during working life

In the case of pensions, the compulsory nature of the insurance is directly related to the problem of myopic behaviour, but not to the problem of adverse selection. The myopic behaviour arises from the inability of individuals to take into account their entire lifespan when they make their current consumption and saving decisions. When the giving-up of the current PAYG systems and their subsequent change to private pension funds is proposed, the need to oblige individuals to sign these insurance-pensions contracts is stressed. The implicit assumption is that, because of the existence of myopia, there exist risks that individuals do not insure against.

At best, the only costs that compulsory insurance can solve are those that arise from a lack of income during the retirement period: that is, it could avoid a fall in retired people's incomes below the poverty threshold. These limited consequences arising from compulsory insurance are due to the fact that this measure only corrects for one of the many ways in which individuals are subject to bounded rationality.

One of the most dramatic consequences of the myopia discussed earlier arises when individuals, in a world of individual accounts, have to face the need to adjust their contributions when there is a gap between estimated and true returns.

Any gap between these leads to changes in the contributions that are necessary in order to avoid any undesirable consequences. If the profitability reached is below that needed to guarantee the pension target, the individuals will have to increase their contributions. If they do not accomplish this, their lack of foresight will lead to a level of retirement consumption that will be lower than they initially wished. One possible option in this case would be to maintain the desired level of consumption by extending their working life. If, however, the rate of return is higher than the planned rate, individuals should reduce their contributions in the next period in order to avoid an excess of savings; unless they do this, their optimal level of consumption will be too low.

This consequence could be *partially* corrected if every year the state set the ranges of compulsory contributions according to the changes that had occurred in the representative financial rates of return. This kind of intervention would have the effect of compulsorily setting the rate of household saving. However, this is more complicated than setting the volume of contributions required for any given expenditure on pensions each year. It is obvious that if there were only individual saving accounts, no state would dare to make such an intervention.

The above solution would only be partial: that is to say, it would only work under the assumption that it is possible to adjust the contributions so that people have enough time to react to any unexpected events. However, if individuals do not have sufficient time, any sudden (downwards) gap between the true and the planned rates of return will lead to a loss of welfare during the retirement period, or to an increase of working life beyond the planned age of retirement. The burden of the adjustment will always fall on the insured person. In a world ruled by funded individual accounts, the most critical ages will be those closest to the retirement age because the room for adjustments is smaller. The problem will not be serious if the deviations are small. Nonetheless, any financial crisis that happens at that critical time can ruin earlier efforts made during working life.

In the current public PAYG systems, there are also risks that are similar to those mentioned above. The notion of 'political risk' is often used to explain the changes that happen to the expected benefits. By political risk, we mean the risk of a change in the promised benefits from the pension system. This change can take several forms: an increase in the number of working years needed to qualify for the pension; changes in the index used to update the pension according to the change in prices; changes in the legal age of retirement; and so on. It is usually argued that this kind of risk occurs only in the current public pension systems, because the benefits provided by these systems are set through a political process.

However, the study of this kind of risk is not as clear-cut as it should be because, too often in the analysis the measures introduced to rationalize the system are confused with arbitrary measures that actually put the sustainability of the system in danger. This confusion has its origin in the notion of political risk. This is usually only identified with changes in the promised benefits. However, it does not take into account the different origins of these changes, the information that those affected have about the consequences of these changes, or their degree of participation in the decision-makings that generates those changes.

In the crises of the social security systems in Latin America, for instance, nobody questions that the unjustified privileges enjoyed by some groups of workers, or even the political use made of the benefits provided, became a permanent source of instability that helped to lead to the failure of the system. The inefficiency of the different administrations of the social security systems also helped to push the system into an irrevocable crisis (Jiménez, 1998). In these cases, it is fully justified to talk of political risk, because the political process did not work to maintain and reinforce the public pension systems.

However, to use the notion of political risk simply to refer to the potential cuts in future benefits as a consequence of the ageing of the population, as does McHale (1999), is far more problematical. The existence of the political risk is explained by the fact that the management of the PAYG systems is developed in the political arena, and therefore it might be influenced by political and electoral factors rather than by non-technical ones. That would result in the management of the PAYG systems, the setting of the amount of benefits, the contributions, and the requirements that generate the entitlement to get a pension being determined purely for political reasons.

The ageing population problem is not an exogenous, non-economic, element that affects to the 'technical' working of the pension system, but an endogenous ('objective') element that influences the technical management process of any pension system. By changing a set of technical elements of any pension system (life expectancy, the ratio of the years spent working and making contributions to the years of retirement, or the ratio of retired population to working population), the ageing process involves the necessary adoption of technical adjustment measures that guarantee the long-term financial sustainability of pension systems. One of these measures could be to cut the size of benefits. Therefore, the implementation of such a measure should not indicate the existence of political risk, if it is done for purely economic reasons.

Throughout this chapter, we have analysed the capacity of the current pension systems to adjust themselves to the demographic change that we are facing. One option would be to keep unchanged the entitlement to receive a pension, allowing the contributions to bear the whole burden of the adjustment arising from the increased expenditure. The second option would be quite the opposite: to adjust the expenditure keeping the contributions constant. The third option would be a mixture of the first two. It is true that the second option predominates in most developed countries. The measures currently implemented, and those currently under debate, are directed towards halting the growth of social security expenditure by cutting the benefits. This does not mean that, in the near future, these other reforms cannot be introduced, especially if the future economic growth rates are not high enough to finance the expected growth of the expenditure on benefits. How should we view the reform: as a risk, or as a guarantee that the public pension system will be able to keep satisfying the income needs of the retired population?

In any case, political risk remains if we ignore the available information and if the reforms needed are not adopted under the premise that the future will solve the problem. But the implementation of radical reforms, promising results that are impossible to guarantee, is also a political risk. It is the responsibility of the administration and the policy-makers to safeguard the future of pensions, and not to cut them.

The active role of the state in the pension system is unavoidable, even for some critics of the current system who wish to reform them by constructing a 'new man'. Regardless of the efforts of this 'new man' and the supervising role played by the public sector, the problems arising from the bounded rationality will be a heavy burden for individuals. Agents have significant computational limitations as regards processing the available information. In many cases, especially in the case of the future events, that information simply does not exist. Therefore, to make the best possible decisions, people need help to obtain and process the information required.

In the private pension systems, the management of the necessary information is made through a direct relation between the company and the insured person, but in the current public systems, this management is made in a collective way through a democratic political process. Both systems need some institutional constraints to guarantee their good management. Any lack of effective management could be considered as a political risk. Both systems, therefore, can be negatively affected by the discretionary behaviour of public authorities.

In the case of the private systems, these constraints affect, first, the working of the market and, second, the working of the companies that manage the pensions. By acting on the market, the intention is to introduce the competition that is needed to avoid excessive administrative costs, although experience does not suggest that this is likely to be successful. By regulating the portfolios of assets in which household savings are invested, the aim is to avoid critical situations for retired workers in the future, although the experience of the recent financial crises of the pension funds does not encourage optimism. In any case, this kind of regulation does not prevent the asymmetric distribution of power between the insured person and the insurance company. This arises, due to their different capacities to process the available information, favouring the latter. In the financial markets, the ultimate effect of this distribution of information does not seem to be in favour of the clients.

In public systems, the guarantee of the democratic control alone is not enough when the administration of social security is opaque and inefficient or when the political decisions are based on short-run electoral considerations. The aim is to remove both sources of perturbation. The requirement of a wide social and political consensus to implement reforms in the pension systems can be a good antidote to political decisions driven by short-term considerations.

However, even the best sort of regulations cannot avoid a pessimistic future scenario. As we mentioned above, the rate of economic growth is the crucial variable in both systems. If the rate of economic growth is not high enough, the ability to minimize the adjustment costs, for the same degree of regulation and administrative efficiency, is higher in the PAYG system compared with the funded system. In the latter system, all the burden of the adjustment falls on the individuals, but in the PAYG system the costs are redistributed among successive generations. We should emphasize that we are talking about a temporary situation: that is, the costs arising from the ageing population will be borne over a certain period. Consequently, the transfer of the costs across generations (via increased contributions and issuing of public debt) is a feasible option that should not significantly change the absolute and relative levels of welfare of the successive cohorts involved.

In this sense, the implementation of a radical reform of the public pension systems to solve a temporary problem is the main problem faced by these systems.

Macroeconomic considerations

Funding, investment and economic growth

The neoclassical relationship between economic growth and pension systems can be presented in two ways: the first shows the positive effects that funded individual accounts could generate for economic activity; and the second focuses on the negative effects arising from the current public systems. In the former, special attention is paid to the positive impact that an insurance system based on individual savings has on the capital markets in addition to the consequences for the savings rate and the labour force. A more narrow perspective, which is the main one in the literature, focuses only on the two first variables mentioned: the impact on savings and capital markets.

From a theoretical point of view, the argument runs as follows. Public pension systems have depressed the rate of national savings and, subsequently, the level of investment and the rate of economic growth. The ultimate effect of these systems has been a lower level of welfare than the one that could have been reached with private systems based on individual savings accounts. The change to funded capital accounts would, therefore, have led to the opposite result.

This relationship is open to a number of criticisms. The first one is: how can we calculate the optimal rate of saving used as a benchmark? The way to calculate the optimal rate of saving that an economy without social security would reach is by aggregating the behaviour of a representative individual. This individual is assumed to behave rationally: that is, he or she has no limit on the ability to process information and always maximizes his or her utility. By definition, there is perfect information available to the individual. In sum, the model is constructed under the assumption of rational expectations. With all these assumptions, the critics of the PAYG system build a model of equilibrium where the rates of saving are optimal. Finally, this virtual world is compared to the real world to identify the differences. If the observed rate of saving is lower than that estimated in the model, the conclusion is that the public systems are squeezing the savings.

This empirical analysis is seen as the key to reaching any conclusion. The empirical research has been very extensive and the only clear conclusion is that there is no a clear answer, because of the conflicting results of those studies. The reason is that this kind of research is based on a false theoretical premise. The estimation of the optimal rate of saving is a purely speculative exercise as it is impossible to test it empirically. The information that it is assumed to be managed by the individuals when they maximize their intertemporal utility is not the available statistical information existing in the real world. In the theoretical models the individuals work with perfect information, but the world we are living in only provides imperfect information. Thus, the optimal rate of saving is arbitrarily calculated, using, for instance, the average income of a certain number of years as a proxy for the life income overall. Obviously, the outcomes reached will be different, depending on the kind of proxies used.

Besides, in the economic models on which the criticisms to the public pension systems are based, the aggregated supply is the dominant economic variable. The investment is constrained by the availability of saving: that is, any increase of saving is automatically transformed into an equivalent increase of investment. In these models, the market economies do not face any long-run demand-side constraint. Aggregated demand is automatically adjusted to the changes in supply. The adjustment can be fast or slow, depending on the degree of rigidities in the goods or inputs markets; but in the long run the economy will always be in equilibrium. The trend to the equilibrium is the outcome of the interactions among individuals who behave in a rational manner.

In this framework, the change from the current PAYG system to a system based on individual accounts will automatically increase the volume of savings and the rates of economic growth. But from a theoretical point of view, there is no clear answer as to what will happen. It could be argued that the outcome would be a recomposition of the different motives for saving, which leaves the aggregated rate of saving unaffected. This rate could also fall as a consequence of the myopic behaviour of individuals. But even assuming there is an increase in the rate of saving, this increase would be transitory, lasting only until the new system matures. At that moment, the lack of saving by the retired population would equal the saving of the working population, thus removing the initial rise in savings and changing the outcome (Toporowski, 2000; Sawyer, 2003).

An increase in the saving rate will not automatically lead to an increase in investment, because the latter depends fundamentally basically on the expectations of profits and not on the current supply of loanable funds. Furthermore, a simple national income accounting shows us that:

$$(S - I) + (T - G) = (X - M) \tag{7.1}$$

and further

$$S = I + (G - T) + (X - M) \qquad (7.2)$$

Therefore, an increase in savings will lead to a similar increase in investment if and only if $(G - T) + (X - M) = 0$. If the increase in savings is not associated with an equivalent increase in investment, the higher rate of savings will necessarily lead to a higher public deficit and/or a surplus in the current account and a deficit in the capital account (Sawyer, 2003). In the first case, the higher public deficit involves, in the short run, a fall in public savings. The fall in public savings will (partially) offset the higher private savings, thus reducing the impact of the increase of private savings on total national savings, the relevant variable. Furthermore, in the long run, the higher public deficit, and the consequent higher debt burden, can lead to a rise in taxes, thus affecting private savings (Cessarato, 2002, 2006; Sawyer, 2003).

If higher savings are not associated with higher investment and/or higher public deficit, they must be associated with a higher current account surplus and, therefore, with a higher deficit in the capital account. The economy will become a net exporter of capital, and in this case those economies with lower savings, those where their savings are below the level of investments, will be the ones who will benefit most from the greater supply of capital.

Expectations, uncertainty and social security

Neoclassical economics has analysed the role played by pension systems, public or private, funded or pay-as-you-go, and their impact in terms of the consequences generated by these systems on the possibility of reaching economic equilibrium. By definition, the public management of PAYG pension systems is seen as an allocation mechanism that is less efficient than a private system based on the individual management of accumulated savings (funded systems). Consequently, the PAYG public pension systems are a source of distortion that causes the economy to deviate from the optimal equilibrium outcome, thus involving costs in terms both of economic activity[14] and individual and collective welfare.

This kind of analysis is based on a set of assumptions including the existence of perfect information or, in its modern version, the rational expectations hypothesis. Perfect information, or the ability to make perfect forecasts with no systematic errors according to the rational expectations hypothesis, is needed for individuals to make an optimal intertemporal allocation of their lifetime resources. However, the existence of uncertainty in a Post Keynesian sense of the term (i.e., the impossibility of predicting future outcomes based on past information in a non-ergodic world: see Davidson, 1991), means that the neoclassical notion of equilibrium disappears. The resource allocation decisions are not optimal and the individual behaviours stop being automatically co-ordinated. In other words, the causal relations among variables are not stable and the people's capacity to predict future events or outcomes disappears, especially in the long term.

In this scenario, institutions become key elements in the analysis of the economic process and in the decision-making processes. They generate relevant information for the decision-making processes that help to stabilize long-term expectations by providing information about the future. Institutions allow individuals to make sensible decisions by temporarily stabilizing the causal relations between economic variables and agents (Ferreiro and Serrano, 2005). Thanks to the information generated by the institutions, individuals can incorporate long-term planning in their current decisions. They can plan for the future, and therefore can make decisions about intertemporal resource allocations.

The stability of these relations gives people the capacity to forecast and, therefore, studying the future on the basis of probabilities is a feasible option. However, this does not mean that we are re-establishing the conditions for efficient-optimal outcomes, as the neoclassical model proposes. Logical time is not synonymous with economic equilibrium, as neoclassical economics states. The economy is not always in equilibrium: that is, the causal relations among variables are not always stable. Moreover, equilibrium, when reached, is not permanent: it lasts only whilst long-term expectations are constant. Furthermore, not all the equilibrium states are *socially* acceptable. Some states can offer acceptable outcomes at a specific time but they can be valued differently at other times. Whether the final outcome is efficient or not is a problem related to the notion of efficiency used, a notion that in any case can only be defined in the normative manner (Ferreiro and Serrano, 2005).

In any case, what is relevant for our analysis is the fact that current economic outcomes are dependant on the type of institutions existing, and therefore these institutions have contributed to the causal relations existing among (public and private) agents and economic variables.

Public pension systems have been in existence for more than a century. It seems clear that they have helped to shape our current consumption and saving patterns, as they have helped individuals to make accurate forecasts about key elements for their decisions about allocating resources. These include, among others, the age of retirement, the years of working life, and the existence of income during the retirement and the value of this income. If the social security system, as we know it nowadays, had not existed, these patterns would be different from the current ones, although we cannot know precisely what they would look like. Without a doubt, the family would have played a more important role in the care and maintenance of elderly people, although retirement-motivated saving could also have played a more important role. In any case, to speculate about what could have happened if past events had been different is a futile exercise.

The certainty about the availability of future income provided by these systems may have reinforced the relationship between current disposable income and current consumption. Besides, these systems might have guided the pattern of consumption towards the consumption of durable goods, helping to create the current pattern of consumption in the developed economies. That is, they have encouraged people to consume, both during the period of working life and when retired, by generating stable expectations about future income. Obviously, stability of the long-term expectations has not been solely the result of the social security systems. The Welfare State, of which the pensions system is a part, has worked as a powerful tool to reach this stability.

In the short run, the stability of long-term expectations has favoured the expansion of demand, which has led to an increase in the rate of investment and the rate of economic growth. What is more relevant, however, is that it has made possible the implementation of the stabilization policies which were needed to correct short-term disequilibria. This kind of economic policy is only effective if the causal relations among variables are stable and predictable. This stability only exists if the long-term expectations are stable.

As we have tried to explain above, the safety net provided by a funded system, because of its higher adjustment costs, is lower than that provided by the current PAYG systems. However, there is one issue that cannot be ignored. The individual accounts require permanent adjustments to the saving rate during the years of working life because of the inevitable gap between the planned and the true rates of return. If there is no degree of compulsion, the adjustments may be only partial. In any case, one result would be that there would be a closer relationship between the business cycle and the fluctuations in the financial system. Financial wealth would be a more important determinant of the decisions made about consumption and saving in each period. Consequently, private consumption would be a less stable expenditure.

If the business and the financial cycles were symmetric, the influence of that variable would be small. Nonetheless, the problems would come from the reallocation of saving that would be needed to get the highest rates of return. The increasing risk it could generate, together with the disconnection between the business cycles in the capital exporting countries and the international financial system (and the national financial system of the receiving countries), would lead to higher instability in the business cycle. A lower stability of long-term expectations would lead to a lower stability in the causal relations among the short-term variables: for instance, it would induce a higher volatility in the decisions about consumption, saving and investment. This lower stability would generate problems for the implementation and effectiveness of stabilization policies.

All the above-mentioned outcomes might not happen. But our knowledge about the working of markets, mainly the international finance markets, lead us to believe that that outcome is more feasible than an efficient international reallocation of saving. If that presumed efficiency actually existed, we would not now be continually talking of financial crises or the need to put the working of the current international financial system in order.

One additional element that could dampen economic activity as a result of a radical reform would be the impact that the effect of a fall in the welfare of retired people would have on the level of aggregated consumption. In a world where there is a higher proportion of the elderly, the relevance of their current consumption on the aggregated demand would be greater than it is nowadays. The fall in their welfare could be the result of a number of elements: a lower number of people covered by pension systems, lower pensions due to insufficient adjustments to changes in the financial rates of return and wages, loss of purchasing power due to unanticipated growth of prices during the period of retirement or to unanticipated changes in life expectancy. All these elements could happen even with higher rates of economic growth, because all of them come from the adjustment costs due to the lack of perfect information.

Conclusions

Neoclassical economists argue for the replacement of the current PAYG public pension system by privately funded pension systems, because of the presumed better micro- and macroeconomic outcomes of the latter. The arguments are, among others, that the rate of return of funded systems is higher that that of PAYG systems, and that the capacity of funded systems to deal with the potential risks during both working life and retirement period is greater. Moreover, it is argued that, because of the effects generated on savings and investments, the level of economic activity and the rate of economic growth will be higher with a funded systems than with a PAYG system, because of the effects generated on savings and investments.

However, as we have seen in this chapter, these conclusions are not fully justified by either theoretical or empirical analysis. First, the true rates of financial returns are lower than those used in many studies. This fact, together with the higher administrative costs of privately funded pension systems, makes the presumed higher profitability of private pensions highly implausible. Second, the capacity of PAYG systems to face the risks that agents can suffer and that affect to their intertemporal resource allocation decisions, such as the unanticipated inflation resulting from the ageing process, is higher than that of privately funded systems. Actually, the capacity of the latter systems to face those risks depends dramatically on the compulsoriness of the insurance, and, consequently, on public intervention in the determination of the benefits and/or the contributions paid. Third, the presumed positive impact of funded systems depends on the stimulus provided both to the rates of savings and investment and to providing greater incentives for the working population. These effects are not straightforward: the change from a PAYG system to a funded system may not necessarily lead to higher private savings and, even if savings do rise, they do not necessarily lead to higher total savings and investments.

In any case, we cannot forget the key role played by institutions, social security among others, in providing information about the future and the decisions made by other agents. Institutions help to reduce uncertainty, to stabilize long-term expectations and to co-ordinate individual behaviours. The current European social security and public pension systems have helped people to plan their consumption and savings decisions for many years; that is to say, these systems have provided agents with the information necessary to make rational choices about their intertemporal resource allocations. A radical reform in these systems would remove the capacity of agents to make these decisions. The rising uncertainty generated by these reforms could lead to a less efficient outcome than that generated with the current systems.

Notes

1 In the case of the European Union, for an overview of the impact of the ageing process on the public finances, and the consequent need of radical reforms of the current public pension systems, see Directorate-General for Economic and Financial Affairs (2005, 2006) and the Presidency conclusions

of the Brussels European Council held on 22 and 23 March 2005 (available at http://register.consilium.eu.int/pdf/en/05/st07/st07619-re01.en05.pdf).

2 We will identify the funded scheme with an insurance system based on individual saving accounts managed by the private sector. This identification is not really true. Nonetheless, mainly because we consider the current debate about public pension systems, the identification is not misleading, since one proposed solution to a hypothetical future crisis of the PAYG schemes is the solution that we are identifying as a funded scheme.

3 An example is the practice of indexing current pensions according to the evolution of a price index, so that the pensions permanently provide a real income that guarantees the access to a set of goods (real consumption).

4 Pension systems can have other objectives besides those emphasised in the text (income redistribution, for example), but a system that is unable to provide a sufficient pension should be judged as an undesirable one.

5 In recent years, most neoclassical studies have assumed that, in a dynamically efficient economy, the financial rates of return are higher than the real rates of return and have consequently rejected Aaron's paradox. The conclusion drawn is that pension funds that invest private savings in financial assets will always provide higher returns than the PAYG schemes.

6 There is another problem: if in the long-run the rate of interest is constantly higher than the rate of economic growth, the share of financial-capital incomes in GDP will be permanently rising, and, therefore, in the long-run capital incomes and GDP will become equivalent.

7 McMorrow and Roeger accept the existence of these costs and their negative impact on the rate of return. Transition costs are estimated to be 1 percentage point, and, therefore, the rate of return of the funded systems would fall from 5.25 per cent to 4.25 per cent. If we apply this cost to the rates estimated by Siller, the rate of return of the funded systems would be lower than that of PAYG system.

8 Some authors (Mitchell, 1996) have argued that the higher costs could be explained by the 'greater and better' services provided by the private insurance companies. This could be true, but the available objective measures of these costs, despite the methodological problems in making such comparisons, show that the administration costs of the current public systems are well below those faced by private systems.

9 We make this assumption for analytical reasons only, and it cannot be considered as the most likely future scenario.

10 It could be argued that the profitability of financial assets does not depend only on the retirement-motivated saving. Financial profitability is also influenced by many other factors. However, to accept this hypothesis would mean to accept that in a world with private pensions funds the retirement-motivated saving would not be the dominant kind of saving, an assumption hard to accept.

11 See Group of Ten (1998).

12 Actually, social contributions are a tax on a wage bill that can change because of both a change in prices and in productivity. Therefore, the system could have a built-in mechanism to update the pensions not only in terms of prices but also in terms of the changes in productivity, sharing the gains in welfare from the increase in productivity with the retired population. One of the most intense

current debates in relation to the reforms of the public pension systems is, indeed, that related to the appropriate index for updating pensions. In some countries (Spain and USA, for instance) the option has been to update pensions according to the changes of prices. That means that the retired worker maintains the purchasing power of the pension received at the age of the retirement, but that she does not share the gains in welfare from the productivity growth.

13   For an in depth analysis of the problems that should be solved in a hypothetical privatization of the social security system and the cover of these risks, see Congressional Budget Office (1988).

14   The negative impact on economic growth would come from the lower rate of savings and investments and from the lower working population.

References

Aaron, H.J. (1966) 'The Social Insurance Paradox', *Canadian Journal of Economics and Political Science*, 32, 371–4.

Barr, N. (2000) 'Reforming Pensions: Myths, Truths and Policy Choices', *IMF Working Paper*, No. 00/139.

Blake, D. (2000) 'Does it Matter What Type of Pension Scheme You Have?', *Economic Journal*, 110, 46–81.

Bloom, D.E., Canning, D. and Sevilla, J. (2001) 'Economic Growth and Demographic Transition', *NBER Working Paper Series*, No. 8685 (Cambridge, MA: NBER).

Cessarato, S. (2002) 'The Economics of Pensions: A Non-Conventional Approach', *Review of Political Economy*, 14(2), 149–77.

Cessarato, S. (2006) 'Transition to Fully Funded Pension Schemes: A Non-Orthodox Criticism', *Cambridge Journal of Economics*, 30(1), 33–48.

Congressional Budget Office (1998) *Social Security Privatization and the Annuities Market* (Washington, DC: Congressional Budget Office).

Davidson, P. (1991) 'Is Probability Theory Relevant for Uncertainty? A Post Keynesian Perspective', *Journal of Economics Perspectives*, 1, 129–43.

Directorate-General for Economic and Financial Affairs (2005) *Public Finance in EMU 2005*(Luxembourg: Office for Official Publications of the EC).

Directorate-General for Economic and Financial Affairs (2006) *The Impact of Ageing on Public Expenditure: Projections for the EU25 Member States on Pensions, Health Care, Long-term Care, Education and Unemployment Transfers* (2004–2050), Special Report No. 1/2006 (document available at the website: http://europe.eu.int/comm/economy_finance/publications/european_economy/2006/eesp106en.pdf).

Fehr, H., Jokisch, S. and Kotlikoff, L. (2004) 'The Role of Immigration in Dealing with the Developed World's Demographic Transition', *NBER Working Paper Series*, No. 10512 (Cambridge, MA: National Bureau of Economic Research).

Feldstein, M. (1997) 'Transition to a Fully Funded Pension System: Five Economic Issues', *NBER Working Paper Series*, No. 6149 (Cambridge, MA: National Bureau of Economic Research).

Ferreiro, J. and Serrano, F. (2005) 'Institutions, Uncertainty and Economic Policy', paper presented at the Conference, 'Macroeconomics and Macroeconomic Policies. Alternatives to the Orthodoxy', 28–29 October, Berlin.

Friedman, B.M. and Warshawsky, M.J. (1990) 'The Cost of Annuities: Implications for Saving Behavior and Bequests', *Quarterly Journal of Economics*, 104(1), 135–54.

Group of Ten (1998) *The Macroeconomic and Financial Implications of Ageing Populations* (Basel: Bank for International Settlements).

Jiménez, Adolfo (1998) 'La Reforma de los Sistemas Públicos en América Latina', *Ekonomiaz*, 42, 132–45.

McHale, J. (1999) 'The Risk of Social Security Benefit Rule Changes: Some International Evidence', *NBER Working Paper Series*, 7031 (Cambridge, MA: National Bureau of Economic Research).

McMorrow, K. and Roeger, W. (2002) 'EU Pension Reform. An Overview of the Debate and An Empirical Assessment of the Main Policy Reform Options', *Economic Papers*, No. 162 (Brussels: Directorate General for Economic and Financial Affairs, European Commission).

Miles, D. and Timmermann, A. (1999) 'Risk Sharing and Transition Costs in the Reform of Pension Systems in Europe', *Economic Policy*, 14(29), 251–86.

Mitchell, O. S. (1996) 'Administrative Costs in Public and Private Retirement Systems', *NBER Working Paper*, No. 5734 (Cambridge, MA: National Bureau of Economic Research).

Mitchell O.S., Poterba, J. M., Warshawsky, M.J. and Brown, J.R. (1999) 'New Evidence on Money's Worth of Individual Annuities', *American Economic Review*, 89(5) (December), 1,299–318.

Murro, E.R. (2004) *El Dilema de la Seguridad Social en el Cono Sur*, Working Paper No. 180 (Lima: Organización Internacional del Trabajo, Oficina Regional de la OIT para América Latina y el Caribe).

Samuelson, P.A. (1958) 'An Exact Consumption-Loan Model of Interest with or without the Social Contrivance of Money', *Journal of Political Economy*, 56, 467–82.

Sawyer, M. (2003) 'An Economic Evaluation of Alternative Arrangements for Retirement Pensions', mimeo, available at http://www.epoc.uni-bremen.de/pdf/Vienna.

Shiller, R.J. (2005) 'The Life-Cycle Personal Accounts Proposal for Social Security: An Evaluation', *NBER Working Paper Series*, 11,300 (Cambridge, MA: National Bureau of Economic Research).

Toporowski, J. (2000) *The End of Finance. Capital Market Inflation, Financial Derivatives and Pension Fund Capitalism* (London: Routledge).

Warshawsky, M.J. (1988) 'Private Annuities Markets in the United States: 1919–1984', *Journal of Risk and Insurance*, 55(3), 518–28.

8
The European Union Budget: The Common Agricultural Policy and European Economic Priorities

Juan Ramón Murua and José Albiac

Introduction

These are hard times for the EU, from both a political and an economic point of view. Over the last few years, the EU has made important strides towards integration and has completed its greatest ever enlargement. At the same time, however, these political achievements pose enormous economic, financial and organizational challenges. The current situation is made all the more difficult because some of the countries that used to act as drivers of the European project are at present experiencing major internal difficulties, which means that their primary concern and interest lies in solving their own domestic problems. Only once this is done, therefore, will they be in a position to give a new boost to the enlarged European project, which will require extra commitment from all its members.

The current European environment is not the best scenario for a calm discussion about the budgetary policy of the enlarged EU. It is a context in which deep discrepancies arise as to the actual purpose and nature of European integration. There appear to be at least two differing conceptions of the future of the EU: one that aspires to a deepening of the integration process of the EU, and another that appears more inclined towards the idea of something more akin to a free trade area, where plans for integration and political institutionalization will gradually give way to economic or merely commercial issues. At the risk of over-simplifying the respective positions, the first might be interpreted as a 'federalist' approach, the second as a 'liberal' one. The recent pronouncement of the British Prime Minister may be an implicit reflection of these two positions.[1]

These differing conceptions regarding the nature of the EU are also reflected in the budget, since deeper integration will obviously mean further development of common policies and thus higher budgets. If the aim is to be directed towards the development of a free trade zone, however, the common policy requirements and budgetary needs will be far fewer.

The crux of the issue is to find the right strategy for the current European and worldwide economic environment, in a global scenario where new economic powers are emerging and there are signs of a shift in the world's economic centre of gravity. How can an economic and political space such as the EU best defend its role and economic and political interests? How can the various member states best defend their own interests? Do they need a solid and increasingly integrated EU, or one that is weak?

As already mentioned, the EU is undergoing major changes that are having a direct impact on both the size and structure of the budget. The inclusion of ten new member states, and the imminent accession of another two, suggests the need to reassess the budgetary commitments adopted through common policies, since the new members have a much lower level of economic development. The aim of the ambitious Lisbon strategy, moreover, was to push through economic reform in order to turn the EU into the most competitive economy in the world by the year 2010.

The debate and subsequent agreement on financial prospects for the period 2007–13 are inscribed within this framework. A significant increase in competitiveness and higher employment in the enlarged EU with growing cohesion seems an extremely difficult target to achieve while decreasing the budgetary endowment. A budget cutback may even endanger the fulfilment of the commitments acquired within the framework of the enlargement agreement and the Treaty of the Union.

The main common policies – that is, the agricultural heading and the structural funds – absorb the bulk of the budget, which largely explains how they come to be at the centre of budgetary disputes and proposals. Despite the apparent weakening of the democratic legitimacy of the current CAP, the options defended in some quarters (to abolish it entirely, reduce it to its least possible expression, or renationalize it along with the regional policies) are debatable to say the least. In the first place, it would be necessary to assess the timeliness and potential of a coherent agro-environmental and rural policy to replace the current CAP,[2] and in some cases supplement the structural funds. Second, the funds liberated by abandoning, minimizing or renationalizing those policies would not be sufficient to adequately cover the competitiveness and growth policies.

The size, structure and source of the EU budget are questioned on various grounds. Several European leaders and echelons, among them the Commissioner for Economic and Monetary Affairs and the European Parliament, have recently been discussing the advisability of adopting a more rational solution for the funding and allocation of resources which would avoid the eternal debate between countries about net contributors and net receivers.

The European Union's budget and economic priorities

The reformulation of EU objectives in the Lisbon strategy is intended to address the urgent need for higher economic growth, job creation and increased competitiveness in world markets, in order to prevent the EU from slipping backwards in the world economic rankings.

The European Commission (European Commission, 2004) describes the Union's economic performance as disappointing. The EU15 has grown by 2.2 per cent since 1995, compared with the 3.2 per cent growth of the United States, and the 3.6 per cent growth of the global economy. Productivity in Europe is growing much more slowly than in the US, and the per capita GDP gap is not getting any narrower (per capita GDP is 70 per cent of that of the US); unemployment in Europe stands at an intolerable level of 20 million. In a global setting, the European economy is undergoing a period of recession or stagnation that can only be overcome by means of a co-ordinated response.

The Commission, logically enough, intends the approved budget to meet the objective of boosting growth, competitiveness and social cohesion, claiming that 'it is not about redistributing resources among member states. It is about how to maximize the impact of our common policies so that we further enhance the added value of every euro spent at European level.'

Financial perspectives are inevitably a reflection of a political project, whatever its level or lack of coherence. The profound discrepancies that exist over European integration are apparent in the debate over the budget, which is the financial side of the European project under discussion. Lack of leadership and a solid project for the EU result in, among other things, the imposition of 'accounting logic' and 'just return' in budget balances. This logic makes it difficult to draw up budgets that are coherent with the objectives adopted as part of a larger project (Le Cacheux, 2005).

In relation to this, Tracy (1993) claimed that the balancing of the budget is the single most important issue when drawing up the Common Agricultural Policy, since it conditions the position of each member state. This attitude, whereby each country's stance towards the budgetary balance is to protect its own individual interests, is what is known as 'accounting logic' or 'just return'. This forces the Commission to design packages in which there is something for everyone, thus increasing the complexity of the CAP and weakening its coherence. The unanimity vote makes it difficult to achieve a reasonable or economically optimal outcome.

The EU budget is not only small, it is also weighted down by inertias of the past. The politics needed to reach approval compromise the coherence and flexibility of the budget. As a consequence, the final outcome fails to address the predefined objectives. It should be mentioned, however, that the EU budget is just over 1 per cent of GDP, whereas national budgets are around the 45 per cent of GDP level.

The rhetoric claims that resources invested in common policies should be aimed at achieving the maximum added value in order to strengthen social and economic cohesion in the EU. Furthermore, the Treaty of the Union, with respect to cohesion policies, is committed to supporting the poorest countries and regions in order to reduce existing income disparities and promote regional convergence. This convergence ultimately contributes to growth and the creation of employment, objectives for which there is a recognized need to allocate more resources.

Working on the grounds of 'accounting logic', every member state without exception tenaciously defends the type of EU budget that will maintain the amount of income it receives, while reducing or freezing the amount it has to contribute. There are even some countries that question the very idea of a strict budget constraint. In December 2002, five of the richest nations (Germany, France, the Netherlands, Austria and the UK) presented a joint request to limit expenditure to 1 per cent of GDP, despite the foreseeable impact of the imminent enlargement. Meanwhile, France and Germany reached an agreement to limit agricultural expenditure and to postpone any significant reform of the CAP. Spain, for its part, has vigorously defended the allocation of structural funds in the current financial perspectives to guarantee its continuation as a net receiver until the year 2013. The UK defends its rebate despite the change in circumstances since it was originally granted. The net receivers, meanwhile, were in favour of increasing the budget in order to cover the enlargement costs in such a way as to prevent the channelling of resources to the new members from eroding away their net balance. Finally, the new members protested against what they saw as an attempt to achieve an enlargement on the cheap, in which they would receive 'second class' treatment, in terms of both CAP aid, and regional and cohesion funds.

Thus, the main battle has been over the size of the enlarged EU budget. While some want to limit it, others argue for it to be increased: the former in an attempt to reduce their own contribution, and the latter with a view to defending the amount of aid received in the past or due to them in the future. The Commission proposed a budget increase of up to 1.15 per cent of GDP in the next financial perspectives for 2007–13, in order to cover the cost of the enlargement and strengthen new common policy areas. The proposed budgetary increase was judged excessive by the net contributors, however, some of whom also denounced the inconsistency of their being forced to make a bigger contribution while at the same being expected to reduce their deficit in order to comply with the Stability Pact.

If we take a look at gross contributions to the budget as a percentage of GDP, we can see that Belgium and the Netherlands contribute more than 1 per cent of their GDP, while the UK, Ireland and Austria contribute the lowest percentages.[3] When it comes to gross contributions per head, the highest are made by Luxembourg, Denmark and Belgium, while the lowest are those of Greece, Portugal, Spain and the UK.

Net budgetary flow or net contribution is only one aspect of the economic impact of integration on the EU, which extends to affect areas as diverse as the advantages to be gained from enlarged markets or intra-community trade flows, business relations, productive factor mobility, competitiveness, and other less tangible political and cultural influences.

Trade flows within the Community reveal that the net contributors (particularly Germany, France, Italy, the Netherlands, Austria, Finland, Sweden and the UK), all of them strong economies, account for 90 per cent of EU15 intra-community exports (Germany's share is 23 per cent). The net recipients export only the remaining 10 per cent. The eastwards enlargement increases the EU market by 100 million people, and 60 per cent of the goods imported by these newcomers are from the EU15 (Ministère de L'Economic des Finances et de L'Industrie, 2004). The British Prime Minister used the volume of trade with the rest of the EU (10.2 per cent of exports within the Community) as one of his arguments to justify his support for the approved financial framework.

The second issue in the discussion revolves around the allocation of funds for the different expenditure headings, which is the mechanism that determines the package of resources to be received by each country. The Commission's proposal involved changes in the names of the main expenditure headings, but contemplated little essential change in their content or structure. At the other extreme, the widely disputed proposal made by Sapir *et al.* (2003) suggested a profound readjustment of expenditure, including a sharp curb on farm spending and a freeze on regional aid; it also argued for deliberately concentrating the allocation of resources on growth and competitiveness in areas with higher growth potential.

The main priority in the proposal made by the Commission was the completion of the internal market, which includes competitiveness and cohesion, as well as natural resource management to enhance sustainable

Table 8.1   Main headings in the current financial framework and the next
(€ billions)

Financial framework	2000–06	2007–13			
		Commission proposal	Luxembourg proposal	UK proposal	Final agreement
Sustainable development	260	458	382	367	380
Competitiveness		122	72	72	72
Cohesion	260	336	310	297	308
Conservation and management of natural resources	331	400	378	367	371
Direct payments and markets	293	301	295	293	293
Foreign affairs	35	63	50	50	50
Administration	38	58	50	49	50
Total[a]	746	994	871	847	862

[a] Including internal policies, security and justice, pre-accession aid, and compensation.
Source: European Commission (2004). Data in 2004 euros, except for 2000–3 spending (given in current euros).

growth. The implementation of the Lisbon strategy is intended to transform the EU into a competitive and dynamic knowledge-based economy, capable of sustainable economic growth and greater social cohesion. The basis of sustainable growth is better management of natural resources, by integrating the agricultural and environmental policies.

Competitiveness is becoming the key factor for growth and job creation, which will promote social cohesion. Competitiveness and cohesion therefore emerge as two mutually reinforcing elements. Making competitiveness the top priority means realigning and co-ordinating budgets with community and national policies.

Nevertheless, little change is apparent in the Commission's proposal for the 2007–13 financial framework, which remains weighed down by past inertia (Table 8.1). Expenditure is just over 1 per cent of EU GDP, an amount that apparently falls short of meeting the immense challenge proposed by the Commission. The expenditure structure largely follows the lines of previous budgets. Though there is some reduction in farm spending, this still accounts for 30 per cent of the total. The cohesion fund remains stable at 33 per cent, despite the accession of ten new members and the imminent accession of Romania and Bulgaria, which will considerably increase demand on the available budget.

The European Union budget and common policies

The EU budget funds the European institutions and the programmes and projects of the European policies, with total annual expenses close to €100 billion. The main headings in the European Union budget are sustainable development, and conservation and management of natural resources, administration, foreign affairs, and internal policies. The funds allocated to sustainable development support the structural policies directed towards the development of poor regions within the EU, and the new Lisbon initiatives to further European competitiveness. Conservation and management of natural resources funds the CAP through direct payments to farmers and rural development support. The largest part of the budget spending goes to the structural policies and the CAP, which receive the same 79 per cent of total spending in both the current financial framework and the next (Table 8.1).

The biggest net recipients of EU funds are Spain and France (who receive close to €15 billion/year), followed by Italy and Germany (close to €10 billion), and the UK, Greece, Portugal and Belgium (close to €5 billion). The EU budget is financed by the member states, at a rate of 1 per cent of each nation's GDP;[4] thus, contributions to the EU budget are determined by the economic size of each country, regardless of its relative wealth. The resulting main net contributions to the EU by country are Germany (€9 billion), the UK (€4 billion), the Netherlands (€3 billion), France (€2 billion), and Italy and Sweden (€1 billion). The countries receiving the main net payments from the EU budget are Spain (€8 billion), Greece and Portugal (€3 billion), and Ireland (€1 billion).

The Common Agricultural Policy was the first common policy implemented by the European Union in 1965. It was followed by structural policies such as the European Regional Development Fund in 1975, and the Cohesion Fund in 1992. Together, these two common policies have accounted for around 80 per cent of budget spending since 1970. The construction of Europe was facilitated by the agricultural and structural common policies. As explained by Baldwin (2005a), support to farmers through the CAP helped European integration, and the structural funds directed to poor regions facilitated economic and monetary integration. Now, however, this author considers that the CAP and the structural funds have become obstacles to integration, because instead of being based on principles, each of these policies serves special interest groups.[5] Nevertheless, agricultural and structural common policies are important tools to advance integration. The issue is further discussed at the end of the section.

This point of view represents the 'liberal' approach, which considers that Europe should simply evolve towards an intergovernmental co-operation scheme. The opposite, 'federalist' approach considers that further policy efforts are important, in order to consolidate Europe as a federation of states. The Common Agricultural Policy has two components. The first supports direct payments to farmers and intervention in agricultural markets, while the second, which is known as the 'second pillar', is directed towards rural development. The share of expenditure on rural development remains small, although rural development funding for the next financial framework (2007–13) has almost doubled from 12 to 21 per cent of CAP funding. The costs of the CAP to taxpayers in the next financial framework is €53 billion per year, and the total cost to consumers and taxpayers is estimated at around €100 billion per year (OECD, 2005).

The direct payments and market intervention vary widely according to type of product, country and farm size. The reason for this uneven treatment is that CAP spending is based on the political power wielded by each country or group of countries. Observing the distribution by product type, continental products in central and northern European countries receive much more support than Mediterranean products of southern Europe.[6] The consequence is that the distribution of direct payments and market intervention support by country benefits central and northern countries much more than it does those of southern Europe.[7] However, CAP aid is also low in several southern European regions that specialize in continental products, such as the Cantabrian coast (Spain), which receive similar amounts as those producing Mediterranean crops (Murua, Albiac and Astorkiza, 1996).

The enormous differences in the amounts received by individual farmers in the form of direct payments weaken the legitimacy of the CAP in the eyes of many observers. As the general public becomes aware that the bulk of the income transfers are going to rich farmers and large landowners, public disagreement may ultimately trigger the collapse of the CAP. It seems that 1.5 per cent of the richer farmers are getting 27 per cent of the direct payments, which amounts to a total of €8 billion per year. This inequality is widespread and affects all countries in the European Union.[8] The only conceivable reason for maintaining payments to rich farmers is that their lobbying effort guarantees the continuity of the current CAP regime, and thus protects the small share of income support that goes to poor farmers. If direct payments to the 1.5 per cent richer farmers and large land owners were scrapped, almost €60 billion would be available for the seven years of the next financial framework. These funds could be redirected towards rural development or other headings of the financial framework, such as sustainable development through funding for R&D and innovation and structural projects in new member countries. Despite the fact that investment in R&D and innovation is critical, funding for the 2007–13 period was cut from the €122 billion proposed by the European Commission to only €72 billion in the final agreement (Table 8.1).[9]

The CAP was substantially modified in the mid-term review of 2003 in order to prepare the European Union for the WTO negotiations and EU enlargement. The objective of the European Commission in the 2003 mid-term CAP review was to reduce prices and decouple subsidy payments. This further shifted the focus of the CAP from agricultural productivity support to farmers' income support.

The implementation of the mid-term review strengthens the EU bargaining position in the WTO negotiations, because support is shifted from the 'blue' to the 'green' box. Currently, the WTO negotiations on agriculture focus on reducing trade distorting subsidies and market support, ending export subsidies, and increasing market access for developing countries. The EU has recently shown its willingness to phase out agricultural export subsidies by 2013, provided that the US also ceases to operate any kind of export support mechanism.

The relationship between the EU budget and trade liberalization has been studied by Kernohan, Nuñez and Schneider (2005). They report that the Uruguay round has changed CAP policies and objectives because of the reduction in tariffs and export subsidies, and the Doha round would also affect the CAP, although it would have little impact on the EU budget. The likely agreement to eliminate €4,000 million of export subsidies will reduce the net balance of countries receiving subsidies, leaving Denmark (−0.08 per cent) and the Netherlands (−0.06 per cent) as the most severely affected.

Since the 2004 enlargement, new members have been receiving only 25 per cent of CAP direct payments, though they are set to receive 100 per cent by 2013. This unequal treatment is compensated to some extent by rural development expenditures, because new members will benefit from rural development funds that have been doubled from €40 to €80 billion for the next financial framework.

The potential gain for new members is the structural funding they are due to receive up until 2013 because, in the new financial framework, the cohesion heading increases by €50 billion, and current structural funding is redirected towards new members. However, this potential gain deserves qualification because, while funding increases by 18 per cent, the eligible population grows by 84 per cent.

As far as structural policies are concerned, the regions of the EU lack homogeneity because of their varying levels of income, employment, education and training, productivity and infrastructure. Regional disparities are inevitable, given the uneven spread of the spatial distribution of economic activities and population. The sectoral mix of economic activities is determined by each region's geographical conditions, natural factor endowment and capacity to adapt to economic change.

There is no natural reason why the costs and benefits of an economic integration process should be evenly distributed among the different regions and countries of the EU; thus, regional actions must be undertaken in the name of equity and solidarity. Growth can have a negative effect on cohesion if regional and personal income inequality is exacerbated by market forces (Sapir, 2006). From the economist's perspective, regional imbalances are due to inefficient use of resources; the most highly developed regions tend to experience problems arising from over-use of fixed social capital and infrastructure which generates rising congestion and pollution costs, while in the less developed regions the problem is one of under-use or lack of social capital and basic infrastructure. Actions oriented towards cohesion allow the more backward regions a share in the wealth generated by economic growth, thus preparing the ground for a gradual but sustained reduction in income inequality.

The approved financial framework differs in some respects from the proposal made by the Commission (Table 8.1). The amount, which is just over 1 per cent of EU GDP (1.045 per cent), is lower than that proposed by the Commission. There are cuts in the cohesion and agricultural policy funds although, at close to 70 per cent, they still account for the bulk of the expenditure. The agricultural heading is set to fall steadily from 35.6 per cent to 32.1 per cent by the end of the period. The approved framework reduces funds for other headings, competitiveness in particular, which is reduced by half.

The cohesion funds grow in absolute terms but there is hardly any variation in their relative importance over the period, which remains stable at 35 per cent. Since the enlargement, the population residing in regions with GDP per head below 75 per cent of that of EU25 practically double (a 84 per cent increase). The cohesion fund would therefore need to increase in the same proportion in order to maintain the same level of aid per recipient population. If we compare the resources allocated to structural and cohesion funds in the previous period (in 1999 euros) with those allocated to cohesion funds in the enlarged Europe, we can see that they have grown by 18 per cent while the eligible population has grown by 84 per cent. Such a marked increase in demand on the available budget means that the scope and achievements of the cohesion policy will be severely diminished.

The cohesion policy plays a fundamental role in the construction of the EU and the general opinion is that this fund should continue to be a vehicle for the transfer of resources between member states through the budget. Its ultimate objective should be to promote sustainable growth and development through investment in physical and human capital.

Interregional solidarity demands that the public sector promote the transfer of resources from richer to poorer regions in order to reduce inequality and drive cohesion (Castells and Espasa, 2002). Regional cohesion policies, however, should be directed at removing the causes of regional income and wealth differentials and thus prevent interregional transfers from becoming a permanent requirement.

Albeit with varying outcomes, the regional and cohesion funds appear to have had considerable impact in terms of real convergence. In the case of Spain, between 1989 and 2006, Structural and Cohesion Funds are estimated to have enabled the country to push income per head up to 89.4 per cent of the EU average: that is, 6 points higher than would have been possible without such aid. According to these estimates, this aid has helped to create almost 300,000 new jobs (Fundación de Estudios Financieros, 2005).

Structural aid has a twofold impact: an immediate effect in the form of income transfers which translate into higher income per head, and a more lagged effect on production factors and endogenous growth potential which in turn boost GDP growth capacity. Furthermore, structural interventions contribute to the overall growth of the EU by promoting trade and integration within the union, since it is estimated that a quarter of this investment reverts back to the EU in the form of increased imports, machinery and capital goods in particular (Torrebadella, 2006).

Though it appeared to meet with little success at the time, Sapir's proposal has nevertheless since been widely used as a reference in economic and academic circles for the budgetary debate (Table 8.2). As mentioned earlier, this proposal considers the budget to be a poor reflection of EU priorities and claims that the financial perspectives should be oriented towards financing the objectives of the Lisbon agenda, which were to create a dynamic knowledge-based economy, and help the new members to catch up with the rest as quickly as possible. It is in this spirit that it calls for a radical reorientation of the EU budget.

In line with the demands of several member states, it is likely to hold the budget below 1 per cent of EU GDP, while acknowledging that this means limited resources. Perhaps in an attempt to offset the lack of resources, it brings up the possibility of co-ordinated action with national budgets, co-ordination arrangements being an obvious requirement in any type of action. It also recommends dividing budget expenditure under

Table 8.2 Budgetary proposal from the Sapir report

Expenditures	% of GDP
1 GROW	0.45
(R&D)	(0.25)
(Education and training)	(0.075)
(Infrastructure)	(0.125)
2 CONVERGENCE	0.35
(New members)	(0.20)
(Old members)	(0.10)
(Phasing out)	(0.05)
3 RESTRUCTURING	0.20
(Displaced workers)	(0.05)
(Agriculture)	(0.05)
(Phasing out)	(0.10)
4 TOTAL	1.00

Source: Sapir *et al.* (2006).

three broad headings: a fund for economic growth, a convergence fund and a restructuring fund.[10]

One of the most striking features of this proposal is the sudden and practically total abolition of the agricultural policy and a similar reduction in the allocation for the convergence fund (similar to that proposed by the Commission). It is beyond discussion that the agricultural sector has little margin for growth or new job creation. It is equally true, however, that it has a ready market of 500 million consumers and provides direct employment for 14 million people. In addition, it is closely linked to a strong agro-industry that represents 13 per cent of the industrial sector and employs 3.4 million workers. To all this, it should added that agriculture is a major part of the economies of the new member states, where it accounts for 3 per cent of GDP, 13 per cent of employment, and approximately 24 million farm holdings.

Though it is hard to find objective economic arguments for setting the budget at a specific level, it is difficult to see (apart from the aim of holding the budget below 1 per cent of GDP) why renationalization is recommended for some common policies, while physical and human capital investment policies are promoted at the EU level. In this respect, Mayhew (2004) suggests that investment aims might be easier to achieve at national or sub-national level rather than at the EU level.

The proposal that was finally agreed does not match the real needs of the enlarged EU, with an economy in need of a strong boost. The approved measures look more like the outcome of a game of short-sighted political bickering between the members of an EU in a state of severe crisis than a set of policies designed to transform and boost the European economy and European society. Since the enlargement, competitiveness and cohesion policies have become much more critical for the future of Europe. These are probably transition policies to postpone the change that is needed, and they are very likely to give way to more radical actions in the future.

The discussion over the budget and the common policies is also permeated by the varying preferences of each member country when it comes to adopting a more 'liberal' or 'federal' social model for the European Union (Massot, 2005). Countries promoting the 'liberal' approach question the CAP and the rest of the common policies, and are willing to slash the budget and maintain only temporary funding for poor new member countries. The Sapir report provides some arguments to support this view, because it states that agricultural support should be redistributed towards funding economic growth, structural funds to poor new members, and restructuring of stagnating sectors, while farmers' support is left to member countries. This 'liberal' approach would convert the European Union into an intergovernmental co-operation scheme, where budget and net contributions are scaled down to a minimum.

The 'federal' approach, meanwhile, considers the main goal to be the successful integration of member countries into the European Union. This requires more, not fewer, common policies, including European funding of research and development, and substantial investments in European infrastructure. A continental Europe willing to unite would need a budget surpassing the current meagre 1 per cent of GDP, in order to expand the growth and cohesion policies while maintaining the structural and rural development policies. Massot (2005) states that the agricultural policy should be more selective and efficient in supporting market regulation in a global and open context. But some of the countries that blocked such an outcome by opposing a transfer of funds from rich farmers to rural development (the UK, Denmark, the Netherlands), are precisely the strongest adversaries of the CAP.

The optimum degree of centralization is a complex issue to decide, and the MacDougall Report (1977) advocated a substantial increase in centralized resources in order to cope with any future asymmetric shocks. Later studies suggest that the EU might even function successfully with lower central budgets, as long as there is sufficient flexibility in national fiscal policies.

There is no doubt that, despite their shortcomings, common policies have made an effective contribution to structuring the European Union.

In the current world context, the best option would be to strengthen and enlarge some common policies, while reducing those that appear to be less well oriented.

Concluding remarks

Due to its unreasonably high budget, the current CAP is a key factor in the flawed accounting logic used by most countries when discussing the European budget. The CAP is an easy prey for those that try to reorient the EU project by dismantling its main common policy, one of the virtues of which has been to facilitate the structuring of the EU.

The democratic legitimacy of the CAP has gradually weakened due to its lack of consistency and perverse effects. Its inherent inconsistencies are used as an argument for scrapping the CAP entirely or redirecting its resources for other purposes. The advisability and correctness of such measures need to be assessed without making prior assumptions.

EU agriculture has a market of 500 million consumers and provides direct employment for 14 million workers. The sector is linked to a powerful agri-food industry that represents 13 per cent of the industrial sector and employs 3.4 million workers. The agricultural sector also plays a key role in environmental conservation and maintenance of the rural environment. The gradual and inevitable decline in the importance of the agricultural sector and the above-mentioned problems relating to the CAP are not sufficient reasons to scrap the common agricultural policy or drain it of all its content. On the contrary; this policy should be redesigned to make it contribute effectively and efficiently to the general objectives of economic growth, higher employment, integration and cohesion in the EU. The budget allocation for regional and cohesion policies is inadequate because of the large funding required by new member countries.

Other economic powers, such as the United States, have not renounced the idea of an active agricultural policy to fulfil the traditional functions, as well as acting as a key factor in its foreign policy.

Re-nationalization and abandonment of the communitarian nature of the agricultural policy cannot be justified for any reason other than as a way to curtail the EU budget. Such a move appears quite inapt following the incorporation of new countries in which agriculture plays an important role in the economy. Furthermore, the severe distortion resulting from re-nationalization would jeopardize the completion of the enlarged internal market.

Any decision to concentrate investment and policy actions in the more dynamic areas, where scale and location economies can be exploited, would end up by deepening existing inequalities and creating new ones. The idea is grounded on the hypothesis of agglomeration economies, since productivity gains leading to economic growth are more effectively achieved by concentrating resources. The suggested strategy is to facilitate factor mobility towards dynamic zones and avoid the spatial dispersion of factors of production and economic activities.

Despite diverse circumstances, the growth of the Spanish economy over the last two decades shows precisely how well cohesion policies can work in regions on the periphery of highly developed areas, when they are correctly implemented and the proper institutions are in place.

The attempt to subordinate any action to achieving the maximum short-term benefit, irrespective of any further consideration, implies abandoning or at least relegating the aim for balanced regional development. This policy, based on concentration of the economy, will result in further regional disparities, the correction of which takes second place to the spread of growth effects from the central to the peripheral regions.

Regional policies are abandoned or postponed, together with efforts to promote social cohesion and convergence. To apply this approach is to display total disregard for its effect on regional development and spatial equilibrium, and thus relegate the reduction of regional inequality in the standard of living.

The total or partial re-nationalization of agricultural and structural policies is a way to liberate funds from the EU budget for other purposes. However, each member state would then have to allocate resources from its own budget to finance these policies, and poorer countries would be hard pressed to do so. Thus, although the budgetary issue would be passed from the EU level to the national level, the problems of rural areas and poor regions would continue to exist and possibly be aggravated. The social cohesion objective would have lost its priority status.

Rich countries have the least need for agricultural and structural aid, since they have well functioning agricultural sectors and fewer regional disparities. These countries can use the 'new approach' to obtain a short-term improvement in their net balance from these policies. Meanwhile, poorer countries, who have a greater need for the aid provided by these policies due to their less developed agricultural sectors and poor regions, would be unable to finance domestically these integration and cohesion policies. This is a strategy under which everyone loses out, because it makes no use of the feedback mechanism by which the economic development of the poorer regions can strengthen that of their richer neighbours.

In short, the economic and social advantages of scrapping the agricultural and regional policies are doubtful, because such a move would mean abandoning policies affecting natural resources and regional imbalances. The task of redressing territorial imbalances would not be seen as being as important as promoting development in high potential growth regions. To give a new boost to common policies, on the other hand, would be to strengthen economic policy guidelines and make an effective contribution towards growth and cohesion. The abandonment of the agricultural and regional policies, moreover, would not liberate sufficient funds to fully finance the competitiveness and growth policies, especially after EU enlargement.

Debate over the size of the budget and the characteristics of the EU project has emerged in light of the apparent inadequacy of the current budget to carry through the policies designed to enhance European integration. The debate is likewise linked to the issue of what kind of European project its members wish to construct, since the mere lifting of import barriers would not require the same measures as those needed for a more federally inspired type of integration.

Several EU echelons, from the European Parliament to the Commission for Economic and Monetary Affairs, advocate a considerable increase of the EU budget by up to 2 per cent of EU GDP (twice the current amount). EU countries need to give careful consideration to selecting the best strategy in the current international scenario. The explosive emergence of China and India as new economic powers in East Asia is shifting the centre of gravity of the world economy, and Europe must decide how to respond to that challenge. Within the framework of the recent negotiations to prepare the Hong Kong summit of the WTO, the EU Trade Commission announced that Europe's negotiating power relies on all its members arguing with one voice.

Individually, the countries of Europe are too small to intervene as key players in the new global order. It therefore makes much more sense for them to enable the EU to grow into a political and economic entity, with the capacity to capitalize on its demographic and economic weight.

Notes

1 In a recent speech the British Prime Minister was heard to say, 'I believe in Europe as a political project . . . I would never accept a Europe that was simply an economic market.'
2 Re-nationalization would not reduce expenditure but redirect it from the European budget to national budgets, thus creating problems with competition between producers in those member states receiving heterogeneous aid.

3   The UK receives a rebate on its contribution, and that of the Netherlands includes import duties on products distributed in central Europe. In addition, the countries with the highest income per head, such as Denmark, Ireland and Sweden, are not the ones who pay the largest contributions as a share of their GDP.

4   Except in the case of the UK, whose contribution is 0.6 per cent of its GDP because of the British rebate (Baldwin, 2005a).

5   The reason given for abolishing policies is that further European integration initiatives would take the form of voluntary co-operation among selected EU countries, which would not need payment programmes or policies in order to proceed.

6   García-Alvarez, Castellano and Sancho (1999) indicate that the PSE/GVA ratio (producer support estimate/gross value added) is above 70 per cent for continental products such as cereals, oilseeds, sugar, dairy products, beef and lamb. But the PSE/GVA ratio is below 15 per cent for Mediterranean products such as fruits, vegetables and wine.

7   The PSE/GVA ratio is above 60 per cent in Sweden, Ireland, Belgium, the UK, Germany and France, and below 40 per cent in Greece, Portugal, Italy and Spain (García-Alvarez, Castellano and Sancho, 1999).

8   Baldwin (2005b) presents the figures for Germany (32 per cent of payments go to 1.2 per cent of farmers), Italy (28 per cent of payments go to 1 per cent of farmers), the UK (28 per cent of payments go to 2.5 per cent of farmers), and France (26 per cent of payments go to 5 per cent of farmers).

9   Massot (2005) indicates that annual EU funding for R&D amounts to €4,100 million, compared with the €86,000 million of national R&D funding by member countries. Member countries with advanced research expertise have always preferred to maintain R&D as an internal policy.

10 The Growth Fund is the most important, since it takes up 45 per cent of total expenditure (0.45 per cent of EU GDP), and is sub-divided into three sub-headings:

(a) research and development: with the aim of investing 3 per cent of GDP in R&D (2 per cent private sector and 1 per cent public sector), the EU budget would contribute 25 per cent of public sector investment (0.25 per cent of GDP);

(b) infrastructure: with an estimated annual cost of €50,000 million, the EU would contribute 25 per cent of estimated annual investment (0.125 per cent of GDP);

(c) education and training: 7.5 per cent of the budget would go to financing 25 per cent of the current gap in public investment in education between the US and the EU.

The Convergence Fund takes up 35 per cent of the budget, which in turn is divided into three broad sub-headings:

(a) new members: 20 per cent of expenditure, after applying the absorption limit on convergence funds (4 per cent of GDP) at the level of the new member states (5 per cent of EU GDP);

(b) existing members: 10 per cent of expenditure based on the eligible population (approximately half the share of the new members);

(c) phasing out: 5 per cent of the expenditure is allocated to finance a period of transition for some macroregions.

The Restructuring Fund takes up the remaining 20 per cent of the budget. This is also broken down into three sub-headings:

(a) aid for displaced workers: 5 per cent, which comprises a subsidy of €5,000 per affected worker as part of a cofunding effort with national policies;
(b) agricultural aid: 5 per cent, assuming that 5–10 per cent of the 14 million workers in the agricultural sector will be affected by restructuring (they are allocated the same subsidy as displaced workers);
(c) phasing out in agriculture: 10 per cent of the funds allocated to financing a period of transition to avoid a sudden termination of the aid previously available through the CAP.

References

Baldwin, R. (2005a) 'The Real Budget Battle. Une crise peut cacher une autre', CEPS Policy Brief No. 75, Centre for European Policy Studies, Brussels.

Baldwin, R. (2005b) 'Who finances the Queen's CAP payments? The CAP as a dooH niboR Scheme', CEPS Policy Brief No. 88, Centre for European Policy Studies, Brussels.

Castells A. and Espasa, M. (2002) 'Desequilibrios territoriales y políticas de cohesión en la Unión Europea en la perspectiva de la ampliación', *Papeles de Economía*, 91, 253–78.

European Commission (2004) *Construir nuestro futuro común. Retos políticas y medios presupuestarios de la Unión ampliada (2007–2013)* (Brussels: European Commission).

Fundación de Estudios Financieros (2005) 'España y las nuevas perspectivas financieras de la Unión Europea 2007–13: Nuevos condicionantes, nuevos objetivos, nuevas estrategias', *Papeles de la Fundación de Estudios Financieros, No. 11*.

García-Alvarez, J., Castellano, E. and Sancho, M. (1999) 'Los efectos redistributivos de la PAC y la cohesión. Un punto de vista mediterráneo', *Revista Asturiana de Economía*, 14, 51–72.

Kernohan, D., Nuñez, J. and Schneider, A. (2005) 'The EU Budget Process and International Trade Liberalisation', CEPS Working Document No. 230, Centre for European Policy Studies, Brussels.

Le Cacheux, J. (2005) 'Le budget européen, victime d'un futur conjugué au passé', *Lettre de l'OFCE*, No. 265.

MacDougall, D. (1977) *Report of the Study Group on the Role of Public Finance in European Integration* (Brussels: Commission of the European Communities).

Massot, A. (2005) 'De la crisis de la Unión a la crisis de la PAC: por un nuevo proyecto para la agricultura europea en un entorno globalizado', Working document DT34/2005 (Madrid: Real Instituto Elcano de Estudios Internacionales y Estratégicos).

Mayhew, A. (2004) 'The Financial Framework of the European Union 2007–2013: New Policies? New Money?', Sussex European Institute, Working Paper No. 78 (Falmer: University of Sussex).

Ministère de l'Economie des Finances et de l'Industrie (2004) 'Elargissement de l'Union européene: un nouveau marché', *DREE Dossiers*, April.

Murua, J. R., Albiac, J. and Astorkiza, I. (1996) 'Contribución financiera de la PAC: Impacto regional en España', Paper presented at the XXII Reunión de Estudios Regionales, Pamplona.

Organisation for Economic Co-operation and Development (2005) *Agricultural Policies in OECD Countries: Monitoring and Evaluation 2005* (Paris: OECD).

Sapir, A. (2006) 'Un Programa para una Europa en Crecimiento. El Informe Sapir', *Papeles de Economía Española*, 107, 3–12.

Sapir, A., Aghion, P., Bertola, G., Hellwing, M., Pisani-Ferrari, J., Rosati, D., Viñals, J. and Wallace, H. (2003) *An Agenda for Growing Europe: Making the EU Economic System Deliver* (Brussels: European Union).

Torrebadella, J. (2006) 'La nueva política de cohesión comunitaria para la Europa ampliada (2007–13)', *Papeles de Economía*, 107, 13–28.

Tracy, M. (1993) *Food and Agriculture in a Market Economy. An Introduction to Theory, Practice and Policy* (Brussels: Agricultural Policy Studies).

9
The European Constitution and (Fiscal) Federalism

Rui Henrique Alves

> The federal system was created with the intention of combining the different advantages which result from the magnitude and the littleness of nations.
>
> (Alexis de Tocqueville, 1945)

Introduction

More than 50 years after the Schuman Declaration, Europe is still far from being a real political union. In fact, Europe faces a critical disparity between the two sides of the integration process, appearing as an important actor on the international economic stage, but as a minor actor in the international political arena.

In this chapter, we begin by arguing that the strategy of 'small steps' which led Europe to the current situation is no longer sufficient to allow the Union to efficiently overcome its present deficits and challenges. While examining these challenges and the main changes proposed by the Treaty establishing a European Constitution, we argue that it seems insufficient to endow the EU with a strong voice in both the political and the economic areas. So we argue that a more radical change in the institutional and economic organization of the EU is required, moving towards a model of largely decentralized federalism.

To this end, we discuss the design of an appropriate institutional framework for the political organization of the EU, presenting an alternative proposal based on the characteristics of a truly federal system, as well as its consequences in what concerns the design and implementation of European economic policies. Finally, we turn our attention to certain other aspects (such as legitimacy, transition, political will or identity) which should be taken into consideration in order to implement this type of model.

The European Union at a crossroads: the main challenges and deficits

Practically all of the studies conducted recently on the European process of integration converge on the idea that the EU is at a crossroads, facing the emergence of a relevant set of fundamental challenges: the need to consolidate the most important results of the economic integration process;[1] the need to provide an effective answer to the questions posed by increasing globalization;[2] the need to boost employment and competitiveness; the need to deal efficiently with the problems arising from enlargement to 25 countries; the need to implement a truly effective common external policy; or the need to promote the participation of its citizens in the process of integration, thus increasing its democratic legitimacy.

In this setting, it is possible to identify three fundamental 'deficits' in the EU. First, a deficit in competitiveness and growth, as it has become clear that the objective of turning Europe into the most competitive area in global terms until the end of this decade (the Lisbon strategy) is far from being achieved.[3] In fact, Europe has undergone a long period of poor economic growth,[4] with grave consequences in social terms, which must be overcome in the near future so as not to endanger some of the results that have in fact been achieved.

Second, there is a deficit of political weight. The weak capacity for joint intervention in the resolution of serious international problems (even those taking place on European territory), together with the lack of a single EU representation at the international level, clearly point to the fact that Europe has relevant economic power yet has failed in creating a solid political core. The causes reside fundamentally in the lack of a truly effective political union and a 'single voice' in the international arena, thus effectively constraining Europe's weight and options in the world. These aspects have been particularly aggravated by the war on Iraq[5] (and, more generally, by the 'war on terrorism') and the division that subsequently arose among the member states.

Finally, there seems to be a deficit in participation, legitimacy and democracy. Factors include a lack of adequate scrutiny concerning the decisions of the Commission and the Council, the restricted scope of the Parliament (even though its powers have been recently reinforced) and the ambiguity that still marks the assignment of competences between member states and the Union.[6] These elements may to a large extent explain why citizens have an inadequate perception of how the Union operates and how responsibilities are assigned to each actor. The consequences of this situation may in fact be found in the growing indifference of most citizens with regard to the process of integration in Europe.

These three deficits give rise to a disquieting idea: six decades after the Second World War and even if several important steps have been taken towards the process of integration, the construction of an area of actual European solidarity and a true feeling of Europeanism (i.e., of being part of a supra-national community) has not by any means been achieved. In fact, nationalisms still carry significant weight in decision-making and that means that the EU's current operational model (based on a strategy of 'small steps', together with a recent trend to intergovernmental deviation), seems impotent to rise to new challenges effectively, and is inefficient at a moment when the EU needs to become not only an important economic voice but also a relevant political voice in the international arena.

The constitutional treaty: an effective response?

Bearing in mind the need to face the challenges and overcome the deficits mentioned above, we will now proceed to analyse the capacity of the proposed Treaty establishing a Constitution for Europe[7] to place Europe on a more developed and solid path.

We will first provide a brief overview of the origins of the Treaty, its original goals and current situation. On 15 December 2001, the European Council in Laeken adopted a declaration on the future of the EU, setting forth its commitment to making the Union more democratic, effective and transparent. The simplification of the Union's instruments and the definition of a clear assignment of competences among the Union, its institutions and the member states were two of its main goals.

A new convention was called upon to play a key role, that of designing a 'Constitution' for Europe. Although, in the first few months, the work of the Convention seemed to be leading the final result towards something very close to a federal model, the ensuing intervention by some countries resulted in a solution that clearly falls short.[8] In October 2004, following some months of tough negotiations among the member countries on the basis of the Draft Constitution (Convenção Europeia, 2004) prepared by the Convention, the member countries signed the European Constitution.[9]

The document was to substitute the Nice Treaty after its ratification by all the member countries. As is well known, the process of ratification was halted after the French and the Dutch rejections in referendum, and at this moment the European Constitution can be considered 'living dead'. In fact, although the text has not yet been abandoned, there are few who believe that it will ever come into force.

However, an analysis of its main proposals for change is still highly relevant, mainly for two reasons: on the one hand, because a number of them
will probably be revived in the ongoing debate on the future of the EU; on
the other hand, the document shows how current consensus could outline
the future orientation of the EU's evolution and we can compare it with a
desired evolution, taking into account present challenges and deficits.

In order to do so, and in light of the conclusions reached in the last
section, we should here point out the most important changes proposed
in the European Constitution:

1 The EU gains juridical personality (Art. 7).
2 The assignment of competences between the Union and the member
   states is bolstered, by defining areas which are exclusively the Union's
   competence (Art. 13), areas of shared competence (Art. 14) and areas
   of support from the Union (Art. 17). The principle of subsidiarity is
   also reinforced (Art. 11 and Protocol on the application of the principles of subsidiarity and proportionality).
3 The Charter of Fundamental Rights is integrated as a 'constitutional'
   text (Part II).
4 The importance of the co-ordination of economic policies is enhanced
   (Art. 15) and a real Common External and Defence Policy (CEDP) is
   called for, ultimately leading to a common defence (Art. 16).
5 An area of European freedom, security and justice is created (Part III,
   chapter IV).
6 The principles for possible entry into the Union are defined, as are
   the procedures possibly required to abandon the Union (Art. 58–60).
7 The basic principles of the EU's institutional framework (Art. 19)
   remain unaltered, although the position of President of the Council
   is created (Art. 22: he or she is elected by peers and responsible for
   co-ordinating the work of this institution and, in some cases, the Union's
   external representation), as also is the position of European Minister
   of Foreign Affairs (Art. 28: he or she is in charge of the proposals and
   the execution of the CEDP); the competences assigned to the European
   Parliament are broadened, namely in matters of co-decision; and a
   reduction in the number of effective commissioners is also called for,
   set at one for each member state until 2014 and at two-thirds of the
   number of member states from then on (Art. 26).
8 There is an increase in the number of areas where decisions are taken
   by a qualified majority and a change in the pattern of this majority,
   introducing more efficient criteria than those of the Nice Treaty
   (Art. 25).

In our opinion, some of these points do certainly represent a step forward in the EU's capacity to deal with the new challenges. However, in some highly relevant areas the advances are still insufficient. Our main criticisms, and which subsequently comprise the main arguments for proposing an alternative view, are as set out below:

1   The excessive length of the proposal:[10] if one of the main goals was to make Community 'law' more accessible and transparent to citizens, it seems to all intents and purposes a huge failure.
2   The length of the Charter of Fundamental Rights is also clearly unwarranted; every possible right envisaged seems to have been contemplated in the proposal, with an excessive amount of secondary issues among those which should clearly be included in the charter.
3   Although an assignment of competences has been set forth, it is not absolutely clear and transparent. They are not as explicitly listed as in the German or Swiss Constitutions, leaving significant margin for misunderstandings and legal problems (despite the clear endorsement of subsidiarity).
4   Moreover, the exclusive competences assigned to the 'centre' do not include several aspects that we could classify as clearly supra-national, such as external policy or fiscal harmonization; furthermore, these matters will continue to be decided by unanimity, meaning that a lack of political international power will undoubtedly persist (i.e., no effective solution for the imbalance between the political and economic sides of integration has in fact been proposed).
5   At the central level, there is still no clear and transparent separation of powers (or a provision for two Parliamentary Chambers). Even with its competences broadened, the European Parliament would still play a minor part in the decision-making process. Given the manner in which the model is designed, there is a high probability that the recent trend towards intergovernmental deviation will persist, ultimately leading to an unacceptable 'directory' of the larger countries; the provision of a President of the European Council and the uneven distribution of votes in this institution are two of the key elements which ultimately mean that this model falls significantly short of a feasible model of federation and they may ultimately drive the EU away from its original idea of equality among nations.
6   At the economic level, the text does not introduce significant changes, and essentially ignores the problem of bolstering financial resources, so maintaining a very short budget; the text does not solve the problem of co-ordinating economic policies, only underlining the idea

that it is an important issue that should be dealt with, but not changing the complex, bureaucratic and barely credible process already established in Maastricht.

In this context, the European Constitution can be regarded as a positive yet insufficient step forward that could bring EU citizens closer to the integration process, provide the EU with a political dimension that is compatible with its status as an economic power and deal effectively with some of the challenges it faces, namely those raised by the recent enlargement or the need for increased competitiveness.[11] In our opinion, there was (and still is) a pressing need to go much further and find a more credible and efficient alternative.

Going for a new model: criteria for an appropriate choice

The first step in finding how the EU might be able to overcome the important imbalance between the economic and the political sides of integration (and thus deal with the above-mentioned deficits) would necessarily involve a credible analysis around a new and appropriate model for the EU, with consequences for its political and economic organization.

The choice of this model should be based on an analysis of the potential that each possible alternative has when confronted with two essential binomials: on the one hand, the binomial 'unity/diversity', corresponding to the need to create efficient conditions leading to a unique intervention in areas that are clearly supra-national, without threatening the preservation of European diversity; and, on the other hand, the binomial 'flexibility/commitment', corresponding to the need to create the capacity in Europe to easily accommodate some relevant changes that may occur in the future (in terms of enlargement or in terms of deepening), without threatening the preservation of some important common values (i.e., those that truly set the European project apart).

Applying these criteria of analysis to a vast set of possible and alternative models[12] for the EU (Europe *à la carte*; multi-speed Europe; European Directory; Europe with variable geometry; Europe with flexible integration; European Federation), we are led to conclude that only the final two models would satisfactorily fulfil these criteria, providing the EU with the necessary force to deal with its major problems (see Figures 9.1 and 9.2). The other models would ultimately lead to the disintegration of the European project or, at best, drive the EU towards a situation of inequality amongst its members, contradicting the very spirit at the origins of the project.

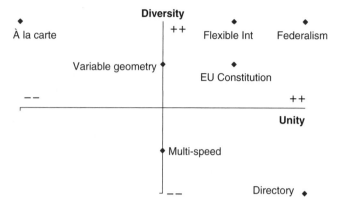

Figure 9.1   Unity/diversity

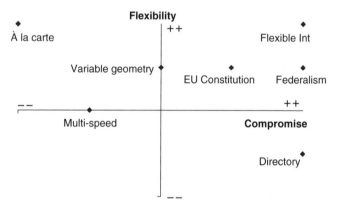

Figure 9.2   Compromise/flexibility

Furthermore, given the clear advantage of federalism over flexible integration in what concerns the formation of a true political entity, the respect that the principles of federalism[13] accord to national autonomy, the success that the implementation of federal models have shown in developed countries and/or in countries with a high level of cultural, ethnic or linguistic diversity, and the presence of a federalist idea in the genesis of the European Communities,[14] it is clear why we have opted for a federal model, convinced that it provides the basis for the necessary change in the EU's institutional and economic organization.

It should also be noted that, when applying the same criteria, the European Constitution could in fact be viewed as a positive step forward, even though it does reveal a number of drawbacks. Based on some of the criticisms mentioned above, we may conclude that it would be worse than the federal solution (or even than the hypothesis of flexible integration).

Indeed, when considering this issue together with the information contained in the next section, the most positive changes included in the project for a European Constitution are apparently those that could in fact bring the EU closer to a true federal model. At the same time, its major drawbacks can be found in those features that clearly represent obstacles in the path towards a Federation. In particular, as we have argued above, progress based on transparency, efficiency in decision-making and accountability, as well as on what concerns co-ordinating economic policies and bolstering the EU's financial resources, would not be entirely achieved with the proposed model.

An alternative proposal

In designing and describing a possible federal model for Europe, we should bear in mind that there is no such thing as one single model of federalism. Even though sharing some important features,[15] the most successful existing federations (such as Switzerland, Germany or the United States) do not share the same political, institutional and economic organization. In fact, the manner in which the principles of federalism are implemented is closely linked to the boundaries of time and space.

The situation of the EU is quite different from those of the above-mentioned 'success cases' and it becomes almost impossible (and certainly not desirable) to radically change the European pattern involving nation states with relevant roles.[16] Thus, a federal European model should necessarily assume an original form,[17] perhaps in line with the idea of a 'Federation of nation states'.[18]

The creation of such a model most certainly implies first and foremost the existence of a truly constitutional text, expressing a clear supremacy of the federal law,[19] together with a clear definition of the Union's main goals, the defence of fundamental human rights and the clear assignment of competences among the various spheres of power.

The model should observe several main features. First of all, it should guarantee a relevant degree of autonomy to its constituting entities, together with a significant measure of decentralization in the assignment of competences. These conditions would thus ensure the maintenance of a reasonable amount of relevance to the traditional nation states, bringing decision-making closer to the citizens and reinforcing democracy in the European project.

The model should also ensure equal treatment among the member states and their citizens, respect for fundamental European values (including, in particular, social values), the development of true European citizenship (leading to the creation of a genuine 'European conscience') and the creation of new financial resources for the Federation (generating a true federal European budget).

We believe that a model of this kind could represent the most adequate solution to maintain the efficiency in an enlarged EU, essential for preserving unity with regard to fundamental questions, together with respect for national, regional and local diversity, and a crucial step towards the further development of the European ideal. In this context, the following points present a brief discussion of some relevant issues concerning a potential European federal model.

Political and institutional organization

The new model should be consecrated in a Constitution defining the EU as a 'Federation of nation states', whose main goals are political and economic stability, peace, prosperity, security, justice, and the defence of liberty and human rights. Underlining these aspects, this Constitution should stress, in its initial chapters, the importance of human rights as well as the respect for political, economic and social values that clearly distinguish the European tradition from the American tradition.

The preamble and the initial chapters of this Constitution should also stress two other elements, because of their symbolism and/or their practical consequences. First, it should be emphasized that the creation of a European Federation corresponds to the will of a broadened union without threatening an enlarged autonomy of national entities and their sovereignty: a formula along the lines of 'the people of Europe and respective Countries (...) establish the following Constitution (...)', similar to the one included in the Swiss Constitution, would be a good start. Second, the consecration of the principles of federalism should be clear, in particular those concerning the autonomy of the constituents, the subsidiarity in public intervention, and the juridical guarantee.

In what concerns the assignment of competences and taking into account the desire of generalized decentralization, only those issues that are clearly supra-national should become the exclusive domain of the federal institutions. Among them, we should include the Union's external policy (including commercial policy), the issues relating to internal security and preservation of the single market (including questions on fiscal harmonization), monetary policy, and the definition and use of the federal (enlarged) budget.

In other areas, the intervention of central power should be possible but subsidiary, taking place only when the matter gains relevance for the common interest or when there are no doubts that positive results can be achieved as a result of central intervention (such as in the conception and financing of European communication and telecommunication networks). Finally, in certain matters, federal power should have the capacity to launch indicative or binding goals, restricting the actions of member states. In any case, federal powers should ensure a wide margin of manoeuvre for member states.

Following the examples mentioned earlier, the assignment of competences should include the explicit consecration of exclusive federal competences and the areas of concurrent competences, leaving all other competences to national (and regional and local) entities; this is the only manner in which to create a largely decentralized federation.

Finally, as regards institutional organization, we are of the opinion that important changes are imperative when considering the current situation. These should clearly observe the principle of separation of powers, being closer to the German or the Swiss model than to the American one, mainly in what concerns executive power.

Legislative power should be entirely the responsibility of a parliamentary institution, here called the 'Federal Assembly' and comprising two Chambers, thus following the example of the main existing Federations. The first Chamber, here called 'European Parliament', would result from the direct transformation of the one existing today. As takes place today, members would be directly elected representatives, according to electoral circumscriptions as defined by the member states. So as to allow for greater efficiency, there would have to be a cut in the number of representatives who currently hold seats in the Parliament. The number of representatives assigned to each country should be proportional to its population. However, so as to avoid the possibility of no representatives from smaller countries, a minimum number of representatives should be set.

The second Chamber, here called the 'European Senate', would comprise an equal number of representatives from each member state.[20] Half of them would be directly elected by national Parliaments and the other half appointed by national governments. This figure should allow each member state to be represented in the legislative process, as well as ensure an increased participation on the part of the national Parliaments, resulting in an evolution from the current European Council.

The 'European Government', comprising a President and a number of ministers, should assume executive power, and command the federal administration. This government (resulting from an evolution of the existing European Commission) and its President would be elected by the Parliament, based on a proposal approved by the Senate. The other Ministers would then be appointed by the President, subject to approval from the Parliament, an institution that would also have the competence to vote on motions of rejection. Even though this procedure to appoint the European Government does to some extent preserve current practices, it nevertheless goes a step further in conferring homogeneity on the entire cabinet and responsibility upon the Parliament.

The President would be in charge of co-ordinating every facet of government and act as representative of the European Union abroad, thus resolving one of the most pressing problems of the current common external policy.

The competence to initiate any legislative process should be assigned to each of the Chambers and to the government. Federal laws (and other juridical instruments) would have to be approved by the two Chambers. If a proposal were approved by the Parliament but rejected by the Senate, it could be resubmitted to the first Chamber, as long as it had been voted for by a majority equal to those that defeated the proposal in the Senate. This Germanic solution could thus better defend European interests. A qualified majority or a simple majority, depending on the issues, would be the rule for decision. Referendums should be permitted but subject to certain constraints regarding the high relevance of the issues in terms of European integration.

Finally, juridical power should follow the German model, in accordance with European tradition. It should comprise the European Constitutional Court, the federal courts included in the Constitution and the national courts. The European Constitutional Court, the result of an evolution of the existing European Court of Justice, would act as the utmost guarantee of the juridical system, interpret the Constitution and decide upon divergences between different jurisdictions.

Consequences for the economic organization

If a change in political organization towards a federal structure did in fact occur, some significant changes would necessarily be required in the way in which the economy is organized. In particular, the definition and the execution of all kinds of public policies would suffer important transformations, as they would have to be adapted to the 'rules' of federalism, in this case, 'fiscal federalism'.[21]

In the area of 'economic federalism' we find a large number of consensual points, even though some challenging ones subsist.[22] In particular, we easily observe that the main conclusions of the 'fiscal federalism' theory[23] would be largely compatible with the political idea of a largely decentralized Federation comprised of the 'former' nation states and with the need to create a 'European economic government' responsible for the competences assigned at this level to the Federation.

The literature also sustains the possibility of obtaining significant welfare gains from the creation of a highly decentralized fiscal system, appropriately designed and focused on efficiency and equity. It should also be noted that 'recent' literature (Inman and Rubinfeld, 1997), when considering political and economic objectives together, stresses the benefits of a largely decentralized federal system, illustrating how the possible reinforcement of political participation, with the related benefits, would outweigh eventual costs in economic efficiency.

In what concerns the supply of public goods, the literature generally favours decentralization with some exceptions, in line with the theorem of Oates (1972). Applying its main ideas to the EU case, large gains are to be expected from high decentralization, taking into account the fact that there are important differences in national demands and preferences, as well as the restricted mobility of families. Centralization would only occur in what concerns public goods of a general and supra-national nature (where defence is a typical example). Also, there could possibly be a need for a greater degree of harmonization/centralization in some other fields, such as in environmental rules or taxation, as a means to avoid the risks of competition driving towards lower standards.

In what relates to redistribution, the literature traditionally favours centralization as a means to promote the geographical neutrality of taxation, following the renowned Tiebout model (1956). However, some works have pointed out the need to combine central competences with sub-central competences, bearing in mind aspects such as the consequences of restricted geographical mobility, concerns about the poorer populations[24] (which is clearly more important when there is greater proximity) and further objectives regarding regional redistribution.[25] Empirical analyses also show that many federations are still adopting redistribution policies at lower levels of government.

If we apply these aspects to the EU case, we can conclude that redistribution policies should be defined as a shared competence of different levels of government. The objectives related to an increased harmonization of income among countries and regions could be achieved by a combination of co-ordination of policies and interregional compensatory transfers.

In what concerns macroeconomic stabilization, the literature traditionally favoured centralization (for instance, the traditional arguments found in the theory of optimal currency areas[26]): a strong central budget serves as an insurance mechanism against the effects of asymmetric or specific shocks, in a context where important instruments of macro-economic national policy have been lost. Some substantial developments have occurred over the last few years, with some works discussing the true role of fiscal policy[27] and many studies on fiscal rules and fiscal discipline (mainly upon the case of the European Monetary Union), as well as the particular case of limited shock-absorber mechanisms.[28]

Applying the relevant literature to the European case and bearing in mind its new challenges, we contend that there should be a significant increase in the European budget, as the only means of providing the federal government with sufficient capacity to deal with macroeconomic stabilization and also to effectively intervene in other fields. Own financial resources should be increased, a goal that could be achieved through the appropriate tax assignment and distribution of revenues among the different levels of government.[29] Structural changes should also be operated on the expenditures side of the budget, with a significant reduction in the importance of the Common Agricultural Policy, together with an improved interest in 'new' common policies.

In the short run, however, some relevant political questions make the problem of increasing the European budget a very difficult one. In this case, an increase in the efficiency with which macroeconomic stabilization is handled requires that the process of economic policy co-ordination be significantly boosted (possibly through the creation of a new supra-national entity, an 'economic government').

The creation of a limited central shock-absorber mechanism, activated in the case of asymmetrical shocks, and a profound and credible reform of the Stability and Growth Pact (SGP), giving more flexibility to the use of fiscal instruments without threatening fiscal discipline, are two of the aspects that, in our opinion, should also be implemented in the very short term, regardless of a possible evolution towards a federal model.

In this context, it should be pointed out that discussions about the SGP have been on the rise in the last few years, particularly owing to the negative economic evolution in the EU and the difficulties that several countries have felt in complying with its rules.[30]

Negotiations around a possible reform have led to important changes, which were agreed upon in March 2005. Some of them (such as: excluding the effects of the economic conjuncture and some investment expenditures; more flexibility in terms of temporal limits for correcting excessive deficits; more attention to the debt criteria and sustainability of public debt, etc.) may be viewed as positive and a step towards the necessary increase in flexibility. However, the problem of credibility persists, particularly if we take into account the high level of subjectivity involved in choosing which public expenditures should be excluded from the relevant deficit. In fact, as agreement in this field has been somewhat *à la carte* in choice, it is not clear whether the reform will ensure the necessary budgetary discipline together with the required increase in flexibility.

Finally, let us consider briefly the instruments of fiscal federalism. Firstly, we should note that the criteria for tax assignment proposed by Musgrave (1983) might be largely applicable, even though they have recently been subject to some criticism, especially if the empirical experience in some federations is taken into account. The European government should be responsible for progressive taxation (because of the perverse effects of excessive migration), for taxes with high mobile bases of calculus (due to the possible effects of distorting decisions on where to locate activities, where the taxes on capital income are a good example) and for taxes whose bases are asymmetrically distributed among regions and countries (because of the possible increase in geographical inequality). National and local governments would in turn be responsible for other types of taxes.

Second, with regard to intergovernmental grants, the relevant literature apparently suggests: the need to promote conditional transfers for internalization of spillover effects; the probable existence of a trade-off between the objectives of harmonizing economic growth and achieving economic and social cohesion and the problems raised by the existence of liquid contributors/receivers, concerning 'fiscal equalization' transfers;[31] and particular care should be taken with the systems of transfers associated to mechanisms of 'revenue sharing', as they should not be too large, so as to avoid a possible increase in fiscal indiscipline.[32]

Concluding remarks

In this chapter, we have argued that the 'small steps' taken by the EU up to the present day, together with a certain degree of intergovernmental deviation over the last few years, is not the most appropriate strategy/model for helping the Union to overcome its present deficits and challenges efficiently. Thus, we have proposed that important changes should be made in the institutional and economic organization of the EU.

We have also argued that the changes which have been proposed by the European Constitution may prove insufficient in establishing the required balance between the political and economic sides of the integration process and in providing the EU with a strong voice in both the political and the economic areas. The model proposed by the European Constitution could fail in certain strategic areas, mainly in what concerns the possibility of having a truly single external policy, the existence of a relevantly-sized common budget, the clarification of competences between the centre and the member states and also among the central institutions, the consecration of true equality in the treatment of all member states and the incentive to encourage participation from European citizens in the process of integration.

To this end, we sought to apply two criteria to some possible models for Europe ('unity/diversity' and 'flexibility/compromise') and argued for a movement towards an actual federal (largely decentralized) system in the European Union, also presenting an alternative proposal for the political, institutional and economic organization of the EU. We argued that this proposal, based on the concept of a 'Federation of nation states', would better provide an efficient answer to the current challenges faced by the EU.

Such a change, resulting ultimately in a federal system, would necessarily have to be legitimated by a European referendum that should take place in each one of the member states. The change would be effective only if approved by a qualified majority of voters and states.

It should also be noted that the proposal is to some degree quite radical and difficult to implement in the very short run. There would probably be a need for progressive evolution, eventually with a first phase based on a model of flexible integration, together with some progressive changes in the economic side, particularly in what concerns the growing weight of the central budget, the institutionalization of a limited common shock-absorber and the reinforcement of the co-ordination of non-monetary policies, as first steps towards the final solutions based on the theory of fiscal federalism.

Finally, note that the success of such a model would largely depend on achieving a sentiment of true European citizenship. In the past, the presence of a feeling of 'belonging' to a supra-national community has proved to be one of the key factors in the success of some federal models (the United States, Germany, Switzerland, etc.), whereas its absence has largely contributed to the disintegration of other supra-national entities[33] (the Soviet Union, Yugoslavia, etc.).

Notes

1 This process has been successful up until now, as Europe almost attained maximum economic integration, with a single currency and the co-ordination

of macroeconomic policies. However, some significant problems persist, such as how to make this co-ordination more effective, issues related to fiscal harmonization or the problems concerning the sustainability of the social welfare system. For a brief review of these matters, see Alves (2001).

2 On the consequences and problems derived from increasing globalization see, for instance, Sassen (1998) and, for a more radical view, Guéhenno (1995).

3 This has been recently recognized by the main political leaders of the member states and has led to a revision of the Lisbon strategy, in an attempt to fulfil its goals (even though the objective of 2010 has been abandoned).

4 Some countries have indeed experienced periods of economic recession.

5 Note, for instance, that during the war in Iraq (March to May 2003) there were no common decisions on the matter, as though it were not the main international problem at the time.

6 Cf. Alesina and Perotti (2004). On legitimacy and democracy see also Scharpf (1999) and Baykal (2004).

7 From now on, and to simplify, it will be referred to as the 'European Constitution'.

8 As Devuyst (2004) notes, the evolution and the results of the negotiations, in particular in the context of the Intergovernmental Conference that followed the Convention, clearly show the objective of rejection of a federal model of organization by the large majority of the member states.

9 Note that the approved text is not very different from the project presented by the Convention: see, for instance, Alves (2004).

10 A simple comparison between the European Constitution and the Constitution of Germany, Switzerland and, in particular, the United States is, at this level, highly suggestive.

11 Some authors (see, e.g., Barry, 2004) have a strongly negative view of the European Constitution, as they consider that it will only allow for growing centralization: 'The purpose of a constitution should be to restrain governments. The proposed EU constitution does not do that – it provides agendas for government action. There is also no mechanism to facilitate jurisdictional competition. As such, if adopted, it will lead to further centralisation and abuse of statutory powers.'

12 For a brief overview of the main features of these models, see Dewatripont *et al.* (1995).

13 Those principles are: autonomy; subsidiarity; participation; co-operation; and guarantee. For a general description, see Héraud (1995).

14 For a history of the federalist idea in Europe, see Sidjanski (2000). In 1950, Schuman, one of the 'founding fathers' of the EU project, considered the creation of the Economic Community of Coal and Steel to be the first concrete step towards a European Federation, which would be 'indispensable to the preservation of peace' (Schuman, 1963).

15 See, for instance, Alves (2004).

16 Cf. Fischer (2000).

17 This originality should not be surprising, as the process of European integration has generally evolved through original steps and there is no general and universal model of federation.

18 Please note that several politicians use(d) this concept, which was first proposed some years ago by Jacques Delors, not always referring to the same model.

19 This is not clear in the European Constitution, and was also not clear in the debate related to it, as there has been a certain amount of discussion on whether the document is actually a Constitution or just one more Treaty, except that in this case the debate is about a Constitutional Treaty, or even whether the European Union really needs a Constitution: see, for instance, Craig (2001).

20 Equality in representation from each member state corresponds more adequately to the ideal that has inspired the process of European integration since its beginning.

21 As Oates (1999) notes, the meaning of 'federalism' in economics is not exactly the same as its meaning in political science. In this area, as observed by the author, it refers to a political system grounded on a Constitution that allows for some degree of autonomy and power to all levels of political jurisdiction. In the area of economics, we note that the public sectors are always 'more or less' federal, in the sense that there are different levels of government supplying public services and performing some power of decision de facto. The subject of 'fiscal federalism' is therefore the set of questions concerning the vertical structure of the public sector (i.e., concerning the intervention of the state itself in the economy at all different levels).

22 Cf. Oates (2001).

23 Development of this subject might be found in Oates (1999) or Spahn (1994).

24 Cf. Pauly (1973).

25 Cf. King (1984).

26 See, for instance, Mundell (1961) and De Grauwe (2003).

27 See Solow (2004).

28 See Italianer and Pisani-Ferry (1994) as an interesting example. Some developments have followed their original work.

29 The European Commission (2004) has already presented a proposal on the issue of 'reforming' the European system of own financial resources. For an interesting evaluation of the current system and of some ways to reform it, see Cieslukowski (2005).

30 For an interesting discussion on the pros and cons of the (original) Pact, see, for instance, Buti *et al.* (2003). It should be noted, though, that these authors largely defend the rules of the Pact. For an interesting alternative, see, for instance, Creel (2003). Buti *et al.* (2005) have recently 'reformulated' their original work, so as to classify the 'new' SGP.

31 See, for instance, McKinnon (1997) and Oates (1999).

32 Cf. Oates (1999).

33 See, for instance, Kux (1996) and Crnobrnja (2002) on, respectively, the former Soviet Union and the recent past and present situation of Yugoslavia.

References

Alesina, Alberto and Perotti, Roberto (2004) 'The European Union: A Politically Incorrect View', NBER Working Paper, No. W10342, March (Washington, DC: NBER).

Alves, Rui Henrique (2001) 'From Single Currency to Political Union?', *Global Economy Quarterly*, II(4) (Oct.–Dec.), 305–42.

Alves, Rui Henrique (2004) 'Europe: Looking for a New Model', in Astengo, Francesca and Neuwahl, Nanette (eds), *A Constitution for Europe? Governance and Policy-Making in the European Union*, Collection 'Etudes Européennes' (Montreal: University of Montreal), 39–55.

Barry, Norman (2004) 'Constitutionalism, Federalism and European Union', *Economic Affairs*, 24(March), 11–16.

Baykal, Sanem (2004) 'Democracy, Legitimacy and Efficiency: Does the Draft Treaty Establishing a Constitution for Europe Get it Right?', in Astengo, Francesca and Neuwahl, Nanette (eds), *A Constitution for Europe? Governance and Policy-Making in the European Union*, Collection 'Etudes Européennes' (Montreal: University of Montreal), 122–35.

Buti, Marco *et al.* (2003) 'Revisiting the Stability and Growth Pact: Grand Design or Internal Adjustment?', CEPR Discussion Paper, No. 3692.

Buti, Marco *et al.* (2005) 'The Stability Pact Pains: A Forward-Looking Assessment of the Reform Debate', CEPR Discussion Paper, No. 5216.

Cieslukowski, Maciej (2005) 'A Rational System of the Own Resources for the European Communities', 4th Annual Conference of EEFS, 19–22 May, Coimbra.

Convenção Europeia (2004) *Tratado que Estabelece uma Constituição para a Europa* (Luxembourg: Serviço das Publicações Oficiais da União Europeia).

Craig, Paul (2001) 'Constitutions, Constitutionalism, and European Union', *European Law Journal*, 7(2) (June), 125–50.

Creel, Jérôme (2003) 'Ranking Fiscal Policy Rules: the Golden Rule of Public Finance vs. the Stability and Growth Pact', *Documents de Travail de l'OFCE*, No. 2003–04, July.

Crnobrnja, Mihailo (2002) 'Yugoslavia', in Griffiths, Ann (ed.), *Handbook of Federal Countries 2002* (Montreal and Kingston: McGill–Queen's University Press, Forum of Federations).

De Grauwe, Paul (2003) *The Economics of Monetary Union* (Oxford: Oxford University Press).

Devuyst, Youri (2004) 'EU Decision-Making after the Treaty Establishing a Constitution for Europe', Policy Paper No. 9, July (Pittsburgh, PA: University Center for International Studies).

Dewatripont, Mathias *et al.* (1995) *Flexible Integration – Towards a More Effective and Democratic Europe*, Monitoring European Integration 6 (London: CEPR).

European Commission (2004) *Relatório sobre Financiamento da União Europeia (Report on Financing the European Union)*, 505, final/2, Vol. I (Brussels: European Commission).

Fischer, Joschka (2000) 'Da Confederação á Federação – reflexões sobre a finalidade da integração europeia' (From Confederation to Federation – on the finality of the European integration), in *Expresso*, 20 May.

Guéhenno, Jean-Marie (1995) *The End of the Nation-State* (Minneapolis: University of Minnesota Press).

Héraud, Guy (1995) *Le Fédéralisme* (Nice: Presses d'Europe).

Inman, Robert and Rubinfeld, David (1997) 'Making Sense of the Antitrust State-Action Doctrine: Balancing Political Participation and Economic Efficiency in Regulatory Federalism', *Texas Law Review*, 75, 1203–99.

Italianer, Alexander and Pisani-Ferry, Jean (1994) 'The Regional-Stabilisation Properties of Fiscal Arrangements', in Mortensen, Jorgen (ed.), *Improving Economic and Social Cohesion in the European Community* (New York: St Martin's Press), 155–94.

King, David (1984) *Fiscal Tiers: The Economics of Multi-level Government* (London: Allen & Unwin).

Kux, Stephen (1996) 'From USSR to CIS: Confederation or Civilized Divorce?', in Hesse, Joachim and Wright, Vincent (eds), *Federalizing Europe – The Costs, Benefits and Preconditions of Federal Political Systems* (Oxford: Oxford University Press).

Mckinnon, Ronald (1997) 'Market-Preserving Fiscal Federalism in the American Monetary Union', in Blejer, Mario and Ter-Minassian, Teresa (eds), *Macroeconomic Dimensions of Public Finance: Essays in Honor of Vito Tanzi* (London: Routledge).

Mundell, Robert (1961) 'A Theory of Optimum Currency Areas', *American Economic Review*, 51 (November).

Musgrave, Richard (1983) 'Who Should Tax, Where and What?', in Mclure, C. (ed.), *Tax Assignment in Federal Countries*, (Canberra: Australian University Press.)

Oates, Wallace (1972) *Fiscal Federalism* (New York: Harcourt Brace Jovanovich).

Oates, Wallace (1999) 'An Essay on Fiscal Federalism', *Journal of Economic Literature*, 37(3) (September), 1120–49.

Oates, Wallace (2001) 'Fiscal Competition and European Union: Contrasting Perspectives', *Regional Science and Urban Economics*, 31(2–3) (April), 133–45.

Pauly, Mark (1973) 'Income Redistribution as a Local Public Good', *Journal of Public Economics*, 2, 35–58.

Sassen, Saskia (1998) *Globalization and its Discontents* (New York: The New Press).

Scharpf, Fritz (1999) *Governing in Europe: Effective and Democratic?* (Oxford: Oxford University Press).

Schuman, Robert (1963) *Pour l'Europe* (Nigel Edit).

Sidjanski, Dusan (2000) *The Federal Future of Europe – From the European Community to the European Union* (University of Michigan Press).

Solow, Robert (2004) 'Is Fiscal Policy Possible?', in Solow, Robert (ed.), *Structural Reform and Macroeconomic Policy* (Basingstoke: Palgrave Macmillan).

Spahn, Paul Bernd (1994) 'Fiscal Federalism: a Survey of the Literature', in Mortensen, Jorgen (ed.), *Improving Economic and Social Cohesion in the European Community* (New York: St Martin's Press), 145–54.

Tiebout, Charles (1956) 'A Pure Theory of Local Expenditures', *Journal of Political Economy*, 64, 416–24.

Tocqueville, Alexis de (1945) *Democracy in America* (New York: Vintage Books Random House; first published in 1838).

Several downloaded documents, including the Constitutions of the United States, Germany and Switzerland and the Treaty Establishing a Constitution for Europe, were also consulted.

Index